Taste *of* Home
Vintage Recipes
MADE EASY

TASTE OF HOME BOOKS • RDA ENTHUSIAST BRANDS, LLC • MILWAUKEE, WI

©2025 RDA Enthusiast Brands, LLC.
1610 N. 2nd St., Suite 102,
Milwaukee WI 53212-3906

Visit us at **tasteofhome.com** for other Taste of Home books and products.

International Standard Book Number:
979-8-88977-100-5

Chief Content Officer:
Jason Buhrmester

Content Director:
Mark Hagen

Creative Director:
Raeann Thompson

Associate Creative Director:
Jami Geittmann

Deputy Editor:
Julie Schnittka

Senior Editor:
Christine Rukavena

Senior Art Director:
Courtney Lovetere

Manager, Production Design:
Satyandra Raghav

Senior Print Publication Designer:
Bipin Balakrishnan

Production Artist:
Nithya Venkatakrishnan

Deputy Editor, Copy Desk:
Ann M. Walter

Copy Editor:
Rayan Naqash

Contributing Copy Editors:
Nancy J. Stohs, Pam Grandy, Dulcie Shoener

Cover Photography
Photographer: Dan Roberts
Set Stylist: Melissa Franco
Food Stylists: Sue Draheim

Pictured on front cover:
Cherry Cola Cake, p. 249

Pictured on back cover:
Sidecar, p. 14; Traditional Meat Loaf, p. 111; Baked Cheddar Eggs & Potatoes, p. 192; Pretzel Gelatin Dessert, p. 312; Country Ham & Potatoes, p. 176; Green Bean Casserole, p. 81

Printed in China
1 3 5 7 9 10 8 6 4 2

285 Classic Recipes Made Easy for Today

Everything old is new again, and that includes the lip-smacking dishes that came from Mom's kitchen. From green bean casserole to golden apple pies, the flavors of yesteryear evoke heartfelt memories of bygone days. Now it's a snap to prepare the foods you love (and miss!) with **Vintage Recipes Made Easy.**

We've simplified the favorites you grew up with, making them quick to prepare. Short ingredient lists, convenience items and modern kitchen appliances mean you can quickly whip up the same foods that originally took hours to make.

Whether hosting a retro cocktail party, serving an old-fashioned Easter brunch or simply baking a chocolate cake like Mom's, you'll find all the classic recipes you adore—each streamlined for the way you cook today. Big on flavor as well as convenience, the specialties in **Vintage Recipes Made Easy** bring back the delicious memories you adore with only a fraction of the work.

Contents

MAI TAI, P. 22

Retro Cocktail Party

Cran & Cherry Punch

This crimson-colored beverage is wonderful for parties and special holidays. It looks festive in a glass punch bowl.
—*Lori Daniels, Beverly, WV*

PREP: 15 min. + freezing
MAKES: 18 servings (3½ qt.)

- ⅓ cup fresh or frozen cranberries
- 2 lemon slices, cut into 6 wedges
- 1 pkg. (3 oz.) cherry gelatin
- 1 cup boiling water
- 3 cups cold water
- 6 cups cranberry juice, chilled
- ¾ cup thawed lemonade concentrate
- 1 liter ginger ale, chilled

1. Place several cranberries and a piece of lemon in each compartment of an ice cube tray; fill with water and freeze.

2. In a punch bowl or large container, dissolve gelatin in boiling water. Stir in the cold water, cranberry juice and lemonade concentrate. Just before serving, stir in ginger ale. Serve over cranberry-lemon ice cubes.

¾ CUP 99 cal., 0 fat (0 sat. fat), 0 chol., 17mg sod., 25g carb. (24g sugars, 0 fiber), 1g pro. **DIABETIC EXCHANGES** 1 starch, ½ fruit.

Lake Charles Dip

Italian salad dressing mix gives this simply delicious dip its wonderful flavor. Serve it with fresh veggies or crackers for an easy appetizer.
—*Shannon Copley, Upper Arlington, OH*

PREP: 15 min. + chilling • **MAKES:** 1½ cups

- 1 cup sour cream
- 2 Tbsp. reduced-fat mayonnaise
- 1 Tbsp. Italian salad dressing mix
- ⅓ cup finely chopped avocado
- 1 tsp. lemon juice
- ½ cup finely chopped seeded tomato
  Optional: Assorted crackers, cucumber slices, julienned sweet red pepper and carrot sticks

In a small bowl, combine the sour cream, mayonnaise and dressing mix. Toss the avocado with lemon juice; stir into sour cream mixture. Stir in tomato. Cover and refrigerate for at least 1 hour. Serve with crackers and assorted vegetables as desired.

¼ CUP 111 cal., 9g fat (5g sat. fat), 27mg chol., 216mg sod., 3g carb. (2g sugars, 1g fiber), 2g pro.

Rumaki Appetizers

Sweet pineapple and crunchy water chestnuts wrapped in bacon and topped with barbecue sauce—yum! These Polynesian-inspired, can't-eat-just-one appetizers are perfect party food. The sauce is also amazing with smoked sausages, so you can set out a whole platter of mixed goodies.
—*Janice Thomas, Milford, NE*

PREP: 30 min. • **BROIL:** 10 min.
MAKES: 14 appetizers

½ cup packed brown sugar
¼ cup mayonnaise
¼ cup chili sauce
14 whole water chestnuts, drained
1 can (8 oz.) pineapple chunks, drained
7 bacon strips, halved

1. In a small saucepan, combine the brown sugar, mayonnaise and chili sauce. Cook and stir over medium heat until mixture comes to a boil; set aside.

2. Place a water chestnut and pineapple chunk on each piece of bacon; roll up bacon and secure with a toothpick. Place on a broiler pan. Broil 4-5 in. from the heat 4-5 minutes on each side or until bacon is crisp. Serve with sauce.

1 APPETIZER 92 cal., 4g fat (1g sat. fat), 4mg chol., 162mg sod., 12g carb. (11g sugars, 0 fiber), 2g pro.

Gimlet

In this classic sweet-tart cocktail, a touch of confectioners' sugar smooths out an otherwise puckery drink. Bring out your inner bartender—try mixing it with vodka instead of gin, or straining it into a chilled cocktail glass and serving it neat.
—Taste of Home *Test Kitchen*

TAKES: 5 min. • **MAKES:** 1 serving

Ice cubes
2 oz. gin
1 oz. lime juice
½ oz. simple syrup
Lime slices

Fill a shaker three-fourths full with ice. Add the gin, lime juice and simple syrup; cover and shake for 10-15 seconds or until condensation forms on outside of shaker. Strain into an ice-filled glass. Garnish with lime.

1 SERVING 196 cal., 0 fat (0 sat. fat), 0 chol., 1mg sod., 18g carb. (15g sugars, 0 fiber), 0 pro.

NOTE You may also strain the Gimlet into a chilled cocktail glass and serve without additional ice.

Bacon-Stuffed Mushrooms

I first tried these broiled treats at my sister-in-law's house. The juicy mushroom caps and creamy filling were so fabulous that I had to get the recipe. It's hard to believe how simple, fast and easy they are.
—*Angela Coffman, Kansas City, MO*

TAKES: 25 min. • **MAKES:** about 2 dozen

- 1   pkg. (8 oz.) cream cheese, softened
- ¼   tsp. garlic powder
- 8   bacon strips, cooked and crumbled
- 1   Tbsp. chopped green onion
- 1   lb. whole fresh mushrooms, stems removed

1. Preheat broiler. Mix the cream cheese and garlic powder. Stir in the bacon and green onion.

2. Place mushrooms in an ungreased 15x10x1-in. pan, stem side up. Fill with cream cheese mixture. Broil 4-6 in. from heat until heated through, 4-6 minutes.

1 STUFFED MUSHROOM 51 cal., 4g fat (2g sat. fat), 12mg chol., 79mg sod., 1g carb. (1g sugars, 0 fiber), 2g pro.

Martini

Whether you're going for a Rat Pack or secret agent vibe, you can't have a cocktail party without a martini on the menu. The choice of gin or vodka is up to you, but either way, this queen-of-the-cocktail-hour drink comes shaken, not stirred.
—Taste of Home *Test Kitchen*

TAKES: 5 min. • **MAKES:** 1 serving

-     Ice cubes
- 3   oz. gin or vodka
- ½   oz. dry vermouth
-     Pimiento-stuffed olives

Fill a shaker three-fourths full with ice. Add gin and vermouth; cover and shake until condensation forms on outside of shaker. Strain into a chilled cocktail glass. Garnish with olives.

⅔ CUP 209 cal., 0 fat (0 sat. fat), 0 chol., 5mg sod., 0 carb. (0 sugars, 0 fiber), 0 pro.

NOTE This recipe makes a dry martini. Use less vermouth for an extra-dry martini; use more for a wet martini. You can also serve the martini over ice in a rocks glass.

APPLE MARTINI Omit vermouth and olives. Reduce vodka to 2 oz. and use 1½ oz. sour apple liqueur and 1½ tsp. lemon juice. Garnish with a green apple slice.

CHOCOLATE MARTINI Omit vermouth and olives. Reduce vodka to 2 oz. and use 2 oz. creme de cacao or chocolate liqueur. Garnish with chocolate shavings.

Best Deviled Eggs

Herbs lend amazing flavor, making these the best deviled eggs you can make!
—Jesse and Anne Foust, Bluefield, WV

TAKES: 25 min. • **MAKES:** 2 dozen

- ½ cup mayonnaise
- 2 Tbsp. 2% milk
- 1 tsp. dried parsley flakes
- ½ tsp. dill weed
- ½ tsp. minced chives
- ½ tsp. ground mustard
- ¼ tsp. salt
- ¼ tsp. paprika
- ⅛ tsp. garlic powder
- ⅛ tsp. pepper
- 12 hard-boiled large eggs
  Minced fresh parsley and additional paprika

In a small bowl, combine the first 10 ingredients. Cut eggs lengthwise in half; remove yolks and set whites aside. In another bowl, mash the yolks; add to mayonnaise mixture, mixing well. Spoon or pipe filling into egg whites. Sprinkle with parsley and additional paprika. Refrigerate until serving.

1 STUFFED EGG HALF 73 cal., 6g fat (1g sat. fat), 108mg chol., 81mg sod., 0 carb. (0 sugars, 0 fiber), 3g pro.

BACON DEVILED EGGS To mayonnaise, mix in 3 crumbled cooked bacon strips, 3 Tbsp. finely chopped red onion, 3 Tbsp. sweet pickle relish and ¼ tsp. smoked paprika.

SMOKIN' HOT DEVILED EGGS To mayonnaise, mix in 3 finely chopped chipotle peppers in adobo sauce, 1 Tbsp. drained capers, 1 Tbsp. stone-ground mustard, ¼ tsp. salt and ¼ tsp. white pepper. Sprinkle stuffed eggs with minced fresh cilantro.

CRABBY DEVILED EGGS Increase the mayonnaise to ⅔ cup. Mix in 1 cup finely chopped imitation crabmeat, ½ cup finely chopped celery, ½ cup chopped slivered almonds, 2 Tbsp. finely chopped green pepper and ½ tsp. salt.

Pineapple Cheese Ball

Pineapple lends a fruity tang to this fun and tasty appetizer. Instead of forming one large cheese ball, you could make two smaller balls—one to serve before a meal and one to take to a party.
—*Anne Halfhill, Sunbury, OH*

PREP: 20 min. + chilling
MAKES: 1 cheese ball

- 2 pkg. (8 oz. each) cream cheese, softened
- 1 can (8 oz.) unsweetened crushed pineapple, drained
- ¼ cup finely chopped green pepper
- 2 Tbsp. finely chopped onion
- 2 tsp. seasoned salt
- 1½ cups chopped walnuts
  Assorted crackers and fresh vegetables

In a small bowl, beat cream cheese, pineapple, green pepper, onion and seasoned salt until blended. Cover and refrigerate for 30 minutes. Shape into a ball (mixture will be soft); coat in walnuts. Cover and refrigerate overnight. Serve with assorted crackers and fresh vegetables if desired.

2 TBSP. 87 cal., 8g fat (2g sat. fat), 10mg chol., 155mg sod., 3g carb. (1g sugars, 1g fiber), 3g pro.

This is the best cheese ball ever! I've made it for over 30 years. I always make an indention with my thumb on top and add a cherry for decoration.
—DEBORAH5620, TASTEOFHOME.COM

Manhattan

Straight up served in a chilled cocktail glass or over ice, this classic New York drink belongs in the hands of whiskey drinkers.
—Taste of Home *Test Kitchen*

TAKES: 5 min. • **MAKES:** 1 serving

  Ice cubes
- 2 oz. whiskey, bourbon or rye
- ½ oz. sweet vermouth
- 2 to 3 dashes bitters, optional
  Maraschino cherries

Fill a pint glass three-fourths full with ice. Add the whiskey, vermouth and, if desired, bitters; stir until well chilled, 20-30 seconds. Strain into a coupe or cocktail glass or an ice-filled rocks glass. Garnish with maraschino cherries.

1 SERVING 151 cal., 0 fat (0 sat. fat), 0 chol., 2mg sod., 2g carb. (2g sugars, 0 fiber), 0 pro.

NOTE You may substitute bourbon for the whiskey if desired. You may also strain the Manhattan into a chilled cocktail glass and serve without additional ice.

Coconut Shrimp

Jumbo shrimp is the perfect vehicle for crunchy, tropical coconut flakes. The fruity salsa is delightful as a dip for this island-influenced appetizer.
—*Marie Hattrup, Sonoma, CA*

PREP: 20 min. • **COOK:** 5 min./batch
MAKES: 1½ dozen

- 18 uncooked jumbo shrimp (about 1 lb.)
- ⅓ cup cornstarch
- ¾ tsp. salt
- ½ tsp. cayenne pepper
- 3 large egg whites
- 2 cups sweetened shredded coconut
  Oil for deep-fat frying

APRICOT-PINEAPPLE SALSA
- 1 cup diced pineapple
- ½ cup finely chopped red onion
- ½ cup apricot preserves
- ½ cup minced fresh cilantro
- 2 Tbsp. lime juice
- 1 jalapeno pepper, seeded and chopped
  Salt and pepper to taste
  Lime wedges, optional

1. Peel and devein shrimp, leaving tails intact. Make a slit down inner curve of each shrimp, starting with the tail; press lightly to flatten. In a shallow dish, combine the cornstarch, salt and cayenne; set aside. In a bowl, beat egg whites until stiff peaks form. Place the coconut in another shallow dish. Coat shrimp with cornstarch mixture; dip into egg whites, then coat with coconut.

2. In an electric skillet or deep-fat fryer, heat oil to 375°. Fry shrimp, a few at a time, 1-1½ minutes on each side or until golden brown. Drain on paper towels.

3. In a bowl, combine the 7 salsa ingredients. Serve with shrimp and, if desired, lime wedges.

NOTE Wear disposable gloves when cutting hot peppers; the oils can burn skin. Avoid touching your face.

1 SHRIMP WITH 1 TBSP. SALSA 141 cal., 7g fat (4g sat. fat), 31mg chol., 170mg sod., 16g carb. (11g sugars, 1g fiber), 5g pro.

Sidecar

Welcome summer with this tart citrus delight. Treat yourself to this sunny drink.
—Taste of Home *Test Kitchen*

TAKES: 5 min. • **MAKES:** 1 serving

- Ice cubes
- 1 oz. brandy
- ⅔ oz. (4 tsp.) triple sec
- 1½ to 3 tsp. lemon juice

OPTIONAL GARNISH
- Lemon twist

1. Fill a shaker three-fourths full with ice. Add the brandy, triple sec and lemon juice. Cover and shake for 15-20 seconds or until condensation forms on outside of shaker.

2. Strain into a chilled cocktail glass. Garnish as desired.

1 SERVING 137 cal., 0 fat (0 sat. fat), 0 chol., 2mg sod., 10g carb. (8g sugars, 0 fiber), 0 pro.

Ham & Cheese Biscuit Stacks

These finger sandwiches are a pretty addition to any spread, yet filling enough to satisfy hearty appetites. I've served them at holidays, showers and tailgate parties.
—*Kelly Williams, Forked River, NJ*

PREP: 1 hour • **BAKE:** 10 min. + cooling
MAKES: 40 appetizers

- 4 tubes (6 oz. each) small refrigerated flaky biscuits (5 count each)
- ¼ cup stone-ground mustard

ASSEMBLY
- ½ cup butter, softened
- ¼ cup chopped green onions
- ½ cup stone-ground mustard
- ¼ cup mayonnaise
- ¼ cup honey
- 10 thick slices deli ham, quartered
- 10 slices Swiss cheese, quartered
- 2½ cups shredded romaine
- 20 pitted ripe olives, drained and patted dry
- 20 pimiento-stuffed olives, drained and patted dry
- 40 decorative toothpicks

1. Preheat oven to 400°. Cut biscuits in half to make half-circles; place 2 in. apart on ungreased baking sheets. Spread mustard over tops. Bake until golden brown, 8-10 minutes. Cool completely on wire racks.

2. Mix the softened butter and green onions. In another bowl, mix mustard, mayonnaise and honey. Split each biscuit into 2 layers.

3. Spread biscuit bottoms with butter mixture; top with ham, cheese, romaine and biscuit tops. Spoon mustard mixture over tops. Thread 1 olive onto each toothpick; insert into stacks. Serve immediately.

1 APPETIZER 121 cal., 7g fat (3g sat. fat), 16mg chol., 412mg sod., 11g carb. (2g sugars, 0 fiber), 4g pro.

NOTES

Old-Fashioned

It's hard to beat a classic cocktail like the old-fashioned. A spear of maraschino cherries makes an appealing garnish.
—*Caroline Stanko, Milwaukee, WI*

TAKES: 5 min. • **MAKES:** 1 serving

- 1 sugar cube or 1 tsp. sugar
- 1-2 dashes Angostura bitters
- 1-2 dashes water
- Ice cubes
- 1½ oz. whiskey
- Optional: Orange peel and maraschino cherries

In a rocks glass, muddle sugar, bitters and water. Add ice and whiskey. Stir until whiskey is chilled. If desired, garnish with orange peel and cherries.

1 SERVING 114 cal., 0 fat (0 sat. fat), 0 chol., 0 sod., 4g carb. (4g sugars, 0 fiber), 0 pro.

Ham & Pickle Wraps

I decided to try making these for my card club, and they loved it. The recipe can be swapped around and changed in so many different ways, and it always turns out. What an easy, great-tasting centerpiece over a hand of cards.
—*Detra Little, Moultrie, GA*

PREP: 10 min. + chilling • **MAKES:** 1 dozen

- 2 oz. cream cheese, softened
- 1½ tsp. spicy ranch salad dressing mix
- 2 slices deli ham
- 2 whole dill pickles

In a small bowl, combine cream cheese and dressing mix. Spread over ham slices. Place a pickle on each ham slice. Roll up tightly; wrap and refrigerate for at least 1 hour or until firm. Cut each wrap into 6 slices.

1 PIECE 24 cal., 2g fat (1g sat. fat), 6mg chol., 243mg sod., 1g carb. (0 sugars, 0 fiber), 1g pro.

Wow! These go back about 30 years. My mom used to make them, and I've made them for gatherings at my home! An oldie but goodie for sure!
—CALECIAN, TASTEOFHOME.COM

SWISS CHEESE
FONDUE

Swiss Cheese Fondue

This rich and fancy fondue is a fantastic appetizer for the holidays. Or let it warm you up on a wintry day. Don't be surprised when the pot is scraped clean!
—Taste of Home *Test Kitchen*

TAKES: 30 min. • **MAKES:** about 4 cups

- 1   garlic clove, halved
- 2   cups white wine, chicken broth or unsweetened apple juice, divided
- ¼   tsp. ground nutmeg
- 7   cups shredded Swiss cheese
- 2   Tbsp. cornstarch
     Cubed bread and assorted fresh vegetables

1. Rub garlic clove over the bottom and side of a fondue pot; discard garlic and set fondue pot aside. In a large saucepan over medium-low heat, bring 1¾ cups wine and nutmeg to a simmer. Gradually add cheese, stirring after each addition until cheese is melted (the cheese will separate from wine).

2. Combine cornstarch and remaining wine until smooth; gradually stir into cheese mixture. Cook and stir until thickened and mixture is blended and smooth. Transfer to prepared fondue pot and keep warm. Serve with bread cubes and vegetables.

¼ CUP 214 cal., 15g fat (9g sat. fat), 44mg chol., 90mg sod., 2g carb. (0 sugars, 0 fiber), 13g pro.

Tequila Sunrise

Everyone loves the pretty sunset layers in this refreshing cocktail classic. It's like a mini vacation in a glass!
—Taste of Home *Test Kitchen*

TAKES: 5 min. • **MAKES:** 1 serving

- 1   to 1¼ cups ice cubes
- 1½ oz. tequila
- 4½ oz. orange juice
- 1½ tsp. grenadine syrup
     Optional garnish: Orange slice and maraschino cherry

Place ice in a Collins or highball glass. Pour the tequila and orange juice into the glass. Slowly pour grenadine over a bar spoon into the center of the drink. Garnish as desired.

¾ CUP 184 cal., 0 fat (0 sat. fat), 0 chol., 0 sod., 17g carb. (15g sugars, 0 fiber), 1g pro.

HOW TO BUILD A RETRO BAR CART
Jazzing things up with a vintage bar cart is a snap!

If you don't have a bar cart, look for retro models at secondhand stores, estate sales and auctions. While you're at it, keep an eye out for cool ice buckets, glasses, martini shakers and bar tool sets.

Add 2-4 bottles of vodka, whiskey, rum, tequila and gin to your cart. It's also good to have a liquor or two on hand for classic cocktails, like vermouth for martinis. Include bitters, simple syrup, grenadine and sour mix.

Add tonic water, club soda, cola and lemon-lime sodas, and fruit juices. Include small bowls of lemon and lime wedges as well as olives and maraschino cherries, and your bar is set!

Watermelon & Blackberry Sangria

This recipe is deliciously pink! Living in the zinfandel wine country of Northern California's Gold Country, I use our local fare in my recipes often. Our scorching summer months of July and August inspired this refreshing, light style of sangria. I like to garnish it with sprigs of mint or basil for personal flair. This easy recipe is perfect for entertaining, and it's especially brunch friendly.
—*Carolyn Kumpe, El Dorado, CA*

PREP: 5 min. + chilling
MAKES: 8 servings

 1 bottle (750 ml) white zinfandel or
    rose wine, chilled
 ¼ cup watermelon schnapps liqueur
 1½ cups cubed seedless watermelon
    (½-in. cubes)
 1 medium lime, thinly sliced
 ½ to 1 cup fresh blackberries, halved
 1 can (12 oz.) lemon-lime soda, chilled
    Ice cubes
    Fresh basil or mint leaves

In a large pitcher, stir together wine and schnapps; add watermelon, lime and blackberries. Chill at least 2 hours. Just before serving, stir in soda. Serve over ice. Garnish with basil or mint.

¾ CUP 119 cal., 0 fat (0 sat. fat), 0 chol., 10mg sod., 12g carb. (8g sugars, 1g fiber), 0 pro.

MIX IT UP
It's easy to mix up this sangria with the summery flavors of peach and raspberry. Simply substitute peach schnapps or raspberry liquor for the melon liquor, and use fresh peaches and raspberries instead of the watermelon and blackberries. You can also add sprigs of fresh herbs to the sangria. Mint, basil, lemon verbena and lemon balm are all tasty yet easy options.

Cheese & Pimiento Spread

My mother made delicious pimiento cheese, but this is a spicy, modern version of her recipe. Serve it stuffed in celery, or spread on crackers or a sandwich.
—*Elizabeth Hester, Elizabethtown, NC*

TAKES: 15 min. • **MAKES:** 2¾ cups

 12 oz. sharp white cheddar cheese
 8 oz. reduced-fat cream cheese,
    softened
 2 tsp. Worcestershire sauce
 2 tsp. white vinegar
 ¼ tsp. white pepper
 ¼ tsp. garlic powder
 ¼ tsp. cayenne pepper
 1 jar (4 oz.) diced pimientos, undrained
    Assorted crackers and vegetables

Shred the cheddar cheese; transfer to a large bowl. Add cream cheese, Worcestershire sauce, vinegar, pepper, garlic powder and cayenne; beat on low speed until blended. Drain pimientos, reserving 2 Tbsp. juice. Stir in pimientos and reserved juice. Serve with crackers and vegetables.

2 TBSP. 90 cal., 7g fat (4g sat. fat), 23mg chol., 150mg sod., 1g carb. (1g sugars, 0 fiber), 5g pro.

Bloody Mary

Horseradish makes this one of the best Bloody Mary recipes in the world. Without the horseradish, you'll have a more traditional drink, and without the alcohol, you'll have a Virgin Mary. Serve with a stalk of celery, dill pickle spear or olives.
—Taste of Home *Test Kitchen*

TAKES: 10 min. • **MAKES:** 1 serving

- ¼ tsp. plus ⅛ tsp. celery salt, divided
- 1½ to 2 cups ice cubes, divided
- 2 oz. vodka
- 1 cup tomato juice, chilled
- 1 Tbsp. lemon juice
- 1½ tsp. lime juice
- ¾ tsp. Worcestershire sauce
- ½ tsp. prepared horseradish, optional
- ⅛ tsp. pepper
- ⅛ tsp. hot pepper sauce

OPTIONAL GARNISHES
Celery rib, pickle spear, green and ripe olives, cucumber slice and/or cocktail shrimp

1. Using water, moisten rim of a highball glass. Sprinkle ¼ tsp. celery salt on a small plate; dip rim into salt. Discard remaining celery salt from plate. Fill a shaker three-fourths full with ice. Place remaining ice in prepared glass.

2. Add vodka, juices, Worcestershire sauce, horseradish if desired, pepper, the remaining celery salt and pepper sauce to shaker; cover and shake until condensation forms on exterior, 10-15 seconds. Strain into prepared glass. Garnish as desired.

1½ CUPS 180 cal., 1g fat (0 sat. fat), 0 chol., 1110mg sod., 12g carb. (7g sugars, 1g fiber), 2g pro.

Mai Tai

This party favorite has been around for quite some time. It's not overly fruity and features a good blend of sweet and sour. For a splash of color, garnish with strawberries and lime.
—Taste of Home *Test Kitchen*

TAKES: 5 min. • **MAKES:** 1 serving

- 1½ to 2 cups ice cubes
- 2 oz. light rum
- ¾ oz. triple sec
- ½ oz. lemon juice
- 1½ tsp. lime juice
- 1½ tsp. amaretto
  Optional garnish: Lime slice, lime twist, edible flowers and fresh pineapple

1. Fill a shaker three-fourths full with ice. Place the remaining ice in a rocks glass; set aside.

2. Add the rum, triple sec, juices and amaretto to shaker; cover and shake for 10-15 seconds or until condensation forms on outside of shaker. Strain into prepared glass. Garnish as desired.

⅔ CUP 241 cal., 0 fat (0 sat. fat), 0 chol., 7mg sod., 15g carb. (13g sugars, 0 fiber), 0 pro.

Oysters Rockefeller

My husband and I delight guests with this classic dish that originated in New Orleans. It's deliciously simple!
—*Beth Walton, Eastham, MA*

PREP: 1¼ hours • **BAKE:** 10 min.
MAKES: 3 dozen

- 1 medium onion, finely chopped
- ½ cup butter, cubed
- 1 pkg. (9 oz.) fresh spinach, torn
- 1 cup grated Romano cheese
- 1 Tbsp. lemon juice
- ⅛ tsp. pepper
- 2 lbs. kosher salt
- 3 dozen fresh oysters in the shell, washed

1. In a large skillet, saute onion in butter until tender. Add spinach; cook and stir until wilted. Remove from the heat; stir in cheese, lemon juice and pepper.

2. Spread kosher salt into 2 ungreased 15x10x1-in. baking pans. Shuck oysters, reserving oyster and its liquid in bottom shell. Lightly press oyster shells down into the salt, using salt to keep oysters level. Top each with 2½ tsp. spinach mixture.

3. Bake, uncovered, at 450° until the oysters are plump, 6-8 minutes. Serve immediately.

1 OYSTER 79 cal., 5g fat (3g sat. fat), 35mg chol., 133mg sod., 3g carb. (0 sugars, 0 fiber), 6g pro.

OYSTERS ROCKEFELLER RECIPE TIPS

How many oysters do you need per person?
If you're serving Oysters Rockefeller as an appetizer, plan on 2 to 3 oysters per guest. For other oyster recipes, serving sizes may vary.

How do you know when oysters are done?
Oysters are done cooking once they become nice and plump, and the edges start to curl.

What goes well with oysters?
A thick, chewy bread always goes well with oysters!

5-MINUTE BEER
P. 37

Best-Loved Snacks & Appetizers

Classic Texas Caviar

I adapted this Texas caviar from one in a cookbook I received a long time ago, and now I can't imagine a get-together at my house without this quick and healthy appetizer.
—*Becky Oliver, Fairplay, CO*

PREP: 20 min. + chilling • **MAKES:** 5 cups

- 2 cans (15½ oz. each) black-eyed peas, rinsed and drained
- 1 can (10 oz.) diced tomatoes and green chiles, drained
- 1 medium green pepper, finely chopped
- 1 cup fresh whole kernel corn or frozen shoepeg corn, thawed
- 1 small red onion, finely chopped
- ½ cup Italian salad dressing
- 2 Tbsp. lime juice
- ¼ tsp. salt
- ¼ tsp. pepper
- 1 medium ripe avocado, peeled and cubed
  Tortilla chips

1. In a large bowl, combine the peas, tomatoes, green pepper, corn and onion. In a small bowl, whisk dressing, lime juice, salt and pepper. Pour over the black-eyed pea mixture and stir to coat. Cover and refrigerate for at least 1 hour.

2. Stir in avocado just before serving. Serve with chips.

¼ CUP 68 cal., 2g fat (0 sat. fat), 0 chol., 200mg sod., 10g carb. (2g sugars, 2g fiber), 3g pro. **DIABETIC EXCHANGES** ½ starch, ½ fat.

Hearty Rye Melts

When we moved from the Midwest to Kentucky, we were invited to a neighborhood gathering where this appetizer was served. Hanky panky—as it's often called around here—is traditionally served at Derby Day parties, but at our home it's become a year-round favorite.
—*Melanie Schlaf, Edgewood, KY*

TAKES: 30 min. • **MAKES:** 2 dozen

- ½ lb. lean ground beef (90% lean)
- ½ lb. bulk pork sausage
- 1½ tsp. chili powder
- 8 oz. Velveeta, shredded
- 24 slices snack rye bread
  Chopped fresh parsley

1. In a large skillet, cook beef and sausage over medium heat until no longer pink, 5-7 minutes, breaking into crumbles; drain. Add chili powder and cheese; cook and stir until cheese is melted. Spread 1 heaping Tbsp. on each slice of bread. Place on a baking sheet.

2. Bake at 350° for 12-15 minutes or until edges of bread begin to crisp. Garnish with parsley. Serve warm.

1 PIECE 88 cal., 6g fat (2g sat. fat), 20mg chol., 231mg sod., 4g carb. (1g sugars, 0 fiber), 5g pro.

PARTY FRANKS

Party Franks

These tiny, tangy appetizers have broad appeal. I prepare them often for holiday gatherings, weddings and family reunions. They're convenient to serve at parties since the sauce can be made ahead and then reheated with the franks before serving.
—Lucille Howell, Portland, OR

PREP: 30 min. • **BAKE:** 20 min.
MAKES: 16 servings

- ¾ cup chopped onion
- 2 Tbsp. canola oil
- 1 cup ketchup
- ½ cup water
- ½ cup cider vinegar
- 2 Tbsp. sugar
- 2 Tbsp. Worcestershire sauce
- 2 Tbsp. honey
- 2 tsp. ground mustard
- 2 tsp. paprika
- ¾ tsp. salt
- ¼ tsp. pepper
- ⅛ tsp. hot pepper sauce
- 1 large lemon, sliced
- 2½ to 3 lbs. miniature hot dogs or smoked sausage links

In a saucepan, saute onion in oil until tender. Stir in the next 11 ingredients. Add lemon. Bring to a boil. Reduce heat; simmer, uncovered, until slightly thickened, 20-25 minutes, stirring occasionally. Discard lemon slices. Place hot dogs in a 13x9-in. baking dish. Top with sauce. Bake, uncovered, at 350° until heated through, 18-20 minutes. Keep warm; serve with toothpicks.

⅓ CUP 268 cal., 21g fat (7g sat. fat), 45mg chol., 1047mg sod., 11g carb. (9g sugars, 0 fiber), 9g pro.

NOTES

_____

_____

_____

_____

_____

_____

_____

Salmon Mousse Canapes

It's so easy to top crunchy cucumber slices with a smooth and creamy salmon filling. Guests rave about the fun presentation, contrasting textures and refreshing flavor.
—Barb Templin, Norwood, MN

TAKES: 30 min. • **MAKES:** about 3 dozen

- 2 English cucumbers
- 1 pkg. (8 oz.) cream cheese, softened
- ½ lb. smoked salmon or lox
- 1 Tbsp. 2% milk
- 1 tsp. lemon-pepper seasoning
- 1 tsp. snipped fresh dill
  Salt and pepper to taste
- ½ cup heavy whipping cream
  Additional snipped fresh dill

1. Peel strips from cucumbers to create a decorative edge; cut cucumbers into ½-in. slices. Using a melon baller, remove a small amount of cucumber from the center, carefully leaving the bottom intact.

2. Place the cream cheese, salmon, milk, lemon pepper and dill in a food processor; cover and process until blended. Transfer to a small bowl and season with salt and pepper. In another bowl, beat cream until stiff peaks form. Fold into salmon mixture.

3. Pipe or dollop mousse onto cucumber slices; garnish with dill. Refrigerate until ready to serve.

1 CANAPE 42 cal., 4g fat (2g sat. fat), 12mg chol., 72mg sod., 1g carb. (1g sugars, 0 fiber), 2g pro.

Cathedral Cookies

Children love the colorful marshmallows in these festive confections. The snacks look like stained glass when they're sliced. They practically light up the room from the serving platter at parties.
—Carol Shaffer, Cape Girardeau, MO

PREP: 10 min. + freezing
COOK: 10 min. + chilling
MAKES: about 5 dozen

- 1   cup semisweet chocolate chips
- 2   Tbsp. butter
- 1   large egg, room temperature, lightly beaten
- 3   cups pastel miniature marshmallows
- ½   cup chopped pecans or walnuts
- 1   cup sweetened shredded coconut

1. In top of a double boiler or a metal bowl over simmering water, melt the chocolate chips and butter over low heat, stirring occasionally. Stir a small amount into the egg, then return all to pan. Cook and stir over low heat for 2 minutes. Pour into a bowl; let cool for 15 minutes. Gently stir in the marshmallows and chopped nuts. Refrigerate for 30 minutes.

2. On a sheet of waxed paper, shape mixture into a 1½-in.-diameter log. Place the coconut on another sheet of waxed paper. Gently roll log over coconut to coat sides. Wrap up tightly in waxed paper, twisting ends to seal.

3. Freeze for 4 hours or overnight. Remove waxed paper. Cut dough into ¼-in. slices. Store in an airtight container in the refrigerator.

1 COOKIE 40 cal., 3g fat (1g sat. fat), 4mg chol., 11mg sod., 5g carb. (4g sugars, 0 fiber), 0 pro.

Cranberry Sauerkraut Meatballs

I tried these meatballs at a birthday party for a friend, and now I make them all the time. They are super easy to make and perfect for a potluck or a Sunday afternoon football game.
—Lisa Castelli, Pleasant Prairie, WI

PREP: 15 min. • **COOK:** 4 hours
MAKES: about 5 dozen

- 1   can (14 oz.) whole-berry cranberry sauce
- 1   can (14 oz.) sauerkraut, rinsed and well drained
- 1   bottle (12 oz.) chili sauce
- ¾   cup packed brown sugar
- 1   pkg. (32 oz.) frozen fully cooked home-style meatballs, thawed
      Minced chives, optional

In a 4-qt. slow cooker, combine the cranberry sauce, sauerkraut, chili sauce and brown sugar. Stir in meatballs. Cover and cook on low until heated through, 4-5 hours. If desired, top with chives to serve.

1 MEATBALL WITH ABOUT 1 TBSP. SAUCE
76 cal., 4g fat (2g sat. fat), 6mg chol., 250mg sod., 8g carb. (6g sugars, 0 fiber), 2g pro.

66
I've had this recipe for years. Frozen meatballs make it easy, but you can make your own. I make my meatballs with ground turkey. It still tastes great, and it's a little healthier.
—IVONSMOM, TASTEOFHOME.COM

Mushroom Bundles

Phyllo dough makes easy work of these impressive appetizers. When I made these crispy bundles for New Year's Eve, they were gone in a flash.
—*Tina Coopman, Toronto, ON*

PREP: 30 min. • **BAKE:** 15 min.
MAKES: 1 dozen

- 1 Tbsp. olive oil
- 1 cup chopped fresh mushrooms
- 1 cup chopped baby portobello mushrooms
- ¼ cup finely chopped red onion
- 2 garlic cloves, minced
- ¼ tsp. dried rosemary, crushed
- ⅛ tsp. pepper
- 4 sheets phyllo dough (14x9-in. size)
- 3 Tbsp. butter, melted
- 2 Tbsp. crumbled feta cheese

1. Preheat oven to 375°. In a large skillet, heat oil over medium-high heat. Add mushrooms and onion; cook and stir 4-5 minutes or until tender. Add garlic, rosemary and pepper; cook 2 minutes longer. Remove from heat.

2. Place 1 sheet of phyllo dough on a work surface; brush with butter. (Keep remaining phyllo sheets covered with a damp towel to prevent them from drying out.) Layer with 3 additional phyllo sheets, brushing each layer. Using a sharp knife, cut the layered sheets into twelve 3-in. squares. Carefully press each stack into an ungreased mini-muffin cup.

3. Stir feta into the mushroom mixture; spoon 1 Tbsp. into each phyllo cup. Form into bundles by gathering edges of phyllo squares and twisting centers to close. Brush tops with remaining butter. Bake 12-15 minutes or until golden brown. Serve warm.

FREEZE OPTION Freeze cooled bundles in freezer containers. To use, reheat bundles on a greased baking sheet in a preheated 375° oven until crisp and heated through.

1 PASTRY 53 cal., 4g fat (2g sat. fat), 8mg chol., 50mg sod., 3g carb. (1g sugars, 0 fiber), 1g pro.

Hot Spinach Spread with Pita Chips

Warm and cheesy, this spread is absolutely scrumptious served on toasted pita wedges. Its colorful appearance makes a stunning addition to any buffet.
—*Teresa Emanuel, Smithville, MO*

PREP: 30 min. • **BAKE:** 20 min.
MAKES: 16 servings (4 cups spread)

- 2 cups shredded Monterey Jack cheese
- 1 pkg. (10 oz.) frozen chopped spinach, thawed and squeezed dry
- 1 pkg. (8 oz.) cream cheese, cubed
- 2 plum tomatoes, seeded and chopped
- ¾ cup chopped onion
- ⅓ cup half-and-half cream
- 1 Tbsp. finely chopped seeded jalapeno pepper
- 6 pita breads (6 in.)
- ½ cup butter, melted
- 2 tsp. lemon-pepper seasoning
- 2 tsp. ground cumin
- ¼ tsp. garlic salt

1. In a large bowl, combine the first 7 ingredients. Transfer to a greased 1½-qt. baking dish. Bake, uncovered, at 375° for 20-25 minutes or until bubbly.

2. Meanwhile, cut each pita bread into 8 wedges. Place in two 15x10x1-in. baking pans. Combine the butter, lemon pepper, cumin and garlic salt; brush over pita wedges.

3. Bake for 7-9 minutes or until crisp. Serve with spinach spread.

NOTE Wear disposable gloves when cutting hot peppers; the oils can burn skin. Avoid touching your face.

¼ CUP SPREAD WITH 3 PITA WEDGES
231 cal., 16g fat (10g sat. fat), 46mg chol., 381mg sod., 15g carb. (1g sugars, 1g fiber), 8g pro.

Cucumber Party Sandwiches

This is one of my favorite appetizers. We have lots of pig roasts here in Kentucky, and these retro sandwiches are perfect to serve while the pig is cooking.
—*Rebecca Rose, Mount Washington, KY*

PREP: 20 min. + standing
MAKES: 2½ dozen

- 1 pkg. (8 oz.) cream cheese, softened
- 2 Tbsp. mayonnaise
- 2 tsp. Italian salad dressing mix
- 30 slices cocktail rye or pumpernickel bread
- 60 thin cucumber slices
  Optional: Fresh dill sprigs, slivered red pearl onions and cracked black pepper

1. Beat cream cheese, mayonnaise and dressing mix until blended; let stand for 30 minutes.

2. Spread cream cheese mixture on bread. Top each with 2 cucumber slices and, if desired, dill, red onion and pepper. Refrigerate, covered, until serving.

1 OPEN-FACED SANDWICH 53 cal., 4g fat (2g sat. fat), 8mg chol., 92mg sod., 4g carb. (1g sugars, 1g fiber), 1g pro.

Down-Home Hush Puppies

Hush puppies are a classic southern treat. The sweet-spicy flavor of these fried bites has delighted friends and family for decades.
—*Gene Pitts, Wilsonville, AL*

PREP: 15 min. + standing • **COOK:** 20 min.
MAKES: 2½ dozen

- 1 cup cornmeal
- 1 cup self-rising flour
- 1½ tsp. baking powder
- ½ tsp. salt
- 1 large onion, chopped
- 2 jalapeno peppers, seeded and diced
- ¼ cup sugar
- 1 large egg, room temperature
- 1 cup buttermilk
  Oil for deep-fat frying

1. In a large bowl, combine the first 7 ingredients. Add the egg and buttermilk; stir just until moistened. Let stand at room temperature for 30 minutes. Do not stir again.

2. In an electric skillet or deep fryer, heat 2-3 in. oil to 375°. Gently drop the batter by rounded tablespoonfuls, a few at a time, into hot oil. Fry until golden brown, about 1½ minutes on each side. Drain on paper towels.

NOTE As a substitute for 1 cup of self-rising flour, place 1½ tsp. baking powder and ½ tsp. salt in a measuring cup. Add all-purpose flour to measure 1 cup. Wear disposable gloves when cutting hot peppers; the oils can burn skin. Avoid touching your face.

1 HUSH PUPPY 73 cal., 3g fat (0 sat. fat), 7mg chol., 132mg sod., 10g carb. (2g sugars, 0 fiber), 1g pro.

Oven-Fried Pickles

Like deep-fried pickles? You'll love this easy unfried version even more. Dill pickle slices are coated with panko bread crumbs and spices, then baked until crispy. Dip them with ranch dressing for an appetizer you won't soon forget.
—*Nick Iverson, Denver, CO*

PREP: 20 min. + standing • **BAKE:** 20 min.
MAKES: 8 servings

- 32 dill pickle slices
- ½ cup all-purpose flour
- ½ tsp. salt
- 2 large eggs, lightly beaten
- 2 Tbsp. dill pickle juice
- ½ tsp. cayenne pepper
- ½ tsp. garlic powder
- ½ cup panko bread crumbs
- 1 Tbsp. snipped fresh dill

1. Preheat oven to 500°. Let pickle slices stand on a paper towel until liquid is almost completely absorbed, about 15 minutes.

2. Meanwhile, in a shallow bowl, combine flour and salt. In another shallow bowl, whisk eggs, pickle juice, cayenne and garlic powder. Combine panko and dill in a third shallow bowl.

3. Dip pickles into flour mixture to coat both sides; shake off excess. Dip into egg mixture, then into crumb mixture, patting to help coating adhere. Transfer to a greased wire rack in a rimmed baking sheet.

4. Bake until golden brown and crispy, 20-25 minutes.

1 PIECE 16 cal., 0 fat (0 sat. fat), 12mg chol., 105mg sod., 2g carb. (0 sugars, 0 fiber), 1g pro.

Orange-Pistachio Divinity

Old-fashioned divinity candy is even yummier with a hint of refreshing orange zest and bits of crunchy pistachios. Store-bought versions just can't compare!
—*Lorri Reinhardt, Big Bend, WI*

PREP: 15 min. • **COOK:** 20 min. + standing
MAKES: about 4 dozen (1⅓ lbs.)

- 2 large egg whites
- 2⅔ cups sugar
- ⅔ cup light corn syrup
- ½ cup water
- 1 tsp. grated orange zest
- 1 tsp. vanilla extract
- ⅔ cup pistachios, coarsely chopped

1. Place egg whites in bowl of a stand mixer; let stand at room temperature for 30 minutes. Meanwhile, line two 15x10x1-in. pans with waxed paper.

2. In a large heavy saucepan, combine sugar, corn syrup and water; cook and stir until sugar is dissolved and mixture comes to a boil. Cook, without stirring, over medium heat until a thermometer reads 252° (hard-ball stage). Just before that temperature is reached, beat the egg whites on medium speed until stiff peaks form.

3. With mixer continuing to run on high speed, slowly add hot sugar mixture in a thin stream over egg whites, beating constantly and scraping sides of bowl occasionally. Add orange zest and vanilla. Beat until candy holds its shape and begins to lose its gloss, 5-6 minutes. (Do not overbeat, or candy will stiffen and crumble.) Immediately fold in the pistachios.

4. Quickly drop the mixture by tablespoonfuls onto prepared pans. Let stand at room temperature until dry to the touch. Store between layers of waxed paper in an airtight container at room temperature.

1 PIECE 68 cal., 1g fat (0 sat. fat), 0 chol., 13mg sod., 15g carb. (15g sugars, 0 fiber), 1g pro.

JUST BEAT IT
Beating divinity can be tricky. It's important to beat the egg whites and sugar syrup sufficiently, but if you overbeat, the whites will break down and the mixture will become grainy. When it just starts to lose its sheen, that's your cue to stop beating. For best results, use a stand mixer. It beats more evenly than a hand mixer and will save wear and tear on your arm!

Bacon Cream Cheese Pinwheels

It's hard to resist a crescent roll, bacon and cream cheese in one bite! Kids, friends—everyone—will scarf down these cream cheese pinwheels. Now I bake a double batch whenever we have a get-together.
—*Krista Munson, Sharpsburg, KY*

TAKES: 30 min. • **MAKES:** 2 dozen

- 3 oz. cream cheese, softened
- 2 Tbsp. finely chopped onion
- 1 tsp. 2% milk
- 1 tube (8 oz.) refrigerated crescent rolls
- 5 bacon strips, cooked and finely chopped

1. Preheat oven to 375°. In a small bowl, mix cream cheese, onion and milk until blended. On a lightly floured surface, unroll the crescent dough into 1 long rectangle; press perforations to seal.

2. Spread with cream cheese mixture; sprinkle with bacon. Roll up jelly-roll style, starting with a long side; pinch seam to seal. Using a serrated knife, cut roll crosswise into twenty-four ½-in. slices. Place on ungreased baking sheets, cut side down.

3. Bake 12-15 minutes or until golden brown. Refrigerate leftovers.

1 APPETIZER 58 cal., 4g fat (2g sat. fat), 6mg chol., 116mg sod., 4g carb. (1g sugars, 0 fiber), 1g pro.

5-Minute Beer Dip

Ranch dressing mix flavors this fast-to-fix mixture packed with shredded cheese and made to go with pretzels. Once you start eating it, you can't stop!
—*Michelle Long, New Castle, CO*

TAKES: 5 min. • **MAKES:** 3½ cups

- 2 pkg. (8 oz. each) cream cheese, softened
- ⅓ cup beer or nonalcoholic beer
- 1 envelope ranch salad dressing mix
- 2 cups shredded cheddar cheese
  Pretzels

In a large bowl, beat the cream cheese, beer and dressing mix until smooth. Stir in cheddar cheese. Serve with pretzels.

2 TBSP. 93 cal., 8g fat (5g sat. fat), 24mg chol., 184mg sod., 2g carb. (1g sugars, 0 fiber), 3g pro.

Super easy and quick to make. I made this a day ahead and served it with mini pretzels. It's a perfect snack to serve when you're having friends over or to take to a party. I used a Pilsner in this recipe, and it was perfect!
—CHRISTINE, TASTEOFHOME.COM

AUNT BETTY'S
BLUEBERRY MUFFINS, P. 52

Golden Breads, Biscuits & More

Mom's Buttermilk Biscuits

These fluffy biscuits are so tasty served warm, slathered with butter or used to mop every last drop of gravy off your plate. I can still see my mom pulling these biscuits out of the oven.
—*Vera Reid, Laramie, WY*

TAKES: 30 min. • **MAKES:** 10 servings

- 2 cups all-purpose flour
- 2 tsp. baking powder
- ½ tsp. baking soda
- ½ tsp. salt
- ¼ cup shortening
- ¾ cup buttermilk

Preheat oven to 450°. In a bowl, combine flour, baking powder, baking soda and salt; cut in shortening until the mixture resembles coarse crumbs. Stir in the buttermilk; knead dough gently. Roll out to ½-in. thickness. Cut with a 2½-in. biscuit cutter and place on a lightly greased baking sheet. Bake until golden brown, 10-15 minutes.

FREEZE OPTION Freeze cooled biscuits in a resealable freezer container. To use, heat in a preheated 350° oven 15-20 minutes.

1 BISCUIT 142 cal., 5g fat (1g sat. fat), 1mg chol., 281mg sod., 20g carb. (1g sugars, 1g fiber), 3g pro.

Swirled Cinnamon Raisin Bread

My mother received this recipe from a friend in West Virginia. We have found that slices of the warm cinnamon bread and a cup of hot tea work wonders for holiday visitors in our home.
—*Joan Ort, Milford, NJ*

PREP: 25 min. + rising • **BAKE:** 45 min.
MAKES: 2 loaves (16 pieces each)

- 2 pkg. (¼ oz. each) active dry yeast
- 2 cups warm water (110° to 115°)
- 1 cup sugar, divided
- ¼ cup canola oil
- 2 tsp. salt
- 2 large eggs
- 6 to 6½ cups all-purpose flour
- 1 cup raisins
  Additional canola oil
- 3 tsp. ground cinnamon

1. In a large bowl, dissolve yeast in warm water. Add ½ cup sugar, oil, salt, eggs and 4 cups flour. Beat until smooth. Stir in enough of the remaining flour to form a soft dough.

2. Turn out onto a floured surface; knead until smooth and elastic, about 6-8 minutes. Place in a greased bowl, turning once to grease top. Cover and let rise in a warm place or until doubled, about 1 hour.

3. Punch dough down. Turn out onto a lightly floured surface; divide in half. Knead ½ cup raisins into each; roll each portion into a 15x9-in. rectangle. Brush with additional oil. Combine cinnamon and remaining ½ cup sugar; sprinkle to within ½ in. of edges.

4. Tightly roll up, jelly-roll style, starting with a short side; pinch seam to seal. Place, seam side down, in 2 greased 9x5-in. loaf pans. Cover and let rise until doubled, about 30 minutes.

5. Preheat oven to 375°. Brush with oil. Bake 45-50 minutes or until golden brown. Remove from pans to wire racks to cool.

1 PIECE 145 cal., 2g fat (0 sat. fat), 12mg chol., 153mg sod., 28g carb. (9g sugars, 1g fiber), 3g pro.

MOM'S BUTTERMILK
BISCUITS

Giant Cinnamon Rolls

As a newlywed, I took it upon myself to make cinnamon rolls because I thought that was the hallmark of a good baker. The rolls were like hockey pucks and flavorless. Our dear black lab, Annie, wouldn't even eat one! So I practiced for months—finally, I entered a contest at the Iowa State Fair, and I won!
—*Cristen Clark, Runnells, IA*

PREP: 45 min. + rising
BAKE: 25 min. + cooling
MAKES: 1 dozen

- 2 pkg. (¼ oz. each) quick-rise yeast
- ½ cup warm water (110° to 115°)
- 2 tsp. honey
- 1½ cups warm 2% milk (110° to 115°)
- ½ cup sugar
- ½ cup butter, softened
- ½ cup mashed potatoes
- 3 large eggs, room temperature, lightly beaten
- 2 tsp. salt
- 7½ to 8 cups all-purpose flour

FILLING
- 1 cup packed brown sugar
- 2 Tbsp. ground cinnamon
- 1½ tsp. all-purpose flour
  Dash salt
- ½ cup butter, softened

VANILLA ICING
- 3 cups confectioners' sugar
- ¼ cup 2% milk
- 1 tsp. vanilla bean paste or vanilla extract
  Dash salt

1. In a small bowl, dissolve yeast in warm water and honey. In a large bowl, combine milk, sugar, butter, potatoes, eggs, salt, yeast mixture and 4 cups flour; beat on medium speed until smooth. Stir in enough remaining flour to form a soft dough (dough will be sticky). Turn out dough onto a floured surface; knead until smooth and elastic, 6-8 minutes. Place in a greased large bowl, turning once to grease the top. Cover and let rise in a warm place until doubled, about 1 hour.

2. For filling, combine brown sugar, cinnamon, flour and salt. Punch down dough. Turn out onto a lightly floured surface; roll out into a 24x12-in. rectangle. Spread butter to within ½ in. of edges; sprinkle with brown sugar mixture. Roll up jelly-roll style, starting with a long side; pinch seam to seal. Cut into 12 slices. Place in 2 greased 13x9-in. baking pans (6 slices per pan), cut side down. Cover with kitchen towels; let rise in a warm place until doubled, about 30 minutes.

3. Preheat oven to 350°. Bake until lightly browned, 25-30 minutes, covering loosely with foil during the last 10 minutes of baking. Cool in pan 30 minutes. In a small bowl, mix icing ingredients; drizzle over rolls.

1 ROLL 695 cal., 18g fat (11g sat. fat), 90mg chol., 588mg sod., 122g carb. (59g sugars, 3g fiber), 11g pro.

Dutch-Oven Bread

This crackling homemade bread requires only 15 minutes of hands-on work. Enjoy the beautiful crusty bread recipe as is, or stir in a few favorites such as cheese, garlic, herbs and dried fruits.
—*Catherine Ward, Mequon, WI*

PREP: 15 min. + rising
BAKE: 45 min. + cooling
MAKES: 1 loaf (16 pieces)

3 to 3½ cups (125 grams per cup) all-purpose flour
1 tsp. active dry yeast
1 tsp. salt
1½ cups water (70° to 75°)

1. In a large bowl, whisk 3 cups flour, yeast and salt. Stir in water and enough remaining flour to form a moist, shaggy dough. Do not knead. Cover and let rise in a cool place until doubled, 7-8 hours.

2. Preheat oven to 450°; place a Dutch oven with lid on center rack and heat for at least 30 minutes. Once Dutch oven is heated, turn out dough onto a generously floured surface. Using a metal scraper or spatula, quickly shape into a round loaf. Gently place on a piece of parchment.

3. Using a sharp knife, make a ¼-in.-deep slash across top of loaf. Using the parchment, immediately lower bread into heated Dutch oven. Cover; bake for 30 minutes. Uncover and bake until bread is deep golden brown and sounds hollow when tapped, 15-20 minutes longer, partially covering if it's browning too much. Remove loaf from pan and cool completely on a wire rack.

1 PIECE 86 cal., 0 fat (0 sat. fat), 0 chol., 148mg sod., 18g carb. (0 sugars, 1g fiber), 3g pro.

TWICE THE TASTE
Double this recipe to make a bread that fills your entire Dutch oven. In a large bowl, whisk 6 cups flour, 2 tsp. active dry yeast and 2 tsp. salt. Stir in 3 cups water to form a soft, shaggy dough. Do not knead. Cover and let rise in a cool place until doubled, 7-8 hours. Proceed with recipe as directed.

Grandma's Sweet Potato Biscuits

The recipe for these mild-tasting biscuits was my grandmother's. They're a family favorite that we always serve at holidays.
—*Nancy Daugherty, Cortland, OH*

TAKES: 30 min. • **MAKES:** 1½ dozen

2½ cups all-purpose flour
1 Tbsp. baking powder
1 tsp. salt
⅓ cup shortening
1 can (15¾ oz.) sweet potatoes, drained
¾ cup 2% milk

1. Preheat oven to 425°. In a large bowl, combine the flour, baking powder and salt. Cut in shortening until mixture resembles coarse crumbs. In another bowl, mash the sweet potatoes and milk. Add to the crumb mixture just until combined.

2. Turn out onto a floured surface; knead 8-10 times. Roll to ½-in. thickness; cut with a 2½-in. biscuit cutter. Place on ungreased baking sheets.

3. Bake until golden brown, 8-10 minutes. Remove to wire racks. Serve warm.

1 BISCUIT 124 cal., 4g fat (1g sat. fat), 1mg chol., 214mg sod., 19g carb. (4g sugars, 1g fiber), 2g pro.

Easy Honey Muffins

I can remember my Grandma Wheeler making these delicious muffins—we'd eat them nice and warm, fresh from the oven! She was a pinch of this and handful of that kind of cook, so getting the ingredient amounts correct for the recipe was a challenge. Now it's a family treasure!
—*Darlis Wilfer, West Bend, WI*

TAKES: 30 min. • **MAKES:** 1 dozen

2 cups all-purpose flour
½ cup sugar
3 tsp. baking powder
½ tsp. salt
1 large egg, room temperature
1 cup 2% milk
¼ cup butter, melted
¼ cup honey

1. Preheat oven to 400°. In a large bowl, combine flour, sugar, baking powder and salt. In a small bowl, combine egg, milk, butter and honey. Stir into dry ingredients just until moistened.

2. Fill greased or paper-lined muffin cups three-fourths full. Bake until a toothpick inserted in center comes out clean, 15-18 minutes. Cool 5 minutes before removing from pan to a wire rack. Serve warm.

FREEZE OPTION Freeze cooled muffins in freezer containers. To use, thaw at room temperature or, if desired, microwave each muffin on high until heated through, 20-30 seconds.

1 MUFFIN 179 cal., 5g fat (3g sat. fat), 29mg chol., 242mg sod., 31g carb. (15g sugars, 1g fiber), 3g pro.

Grandma's Rosemary Dinner Rolls

My grandma used to make these in her coal oven. How she regulated the temperature is beyond me! She always made extra rolls for the neighbors to bake in their own ovens. My mom and aunts would go around delivering the formed rolls at lunchtime.
—*Charlotte Hendershot, Hudson, PA*

PREP: 35 min. + rising • **BAKE:** 20 min.
MAKES: 1 dozen

- 1 pkg. (¼ oz.) active dry yeast
- ¼ cup warm water (110° to 115°)
- 3 cups bread flour
- 2 Tbsp. sugar
- 1 Tbsp. minced fresh rosemary, divided
- ¾ tsp. salt
- ⅔ cup warm 2% milk (110° to 115°)
- 1 large egg, room temperature
- ¼ to ⅓ cup canola oil

EGG WASH
- 1 large egg yolk
- 2 Tbsp. 2% milk

1. In a small bowl, dissolve yeast in warm water. Place the flour, sugar, 2 tsp. rosemary and salt in a food processor; pulse until blended. Add the warm milk, egg and yeast mixture; cover and pulse 10 times or until almost blended.

2. While processing, gradually add oil just until dough pulls away from sides and begins to form a ball. Process 2 minutes longer to knead dough (dough will be very soft).

3. Transfer dough to a greased bowl, turning once to grease the top. Cover and let rise in a warm place until doubled, about 1 hour.

4. Punch down dough. Turn out onto a lightly floured surface; divide and shape into 12 balls. Roll each into a 15-in. rope. Starting at 1 end, loosely wrap dough around itself to form a coil. Tuck end under; pinch to seal.

5. Place 2 in. apart on greased baking sheets. Cover and let rise until doubled, about 30 minutes.

6. For egg wash, in a small bowl, whisk egg yolk and milk; brush over rolls. Sprinkle with remaining 1 tsp. rosemary. Bake at 350° until golden brown, 18-22 minutes. Remove from pans to wire racks; serve warm.

1 ROLL 194 cal., 6g fat (1g sat. fat), 32mg chol., 163mg sod., 28g carb. (3g sugars, 1g fiber), 6g pro.

NOTES

Old-Fashioned Batter Rolls

The first thing my guests ask when they come for dinner is if I'm serving these old-time dinner rolls. The buns are so light, airy and delicious that I'm constantly asked for the recipe.
—*Thomasina Brunner, Gloversville, NY*

PREP: 30 min. + rising • **BAKE:** 15 min.
MAKES: 1 dozen

- 3 cups all-purpose flour
- 2 Tbsp. sugar
- 1 pkg. (¼ oz.) active dry yeast
- 1 tsp. salt
- 1 cup water
- 2 Tbsp. butter
- 1 large egg, room temperature
  Melted butter

1. In a large mixer bowl, combine 2 cups flour, sugar, yeast and salt. In a saucepan, heat water and butter to 120°-130°. Add to dry ingredients; beat until blended. Add egg; beat on low speed for 30 seconds, then on high for 3 minutes. Stir in enough remaining flour to form a stiff dough. Do not knead. Cover and let rise in a warm place until doubled, about 30 minutes.

2. Stir dough down. Fill 12 greased muffin cups half full. Cover and let rise until doubled, about 15 minutes.

3. Bake at 350° until golden brown, 15-20 minutes. Cool 1 minute before removing from pan to a wire rack. Brush tops with melted butter.

FREEZE OPTION Freeze cooled rolls in airtight containers. To use, microwave each roll on high until warmed, 30-45 seconds.

1 ROLL 147 cal., 3g fat (1g sat. fat), 21mg chol., 219mg sod., 26g carb. (2g sugars, 1g fiber), 4g pro.

Poppy Seed Cheese Bread

This easy bread goes well with a salad lunch or a casserole dinner. But I especially like to serve it with spaghetti and pasta dishes.
—*Elaine Mundt, Detroit, MI*

PREP: 20 min. + rising • **BAKE:** 15 min.
MAKES: 15 servings

- 1 pkg. (¼ oz.) active dry yeast
- 2 tsp. sugar
- ¼ cup warm water (110° to 115°)
- ¾ cup warm whole milk (110° to 115°)
- 2 Tbsp. shortening
- 1 tsp. salt
- 2¼ to 2½ cups all-purpose flour

TOPPING
- 2 cups shredded cheddar cheese
- 1 large egg
- ⅓ cup whole milk
- 1 tsp. finely chopped onion
  Poppy seeds

1. Dissolve yeast and sugar in water. Combine milk, shortening and salt; stir into yeast mixture. Add enough flour to form a soft dough. Turn onto a floured surface; knead until smooth and elastic, about 3 minutes. Place in a greased bowl, turning once to grease the top. Cover and let rise in a warm place until doubled, about 1½ hours.

2. Punch down dough; press into a greased 13x9-in. baking pan. Cover and let rise in a warm place until doubled, about 45 minutes.

3. Preheat oven to 425°. Combine cheese, egg, milk and onion; spread over dough. Sprinkle with poppy seeds. Bake 15-20 minutes. Cut into squares; serve warm.

1 PIECE 163 cal., 8g fat (4g sat. fat), 30mg chol., 267mg sod., 16g carb. (2g sugars, 1g fiber), 7g pro.

Best-Ever Banana Bread

Whenever I pass a display of bananas in the grocery store, I can almost smell the wonderful aroma of this quick bread.
—*Gert Kaiser, Kenosha, WI*

PREP: 15 min. • **BAKE:** 1¼ hours + cooling
MAKES: 1 loaf (16 pieces)

1¾ cups all-purpose flour
1½ cups sugar
1 tsp. baking soda
½ tsp. salt
2 large eggs, room temperature
2 medium ripe bananas, mashed
  (1 cup)
½ cup canola oil
¼ cup plus 1 Tbsp. buttermilk
1 tsp. vanilla extract
1 cup chopped walnuts, optional

1. Preheat oven to 350°. In a large bowl, stir together flour, sugar, baking soda and salt. In another bowl, combine the eggs, bananas, oil, buttermilk and vanilla; add to flour mixture, stirring just until combined. If desired, fold in nuts.

2. Pour into a greased or parchment-lined 9x5-in. loaf pan. Bake until a toothpick comes out clean, 1¼ to 1½ hours. Cool in pan 15 minutes before removing to a wire rack.

1 PIECE 257 cal., 13g fat (1g sat. fat), 23mg chol., 171mg sod., 34g carb. (21g sugars, 1g fiber), 4g pro.

Quick Zucchini Bread

My zucchini bread is filled with great cinnamon flavor. It makes two loaves. Have one now and give the second one to a neighbor or freeze for later.
—*Britt-Marie Knoblock, Lisle, IL*

PREP: 15 min. • **BAKE:** 1 hour
MAKES: 2 loaves (12 slices each)

½ cup plus 2 Tbsp. orange juice
½ cup canola oil
½ cup unsweetened applesauce
3 large eggs, room temperature, lightly beaten
2 tsp. vanilla extract
3 cups all-purpose flour
2 cups sugar
4½ tsp. ground cinnamon
1¼ tsp. baking powder
1 tsp. salt
½ tsp. baking soda
2 cups shredded zucchini
1 cup chopped pecans

1. Preheat oven to 350°. In a bowl, combine orange juice, oil, applesauce, eggs and vanilla. In a large bowl, combine flour, sugar, cinnamon, baking powder, salt and baking soda; mix well. Add orange juice mixture; stir until just combined. Fold in zucchini and pecans.

2. Pour into two 8x4-in. loaf pans coated with cooking spray. Bake 60-65 minutes or until a toothpick inserted in center comes out clean.

ZUCCHINI CHIP BREAD Stir in 1 cup semisweet chocolate chips.

Great recipe to use up all that zucchini in the garden! I make this in mini bread pans and freeze the extras.

—MOMTOMATT, TASTEOFHOME.COM

Wild Rice Bread with Sunflower Seeds

Every chance I got I skipped the boring school cafeteria meals and headed to my grandma's house for lunch. The ingredients in this hearty loaf reflect northeastern Minnesota, where she spent most of her life. It's good plain, but try it in your holiday stuffing, too.
—*Crystal Schlueter, Northglenn, CO*

PREP: 35 min. + rising • **BAKE:** 35 min.
MAKES: 2 loaves (16 pieces each)

- 2 pkg. (¼ oz. each) active dry yeast
- 1 cup warm water (110° to 115°)
- 1 pkg. (8.8 oz.) ready-to-serve long grain and wild rice
- 1 cup plus 1 Tbsp. unsalted sunflower kernels, divided
- 1 cup warm fat-free milk (110° to 115°)
- ⅓ cup honey or molasses
- ¼ cup butter, softened
- 2 Tbsp. ground flaxseed
- 2 tsp. salt
- 3 cups whole wheat flour
- 2¾ to 3¼ cups all-purpose flour
- 1 large egg white, lightly beaten
- 1 Tbsp. toasted wheat germ, optional

1. In a small bowl, dissolve yeast in warm water. In a large bowl, combine rice, 1 cup sunflower kernels, milk, honey, butter, flaxseed, salt, yeast mixture, whole wheat flour and 1 cup all-purpose flour; beat on medium speed until combined. Stir in enough remaining flour to form a stiff dough (dough will be sticky).

2. Turn out dough onto a floured surface; knead until elastic, 6-8 minutes. Place in a greased bowl, turning once to grease the top. Cover and let rise in a warm place until doubled, about 1¼ hours.

3. Punch down dough. Turn out onto a lightly floured surface; divide in half. Roll out each half into a 12x8-in. rectangle. Roll up jelly-roll style, starting with a short side; pinch seam and ends to seal. Place each in a 9x5-in. loaf pan coated with cooking spray, seam side down.

4. Cover with kitchen towels; let rise in a warm place until almost doubled, about 45 minutes. Preheat oven to 375°.

5. Brush loaves with egg white; sprinkle with remaining 1 Tbsp. sunflower kernels and, if desired, wheat germ. Bake 35-45 minutes or until dark golden brown. Cool in pans 5 minutes. Remove to a wire rack to cool completely.

1 PIECE 142 cal., 4g fat (1g sat. fat), 4mg chol., 205mg sod., 23g carb. (4g sugars, 2g fiber), 4g pro. **DIABETIC EXCHANGES** 1½ starch, ½ fat.

Aunt Betty's Blueberry Muffins

My Aunt Betty bakes many sweet treats, but I look forward to these mouthwatering muffins the most.
—*Sheila Raleigh, Kechi, KS*

PREP: 15 min. • **BAKE:** 20 min.
MAKES: about 1 dozen

- ½ cup old-fashioned oats
- ½ cup orange juice
- 1 large egg, room temperature
- ½ cup canola oil
- ½ cup sugar
- 1½ cups all-purpose flour
- 1¼ tsp. baking powder
- ½ tsp. salt
- ¼ tsp. baking soda
- 1 cup fresh or frozen blueberries

TOPPING
- 2 Tbsp. sugar
- ½ tsp. ground cinnamon

1. In a large bowl, combine oats and orange juice; let stand for 5 minutes. Beat in the egg, oil and sugar until blended. Combine the flour, baking powder, salt and baking soda; stir into oat mixture just until moistened. Fold in blueberries.

2. Fill greased or paper-lined muffin cups two-thirds full. Combine topping ingredients; sprinkle over batter. Bake at 400° until a toothpick inserted in the center comes out clean, 20-25 minutes. Cool for 5 minutes before removing from pan to a wire rack. Serve warm.

NOTE If using frozen blueberries, use without thawing to avoid discoloring the batter.

1 SERVING 208 cal., 10g fat (1g sat. fat), 18mg chol., 172mg sod., 28g carb. (13g sugars, 1g fiber), 3g pro.

Pumpkin Bread

I keep my freezer stocked for our harvest crew with home-baked goodies like this deliciously spicy, easy pumpkin bread.
—*Joyce Jackson, Bridgetown, NS*

PREP: 15 min. • **BAKE:** 65 min. + cooling
MAKES: 16 pieces

- 1⅔ cups all-purpose flour
- 1½ cups sugar
- 1 tsp. baking soda
- 1 tsp. ground cinnamon
- ¾ tsp. salt
- ½ tsp. baking powder
- ½ tsp. ground nutmeg
- ¼ tsp. ground cloves
- 2 large eggs, room temperature
- 1 cup canned pumpkin
- ½ cup canola oil
- ½ cup water
- ½ cup chopped walnuts
- ½ cup raisins, optional

1. Preheat oven to 350°. Combine the first 8 ingredients. Whisk together eggs, pumpkin, oil and water; stir into dry ingredients just until moistened. Fold in walnuts and, if desired, raisins.

2. Pour into a greased 9x5-in. loaf pan. Bake until a toothpick inserted in center comes out clean, 65-70 minutes. Cool in pan for 10 minutes before removing to a wire rack to cool completely.

1 PIECE 221 cal., 10g fat (1g sat. fat), 23mg chol., 212mg sod., 31g carb. (20g sugars, 1g fiber), 3g pro.

Lemon-Thyme Bread

Lemon and thyme go together like milk and cookies. Fresh thyme is best, but if you have only dried available, reduce the amount to 1 tablespoon and crush it between your fingers before adding it to the batter.
—*Cathy Tang, Redmond, WA*

PREP: 25 min. • **BAKE:** 40 min. + cooling
MAKES: 1 loaf (12 pieces)

- ½ cup butter, softened
- ¾ cup sugar
- 1 large egg, room temperature
- ½ cup buttermilk
- ½ cup sour cream
- 1¾ cups all-purpose flour
- 2 Tbsp. minced fresh thyme
- 1 Tbsp. grated lemon zest
- ½ tsp. baking soda
- ¼ tsp. salt
  Confectioners' sugar

1. In a large bowl, cream butter and sugar until light and fluffy, 5-7 minutes. Beat in egg. Combine buttermilk and sour cream. Combine the flour, thyme, lemon zest, baking soda and salt; add to the creamed mixture alternately with buttermilk mixture, beating well after each addition.

2. Transfer to a greased 8x4-in. loaf pan. Bake at 350° until a toothpick inserted in the center comes out clean, 40-50 minutes. Cool for 10 minutes before removing from pan to a wire rack to cool completely. Sprinkle with confectioners' sugar.

1 PIECE 212 cal., 10g fat (6g sat. fat), 45mg chol., 176mg sod., 27g carb. (14g sugars, 1g fiber), 3g pro.

LEMON-THYME MINI LOAVES Use 3 greased 5¾x3x2-in. loaf pans. Bake at 350° until a toothpick comes out clean, 25-30 minutes.

LEMON-THYME MUFFINS Make batter as directed; fill 12 greased or paper-lined muffin cups two-thirds full. Bake at 400° until a toothpick comes out clean, 16-20 minutes. Yield: 1 dozen muffins.

LEMON-THYME MINIATURE MUFFINS Make batter as directed; fill greased or paper-lined muffin cups two-thirds full. Bake at 400° until a toothpick comes out clean, 10-12 minutes. Yield: 4 dozen miniature muffins.

LEMON-THYME ICING In a small bowl, combine ½ cup confectioners' sugar, ½ tsp. minced fresh thyme and 3-4 tsp. lemon juice, as needed, to reach a drizzling consistency. Yield: 2 Tbsp.

LEMONY CREAM CHEESE In a small bowl, beat 8 oz. softened cream cheese until fluffy. Add ⅓ cup confectioners' sugar, 4 tsp. lemon juice and 1 tsp. grated lemon zest; beat until smooth. Yield: 1 cup.

NOTES

Rustic Rye Bread

This gorgeous rye bread has just a touch of sweetness and the perfect amount of caraway seeds. With a crusty top and firm texture, it holds up well for sandwiches.
—*Holly Wade, Harrisonburg, VA*

PREP: 25 min. + rising • **BAKE:** 30 min.
MAKES: 2 loaves (12 pieces each)

- 1   pkg. (¼ oz.) active dry yeast
- 1¾ cups warm water (110° to 115°), divided
- ¼   cup packed brown sugar
- ¼   cup light molasses
- 3   Tbsp. caraway seeds
- 2   Tbsp. canola oil
- 1   Tbsp. salt
- 1¾ cups rye flour
- ¾   cup whole wheat flour
- 2½ to 3 cups all-purpose flour

1. In a large bowl, dissolve yeast in ¼ cup warm water. Stir in brown sugar, molasses, caraway seeds, oil, salt and remaining 1 ½ cups water. Add rye flour, whole wheat flour and 1 cup all-purpose flour; beat on medium speed until smooth. Stir in enough remaining all-purpose flour to form a firm dough.

2. Turn dough out onto a floured surface; knead until smooth and elastic, 6-8 minutes. Place in a greased bowl, turning once to grease the top. Cover and let rise in a warm place until doubled, about 1½ hours.

3. Punch down dough. Turn out onto a lightly floured surface; divide in half. Shape each into a round loaf; place on a baking sheet coated with cooking spray. Cover with kitchen towels; let rise in a warm place until almost doubled, about 1½ hours. Preheat oven to 350°.

4. Bake until golden brown, 30-35 minutes. Remove from pan to wire racks to cool.

1 PIECE 118 cal., 2g fat (0 sat. fat), 0 chol., 298mg sod., 24g carb. (5g sugars, 2g fiber), 3g pro.

Oven-Fried Cornbread

Nothing says good southern cooking like a crisp cornbread baked in a cast-iron skillet. This old family recipe has been passed down to each generation.
—*Emory Doty, Jasper, GA*

PREP: 20 min. • **BAKE:** 15 min.
MAKES: 8 servings

- 4 Tbsp. bacon drippings or vegetable oil, divided
- 1½ cups finely ground white cornmeal
- 2 tsp. baking powder
- 1 tsp. baking soda
- 1 tsp. salt
- ¼ cup sugar, optional
- 2 large eggs, room temperature
- 2 cups buttermilk

1. Place 2 Tbsp. bacon drippings or oil in a 10-in. cast-iron skillet; place in oven. Preheat oven to 450°. Whisk together cornmeal, baking powder, baking soda, salt and sugar, if using. In another bowl, whisk together eggs, buttermilk and remaining 2 Tbsp. oil. Add to cornmeal mixture; stir just until moistened.

2. Carefully remove hot skillet from oven. Add batter; bake until golden brown and a toothpick inserted in center comes out clean, 15-20 minutes. Cut into wedges; serve warm.

1 PIECE 238 cal., 9g fat (1g sat. fat), 49mg chol., 709mg sod., 33g carb. (10g sugars, 1g fiber), 6g pro.

Grandma's Yeast Rolls

My grandmother used to make these rolls for family get-togethers and holidays. The applesauce may be an unexpected ingredient, but it adds so much flavor.
—*Nancy Spoth, Festus, MO*

PREP: 20 min. + rising • **BAKE:** 15 min.
MAKES: 2 dozen

- 1 pkg. (¼ oz.) active dry yeast
- 1 cup 2% milk (110° to 115°)
- ¼ cup sugar
- ¼ cup unsweetened applesauce
- 2 large egg whites, room temperature, beaten
- 1 tsp. salt
- 3½ to 4 cups all-purpose flour

1. In a large bowl, dissolve yeast in warm milk. Add the sugar, applesauce, egg whites, salt and 2 cups flour; beat until smooth. Stir in enough remaining flour to form a soft dough.

2. Turn out onto a lightly floured surface; knead until smooth and elastic, 6-8 minutes (dough will be slightly sticky). Place in a bowl coated with cooking spray, turning once to coat the top. Cover; let rise in a warm place until doubled, about 1 hour.

3. Turn out dough onto a lightly floured surface; divide into 24 pieces. Shape each portion into an 8-in. rope; tie into a knot. Place on 2 baking sheets coated with cooking spray.

4. Cover and let rise until doubled, about 30 minutes. Bake at 375° until golden brown, 12-16 minutes. Remove from pans to wire racks to cool.

1 ROLL 83 cal., 1g fat (1g sat. fat), 1mg chol., 109mg sod., 17g carb. (0 sugars, 1g fiber), 3g pro. **DIABETIC EXCHANGES** 1 starch.

BAKED POTATO SOUP, P. 65

Heartwarming Soups

Comforting Chicken Noodle Soup

A good friend made us this rich, comforting soup after the birth of our son. It was such a help to have dinner taken care of until I was back on my feet. This yummy dish is so simple to fix that now I give a pot of it (along with the recipe) to other new mothers.
—*Joanna Sargent, Sandy, UT*

TAKES: 25 min.
MAKES: 12 servings (3 qt.)

  2 qt. water
  8 tsp. chicken bouillon granules
6½ cups uncooked wide egg noodles
  2 cans (10¾ oz. each) condensed cream of chicken soup, undiluted
  3 cups cubed cooked chicken
  1 cup sour cream
     Minced fresh parsley

1. In a large saucepan, bring water and bouillon to a boil. Add noodles; cook, uncovered, 10 minutes or until tender. Do not drain. Add soup and chicken; heat through.

2. Remove from the heat; stir in the sour cream. Sprinkle with minced parsley.

1 CUP 218 cal., 9g fat (4g sat. fat), 67mg chol., 980mg sod., 18g carb. (2g sugars, 1g fiber), 15g pro.

FROZEN FLAIR
Use frozen egg noodles to give homemade soup an added flair. They are more rustic and thick than dried noodles and require a bit more cooking. Look for the noodles near the frozen pasta.

Ground Beef Barley Soup

I first tasted this soup when a friend shared it with us one Sunday after church. It's now a favorite with our family, especially our three children.
—*Maggie Norman, Gaithersburg, MD*

PREP: 5 min. + chilling.
COOK: 2 hours 40 min.
MAKES: 8 servings (2 qt.)

  2 qt. water
  2 meaty beef soup bones
  2 beef bouillon cubes or 2 tsp. beef bouillon granules
  1 lb. ground beef
¼ to ½ cup medium pearl barley
  1 large carrot, diced
  1 small onion, chopped
  3 to 4 medium potatoes, peeled and diced
  2 tsp. garlic salt
  1 tsp. onion powder
  2 tsp. dried parsley
  1 tsp. salt
  1 tsp. pepper

1. In a large Dutch oven, bring water and soup bones to a rapid boil; add bouillon. Stir in ground beef in small amounts. Reduce heat; cover and simmer for 1½ hours or until the meat easily comes off the bones.

2. Remove bones. Strain broth; cool and refrigerate. Skim off fat. Remove meat from bones; dice and return to broth along with remaining ingredients. Bring to a boil. Reduce heat; cover and simmer 1 hour or until vegetables are tender.

1 CUP 295 cal., 13g fat (5g sat. fat), 70mg chol., 1068mg sod., 18g carb. (2g sugars, 2g fiber), 25g pro.

Old-Time Oxtail Stew

This wonderfully rich meal will warm your soul and your taste buds. Oxtail stew is a favorite family heirloom recipe. Don't let the name of this dish turn you off. Oxtail describes the meaty part of the tail of an ox (now commonly cow). The meat is delicious, but requires long and slow cooking.
—*Bobbie Keefer, Byers, CO*

PREP: 20 min. • **COOK:** 10 hours
MAKES: 8 servings (3 qt.)

- 2 lbs. oxtails, trimmed
- 2 Tbsp. olive oil
- 4 medium carrots, sliced (about 2 cups)
- 1 medium onion, chopped
- 2 garlic cloves, minced
- 2 cans (14½ oz. each) diced tomatoes, undrained
- 1 can (15 oz.) beef broth
- 3 bay leaves
- 1 tsp. salt
- 1 tsp. dried oregano
- ½ tsp. dried thyme
- ½ tsp. pepper
- 6 cups chopped cabbage

1. In a large skillet, brown oxtails in oil over medium heat. Remove from pan; place in a 5-qt. slow cooker.

2. Add carrots and onion to drippings; cook and stir until just softened, 3-5 minutes. Add garlic; cook 1 minute longer. Transfer vegetable mixture to slow cooker. Add tomatoes, broth, bay leaves, salt, oregano, thyme and pepper; stir to combine.

3. Cook, covered, on low 8 hours. Add cabbage; cook until cabbage is tender and meat pulls away easily from bones, about 2 hours longer. Remove oxtails; set aside until cool enough to handle. Remove meat from bones; discard bones and shred meat. Return meat to soup. Discard bay leaves.

FREEZE OPTION Freeze cooled stew in freezer containers. To use, partially thaw in refrigerator overnight. Heat through in a saucepan, stirring occasionally; add broth or water if necessary.

1½ CUPS 204 cal., 10g fat (3g sat. fat), 34mg chol., 705mg sod., 14g carb. (8g sugars, 5g fiber), 16g pro.

IT'S SO EASY!

How do I trim oxtails?
Oxtails can be tough to cut, so it's best to ask the butcher to slice them into pieces (if they aren't already). Trimming the thick pieces of excess fat off the oxtails before cooking will ensure a stew that's flavorful with a velvety mouthfeel.

How can I make oxtail soup less oily?
Oxtails are rich in fat—and while fat means flavor, the stew can get a bit oily. Trimming off any large pieces of fat before cooking will help reduce the oil in the finished stew. After cooking, skim off excess fat from the surface with a shallow ladle or large serving spoon. If you're cooking a day ahead, refrigerate the stew, then remove the solidified excess fat before reheating.

What else can I put in oxtail soup?
Potatoes are a natural addition to oxtail soup. Add them 30 minutes before the stew is done cooking, and they will be flavored with the rich cooking juices of the stew.

Rustic Ham & Bean Soup

This old-fashioned version of ham and bean soup starts with dried navy beans, but you could start with great northern beans instead. The first soak of the beans softens them, but they won't get tender until after they are simmered in the second step.
—Taste of Home *Test Kitchen*

PREP: 15 min. + soaking • **COOK:** 1½ hours
MAKES: 10 servings (2½ qt.)

1   lb. dried navy beans
1   Tbsp. canola oil
2   medium onions, chopped
2   celery ribs, chopped
8   cups water
1   medium carrot, chopped
2   bay leaves
1   tsp. dried thyme
½   tsp. pepper
2   smoked ham hocks
2   cups cubed fully cooked ham
½   tsp. salt

1. Place beans in a Dutch oven; add water to cover by 2 in. Bring to a boil; boil for 2 minutes. Remove from the heat; cover and let stand for 1-4 hours or until beans are softened. Drain and rinse the beans, discarding liquid.

2. In the same pan, heat oil over medium heat; add onions and celery. Cook and stir until crisp-tender, 3-5 minutes. Stir in softened beans, 8 cups water, carrot, bay leaves, thyme and pepper. Add ham hocks. Bring to a boil. Reduce heat; cover and simmer for 1¼-1½ hours or until beans are tender.

3. Discard bay leaves. Remove ham hocks; set aside until cool enough to handle. Remove ham from bones and cut into cubes. Discard bones. Return ham to soup. Stir in cubed ham and salt; heat through.

1 CUP 230 cal., 4g fat (1g sat. fat), 25mg chol., 521mg sod., 31g carb. (3g sugars, 8g fiber), 20g pro. **DIABETIC EXCHANGES** 2 starch, 2 lean meat.

BEAT THE CLOCK
Canned beans make a smart shortcut for this soup. Simply use them in place of the dried beans, but it's best to add them in the last 30 minutes of simmering the soup. If overcooked, the beans won't retain their shape and will become mushy.

Parsnip & Celery Root Bisque

With its smooth texture and earthy vegetable flavors, this soup makes a simple yet elegant first course. Try chives and pomegranate seeds on top.
—*Merry Graham, Newhall, CA*

PREP: 25 min. • **COOK:** 45 min.
MAKES: 8 servings (2 qt.)

- 2   Tbsp. olive oil
- 2   medium leeks (white portion only), chopped (about 2 cups)
- 1½ lbs. parsnips, peeled and chopped (about 4 cups)
- 1   medium celery root, peeled and cubed (about 1½ cups)
- 4   garlic cloves, minced
- 6   cups chicken stock
- 1½ tsp. salt
- ¾   tsp. coarsely ground pepper
- 1   cup heavy whipping cream
- 2   Tbsp. minced fresh parsley
- 2   tsp. lemon juice
- 2   Tbsp. minced fresh chives
      Pomegranate seeds, optional

1. In a large saucepan, heat the oil over medium-high heat; saute the leeks for 3 minutes. Add parsnips and celery root; cook and stir 4 minutes. Add garlic; cook and stir 1 minute. Stir in stock, salt and pepper; bring to a boil. Reduce heat; simmer, covered, until vegetables are tender, 25-30 minutes.

2. Puree soup using an immersion blender. Or cool slightly and puree soup in batches in a blender; return to pan. Stir in cream, parsley and lemon juice; heat through. Serve with chives and, if desired, pomegranate seeds.

1 CUP 248 cal., 15g fat (7g sat. fat), 34mg chol., 904mg sod., 25g carb. (8g sugars, 5g fiber), 6g pro.

Baked Potato Soup

I found our favorite soup in an unexpected place—a children's cookbook! This creamy comfort food is not only delicious but it's also scaled down to make an amount that's perfect for my husband and me.
—*Linda Mumm, Davenport, IA*

TAKES: 20 min. • **MAKES:** 2 servings

- 2   medium potatoes, baked and cooled
- 1   can (14½ oz.) chicken broth
- 2   Tbsp. sour cream
- ⅛   tsp. pepper
- ¼   cup shredded cheddar cheese
- 1   Tbsp. crumbled cooked bacon or bacon bits
- 1   green onion, sliced

Peel potatoes and cut into ½-in. cubes; place half in a blender. Add broth; cover and process until smooth. Pour into a saucepan. Stir in sour cream, pepper and the remaining potatoes. Cook over low heat until heated through (do not boil). Garnish with cheese, bacon and onion.

1 CUP 277 cal., 8g fat (5g sat. fat), 28mg chol., 1061mg sod., 41g carb. (5g sugars, 4g fiber), 11g pro.

A favorite! You can make this for any number of servings without much extra work. A great recipe any time of year!
—FACSTEACHER, TASTEOFHOME.COM

Pasta Fagioli Soup

My husband enjoys my version of this classic soup so much that he stopped ordering it at restaurants. He'd rather savor the version we can have in the comfort of home. It's so easy to make, yet hearty enough to be a full dinner.
—*Brenda Thomas, Springfield, MO*

TAKES: 30 min. • **MAKES:** 5 servings

- ½ lb. Italian turkey sausage links, casings removed, crumbled
- 1 small onion, chopped
- 1½ tsp. canola oil
- 1 garlic clove, minced
- 2 cups water
- 1 can (15½ oz.) great northern beans, rinsed and drained
- 1 can (14½ oz.) diced tomatoes, undrained
- 1 can (14½ oz.) reduced-sodium chicken broth
- ¾ cup uncooked elbow macaroni
- ¼ tsp. pepper
- 1 cup fresh spinach leaves, cut as desired
- 5 tsp. shredded Parmesan cheese

1. In a large saucepan, cook sausage over medium heat until no longer pink; drain, remove from pan and set aside. In the same pan, saute onion in oil until tender. Add garlic; saute 1 minute longer.

2. Add the water, beans, tomatoes, broth, macaroni and pepper; bring to a boil. Cook, uncovered, until macaroni is tender, 8-10 minutes.

3. Reduce heat to low; stir in sausage and spinach. Cook until spinach is wilted, 2-3 minutes. Garnish with cheese.

1⅓ CUPS 228 cal., 7g fat (1g sat. fat), 29mg chol., 841mg sod., 27g carb. (4g sugars, 6g fiber), 16g pro. **DIABETIC EXCHANGES** 1½ starch, 1 vegetable, 1 lean meat, ½ fat.

NOTES

Traditional New England Clam Chowder

I left a cruise ship with a wonderful souvenir: the recipe for this splendid chowder! It's a traditional soup that stands the test of time.
—*Agnes Ward, Stratford, ON*

PREP: 40 min. • **COOK:** 15 min.
MAKES: 7 servings

- 12 fresh cherrystone clams
- 3 cups cold water
- 2 bacon strips, diced
- 1 small onion, chopped
- 2 medium potatoes, peeled and finely chopped
- ¼ tsp. salt
- ¼ tsp. pepper
- 2 Tbsp. all-purpose flour
- 1 cup whole milk
- ½ cup half-and-half cream

1. Tap clams; discard any that do not close. Place clams and water in a large saucepan. Bring to a boil. Reduce heat; cover and simmer for 5-6 minutes or until clams open.

2. Remove meat from clams; chop meat and set aside. Strain liquid through a cheesecloth-lined colander; set aside.

3. In a large saucepan, cook bacon over medium heat until crisp. Using a slotted spoon, remove to paper towels. Saute onion in drippings until tender.

4. Return bacon to the pan; add clam meat and reserved liquid. Stir in the potatoes, salt and pepper. Bring to a boil. Reduce heat; cover and simmer for 10-12 minutes or until potatoes are tender.

5. Combine flour and milk until smooth; gradually stir into soup. Bring to a boil; cook and stir for 2 minutes or until thickened. Gradually stir in cream; heat through (do not boil).

1 CUP 138 cal., 6g fat (3g sat. fat), 24mg chol., 175mg sod., 14g carb. (3g sugars, 1g fiber), 6g pro. **DIABETIC EXCHANGES** 1 starch, 1 lean meat, ½ fat.

NOTES

Grandma's Pea Soup

My grandma's pea soup was a family favorite. What makes it different from any other pea soups I have tried is the addition of whole peas, spaetzle-like dumplings and sausage. Try it once and you'll be hooked.
—*Carole Talcott, Dahinda, IL*

PREP: 15 min. + soaking • **COOK:** 2½ hours • **MAKES:** 16 servings (4 qt.)

- ½ lb. dried whole peas
- ½ lb. dried green split peas
- 1 meaty ham bone
- 3 qt. water
- 1 large onion, chopped
- 1 medium carrot, chopped
- 2 celery ribs, chopped
- ½ cup chopped celery leaves
- 1 tsp. bouquet garni (mixed herbs)
- 1 Tbsp. minced fresh parsley
- 1 bay leaf
- 1 tsp. salt
- ¼ tsp. pepper
- ½ lb. smoked sausage, chopped, optional

SPAETZLE DUMPLINGS
- 1 cup all-purpose flour
- 1 large egg, beaten
- ⅓ cup water

1. Cover peas with water and soak overnight. Drain, rinse and place in a Dutch oven.

2. Add ham bone, water and remaining soup ingredients except sausage and dumplings. Bring to a boil. Reduce heat; cover and simmer 2-2½ hours.

3. Remove ham bone and skim fat. Remove meat from bone; dice. Add ham and, if desired, sausage to pan.

4. For dumplings, place flour in a small bowl. Make a depression in the center of the flour; add egg and water and stir until smooth.

5. Place a colander with ³⁄₁₆-in.-diameter holes over simmering soup; transfer dough to the colander and press through with a wooden spoon. Cook, uncovered, 10-15 minutes. Discard bay leaf.

FREEZE OPTION Prepare soup without dumplings and freeze in serving-sized portions to enjoy for months to come.

1 CUP 155 cal., 2g fat (1g sat. fat), 20mg chol., 171mg sod., 26g carb. (2g sugars, 6g fiber), 9g pro.

Hearty Beef & Vegetable Soup

When you need to feed a crowd, consider this beefy favorite made easy with lots of frozen veggies.
—*Sue Straughan, Prattville, AL*

PREP: 1¾ hours • **COOK:** 2¼ hours
MAKES: 26 servings (9¾ qt.)

- 2 to 4 Tbsp. canola oil
- 4 lbs. beef stew meat
- 8 medium onions (2¼ lbs.), halved and thinly sliced
- 12 cups water
- 1 can (28 oz.) diced tomatoes, undrained
- 1 can (15 oz.) tomato sauce
- 1⅓ cups Worcestershire sauce
- ½ cup beef bouillon granules
- 12 medium red potatoes (about 3½ lbs.), cubed
- ½ large head cabbage, chopped
- 1 lb. carrots, thinly sliced
- 6 celery ribs, thinly sliced (3 cups)
- 3 cups (about 15 oz.) frozen corn
- 3 cups (about 12 oz.) frozen peas
- 3 cups (about 12 oz.) frozen cut green beans
- 1½ cups (about 15 oz.) frozen lima beans
- 1 bay leaf
- 3 tsp. dried marjoram
- 3 tsp. dried thyme
- 1 tsp. salt
- 1 tsp. pepper
- 1½ cups (6 oz.) frozen sliced okra

1. In a large stockpot, heat 1 Tbsp. oil over medium heat. Brown beef in batches, adding additional oil as necessary. Remove with a slotted spoon. Add onions to drippings; cook and stir until tender. Discard drippings; return beef to pot. Stir in water, tomatoes, tomato sauce, Worcestershire sauce and bouillon. Bring to a boil. Reduce heat; simmer, covered, 45 minutes.

2. Stir in potatoes, cabbage, carrots, celery, corn, peas, green beans, lima beans and seasonings. Return to a boil. Reduce heat; simmer, covered, for 35 minutes. Stir in okra; cook until beef and vegetables are tender, 15-20 minutes longer. Discard bay leaf.

1½ CUPS 245 cal., 6g fat (2g sat. fat), 42mg chol., 1090mg sod., 31g carb. (9g sugars, 6g fiber), 18g pro.

Turkey & Wild Rice Soup

A dear friend shared this recipe with me several years ago before she passed, and I've been making it my own ever since. I prepare this soup whenever I think of her. Sometimes I will add a cup of cheddar cheese at the end and melt it in for an extra measure of comfort.
—Carol Brault, Henderson, NC

PREP: 20 min. • **COOK:** 65 min.
MAKES: 8 servings (2½ qt.)

- ½ cup uncooked wild rice
- 4 cups water
- ½ cup butter, cubed
- 8 oz. red potatoes (about 2 medium), chopped
- 1 medium onion, chopped
- 1 celery rib, chopped
- 1 medium carrot, chopped
- 2 garlic cloves, minced
- ½ cup all-purpose flour
- 3 cups chicken broth
- 2 cups half-and-half cream
- 1 tsp. salt
- ½ tsp. dried rosemary, crushed
- 2 cups cubed cooked turkey or chicken

1. In a saucepan, combine rice and water; bring to a boil over high heat. Reduce heat; simmer, covered, 30 minutes.

2. Meanwhile, in a Dutch oven, heat butter over medium heat. Add potatoes, onion, celery and carrot; cook and stir 6-8 minutes or until almost tender. Add garlic; cook 1 minute longer.

3. Stir in flour until blended; cook and stir 2 minutes. Gradually stir in broth and undrained rice. Bring to a boil over medium-high heat; cook and stir 1-2 minutes or until slightly thickened.

4. Add cream, salt and rosemary; return to a boil. Simmer, uncovered, 15-20 minutes or until rice is tender, stirring occasionally. Stir in turkey; heat through.

1¼ CUPS 338 cal., 19g fat (12g sat. fat), 98mg chol., 832mg sod., 23g carb. (4g sugars, 2g fiber), 16g pro.

Quick Tomato Soup

This recipe is one of my grandmother's favorites, simplified for busy nights. Gram had this delicious soup cooking on the stove every time I visited. She enjoyed making this and other wonderful dishes for family and friends, and she made everything with love.
—Gerri Sysun, Narragansett, RI

TAKES: 15 min. • **MAKES:** 2 servings

- 2 Tbsp. butter
- 1 Tbsp. all-purpose flour
- 2 cups tomato juice
- ½ cup water
- 2 Tbsp. sugar
- ⅛ tsp. salt
- ¾ cup cooked wide egg noodles
  Chopped fresh parsley, optional

In a saucepan over medium heat, melt butter. Add flour; stir to form a smooth paste. Gradually add the tomato juice and water, stirring constantly; bring to a boil. Cook and stir 2 minutes or until thickened. Add sugar and salt. Stir in egg noodles and heat through. If desired, sprinkle with parsley.

1 CUP 259 cal., 12g fat (7g sat. fat), 44mg chol., 1144mg sod., 36g carb. (20g sugars, 1g fiber), 4g pro.

Hearty Navy Bean Soup

Use thrifty dried beans and a ham hock to create this comfort-food classic. Bean soup is a family favorite that I make often.
—*Mildred Lewis, Temple, TX*

PREP: 30 min. + soaking • **COOK:** 1¾ hours
MAKES: 10 servings (2½ qt.)

- 3 cups (1½ lbs.) dried navy beans
- 1 can (14½ oz.) diced tomatoes, undrained
- 1 large onion, chopped
- 1 meaty ham hock or 1 cup diced cooked ham
- 2 cups chicken broth
- 2½ cups water
  Salt and pepper to taste
  Minced fresh parsley, optional

1. Rinse and sort beans; soak according to package directions.

2. Drain and rinse beans, discarding liquid. Place in a Dutch oven. Add the tomatoes with juice, onion, ham hock, broth, water, salt and pepper. Bring to a boil. Reduce heat; cover and simmer until beans are tender, about 1½ hours.

3. Add more water if necessary. Remove ham hock and let it stand until cool enough to handle. Remove meat from bone; discard bone. Cut meat into bite-sized pieces; set aside. (For a thicker soup, cool slightly, then puree beans in a food processor or blender and return to pan.) Return ham to soup and heat through. Garnish with parsley if desired.

1 CUP 244 cal., 2g fat (0 sat. fat), 8mg chol., 410mg sod., 42g carb. (5g sugars, 10g fiber), 18g pro. **DIABETIC EXCHANGES** 3 starch, 2 lean meat, 1 vegetable.

SOUPY SECRETS

How do I thicken navy bean soup?
To thicken navy bean soup, let it cool slightly, then transfer the beans in a food processor or blender to puree. Return mixture back to the soup and stir to combine.

Are great northern beans the same as navy beans?
They are different but do share a few similarities. Both are white beans, but navy beans are smaller in size and require long, slow cooking. Navy beans are one of the central ingredients in canned pork and beans, though they can be used in various dishes that call for navy beans.

CLASSIC MACARONI
SALAD, P. 89

Timeless Sides & Salads

Grandma's Poultry Dressing

Every family seems to have its own favorite dressing recipe that becomes a tradition, and this is ours. It came from Grandma, who passed it down to my mother. Now our children have carried it into their kitchens. This is truly a good old-fashioned recipe!
—Norma Howland, Joliet, IL

PREP: 20 min. • **BAKE:** 40 min.
MAKES: 6 cups

- 1 lb. bulk pork sausage
- 1 cup 2% milk
- 7 cups coarse dry bread crumbs
- 1 cup diced celery
- 2 large eggs
- 2 to 3 Tbsp. minced fresh parsley
- 2 Tbsp. diced onion
- ½ tsp. salt or salt to taste

1. Preheat oven to 350°. In a large skillet, brown the sausage. Drain sausage, discarding drippings. Meanwhile, in a small saucepan, heat milk over medium heat until bubbles form around side of pan. In a large bowl, combine sausage, milk and remaining ingredients.

2. Transfer to a greased 2-qt. baking dish. Cover and bake until lightly browned, about 40 minutes.

½ CUP 352 cal., 12g fat (4g sat. fat), 52mg chol., 826mg sod., 48g carb. (3g sugars, 2g fiber), 12g pro.

Dad's Creamed Peas & Pearl Onions

When I was growing up, it was a family tradition to make creamed peas with pearl onions for every Thanksgiving and Christmas dinner. My dad would not be a happy camper if he didn't see this dish on the table. It was his favorite! I made it for my own family while our kids were growing up; my daughter now makes this dish for her family.
—Nancy Heishman, Las Vegas, NV

TAKES: 25 min. • **MAKES:** 6 servings

- 5 cups frozen peas (about 20 oz.), thawed and drained
- 2 cups frozen pearl onions (about 9 oz.), thawed and drained
- 2 celery ribs, finely chopped
- ¾ cup chicken broth
- ½ tsp. salt
- ½ tsp. pepper
- ½ tsp. dried thyme
- ½ cup sour cream
- 10 bacon strips, cooked and crumbled
- ¾ cup salted cashews

In a large skillet, combine the first 7 ingredients; bring to a boil. Reduce heat to medium; cook, uncovered, until onions are tender and most of liquid is evaporated, 8-10 minutes, stirring occasionally. Remove from heat; stir in sour cream. Top with bacon and salted cashews.

¾ CUP 322 cal., 18g fat (6g sat. fat), 19mg chol., 783mg sod., 26g carb. (10g sugars, 7g fiber), 14g pro.

Marmalade-Glazed Carrots

This side dish is ideal when you'd like to serve your vegetables in a different way for a special dinner. Cinnamon and nutmeg season carrots that are simmered with orange marmalade and brown sugar.
—Barb Rudyk, Vermilion, AB

PREP: 10 min. • **COOK:** 5½ hours
MAKES: 6 servings

- 2 lbs. fresh carrots halved lengthwise and cut into 2-in. pieces
- ½ cup orange marmalade
- 3 Tbsp. cold water, divided
- 2 Tbsp. brown sugar
- 1 Tbsp. butter, melted
- ½ tsp. ground cinnamon
- ¼ tsp. salt
- ¼ tsp. ground nutmeg
- ⅛ tsp. pepper
- 1 Tbsp. cornstarch

1. In a 3-qt. slow cooker, combine the carrots, marmalade, 1 Tbsp. water, brown sugar, butter and seasonings. Cover and cook on low until carrots are tender, 5-6 hours.

2. In a small bowl, combine cornstarch and remaining water until smooth; stir into carrot mixture. Cover and cook on high until thickened, about 30 minutes. Serve with a slotted spoon.

1 SERVING 159 cal., 2g fat (1g sat. fat), 5mg chol., 252mg sod., 36g carb. (29g sugars, 3g fiber), 1g pro.

This is an awesome recipe and is so easy to get ready. I think it would make a great alternative to potatoes.
—ALOHAMRYAN, TASTEOFHOME.COM

Green Bean Casserole

This classic green bean casserole is a breeze to put together and is one of my all-time favorite dishes! You can make it before any guests arrive and keep it refrigerated until baking time.
—Anna Baker, Blaine, WA

PREP: 15 min. • **BAKE:** 30 min.
MAKES: 10 servings

- 2 lbs. fresh green beans, trimmed
- 2 cans (10¾ oz. each) condensed cream of mushroom soup, undiluted
- 1 cup 2% milk
- 2 tsp. soy sauce
- ⅛ tsp. pepper
- 1 can (6 oz.) french-fried onions

1. In a large saucepan, bring 8 cups water to a boil. Add the green beans; cook, uncovered, just until crisp-tender, 3-4 minutes. Drain and set aside.

2. In a bowl, combine the soup, milk, soy sauce and pepper. Gently stir in beans. Spoon half the mixture into a 13x9-in. baking dish. Sprinkle with half the onions. Spoon remaining bean mixture over the top. Sprinkle with remaining onions.

3. Bake at 350° until heated through and onions are brown and crispy, 30-35 minutes.

¾ CUP 163 cal., 11g fat (3g sat. fat), 5mg chol., 485mg sod., 14g carb. (2g sugars, 1g fiber), 2g pro.

Easy German Potato Salad

This tangy potato salad stirs memories of my grandma, who made it for us.
Now my mom makes it with brats and sauerkraut—truly the best meal!
—*Devin Mulertt, Cedarburg, WI*

PREP: 35 min. • **COOK:** 40 min. + cooling
MAKES: 16 servings

- 5 lbs. potatoes (about 12 medium), peeled
- 8 bacon strips, cooked and crumbled
- 1 small onion, chopped
- 3 green onions, thinly sliced
- 1½ cups water
- ½ cup white vinegar
- ⅓ cup canola oil
- 1¼ tsp. salt
- ½ tsp. pepper

1. Place potatoes in a stock pot; add water to cover. Bring to a boil. Reduce heat; cook, uncovered, 15-20 minutes or until tender. Drain potatoes; cool slightly.

2. Cut potatoes into slices. Place in a large bowl. Stir in bacon, onion and green onions.

3. In a small bowl, whisk the remaining ingredients until blended; pour over salad and toss gently to coat. Serve warm. Refrigerate leftovers.

¾ CUP 147 cal., 6g fat (1g sat. fat), 4mg chol., 260mg sod., 20g carb. (2g sugars, 1g fiber), 3g pro. **DIABETIC EXCHANGES** 1½ starch, 1 fat.

Creamy Dilled Cucumber Salad

A Norwegian favorite, this crunchy side dish was a staple at all of our family get-togethers.
I'm happy to say that the tradition continues to this day!
—*Patty LaNoue Stearns, Traverse City, MI*

PREP: 20 min. + chilling
MAKES: 6 servings

- 2 English cucumbers, thinly sliced
- 1 tsp. salt
- 1½ cups sour cream
- ¼ cup thinly sliced red onion
- ¼ cup snipped fresh dill
- 2 Tbsp. white wine vinegar
- 2 garlic cloves, minced
- 1 tsp. sugar
- 1 tsp. coarsely ground pepper

1. Place cucumbers in a colander over a bowl; sprinkle with salt and toss. Let stand 15 minutes. Squeeze and blot dry with paper towels.

2. In a large bowl, combine the remaining ingredients; stir in the cucumbers. Refrigerate, covered, at least 1 hour.

⅔ CUP 143 cal., 12g fat (7g sat. fat), 42mg chol., 416mg sod., 8g carb. (5g sugars, 1g fiber), 3g pro.

CUCUMBER CLUES
The first step in this recipe is to toss the cucumber slices with salt. The salt draws out some of the water to help prevent the slices from becoming watery. Don't skip this step! After letting the slices stand with salt, the salt is rinsed off and slices are patted dry to get rid of extra moisture.

Marinated Three-Bean Salad

Fresh herbs and cayenne pepper provide the fantastic flavor in this marinated salad featuring fresh veggies and canned beans.
—*Carol Tucker, Wooster, OH*

PREP: 20 min. + chilling
MAKES: 8 servings

- 1   can (15½ oz.) great northern beans, rinsed and drained
- 1   can (15 oz.) garbanzo beans or chickpeas, rinsed and drained
- 1   can (15 oz.) black beans, rinsed and drained
- 1   medium tomato, chopped
- 1   medium onion, chopped
- 1   celery rib, chopped
- ⅓ cup each chopped green, sweet red and yellow pepper
- ½ cup water
- 3   Tbsp. minced fresh basil or 1 Tbsp. dried basil
- 2   Tbsp. minced fresh parsley
- 2   Tbsp. lemon juice
- 2   Tbsp. olive oil
- 1½ tsp. minced fresh oregano or ½ tsp. dried oregano
- ½ tsp. salt
- ½ tsp. pepper
- ¼ tsp. cayenne pepper

In a large bowl, combine the beans, tomato, onion, celery and peppers. In a small bowl, whisk the remaining ingredients; gently stir into the bean mixture. Cover and refrigerate for 4 hours, stirring occasionally.

1 CUP 184 cal., 5g fat (0 sat. fat), 0 chol., 452mg sod., 28g carb. (4g sugars, 8g fiber), 8g pro.

NOTES

Southern Fried Okra

Golden brown with a little fresh green showing through, these okra nuggets are crunchy and addicting! My sons like to dip them in ketchup.
—*Pam Duncan, Summers, AR*

TAKES: 30 min. • **MAKES:** 2 servings

1½ cups sliced fresh or frozen okra, thawed
3 Tbsp. buttermilk
2 Tbsp. all-purpose flour
2 Tbsp. cornmeal
¼ tsp. salt
¼ tsp. garlic herb seasoning blend
⅛ tsp. pepper
 Oil for deep-fat frying
 Additional salt and pepper, optional

1. Pat okra dry with paper towels. Place buttermilk in a shallow bowl. In another shallow bowl, combine flour, cornmeal, salt, seasoning blend and pepper. Dip the okra in buttermilk, then roll in the cornmeal mixture.

2. In an electric skillet or deep-fat fryer, heat 1 in. oil to 375°. Fry okra, a few pieces at a time, 1½-2½ minutes on each side or until golden brown. Drain on paper towels. Season with additional salt and pepper if desired.

¾ CUP 200 cal., 12g fat (1g sat. fat), 1mg chol., 430mg sod., 20g carb. (4g sugars, 3g fiber), 5g pro.

FRESH OR FROZEN?
For the best texture and flavor, use fresh okra. If using frozen, thaw the okra first, and thoroughly drain and pat dry. It will have a softer texture than fresh. For some okra recipes, like those that are stewed, frozen okra works just fine as is.

Red Roasted Potatoes

Some fragrant rosemary, fresh or dried, gives these roasted potatoes a distinctive and subtle taste. This dish is simple to prepare, yet elegant in color and flavor. It's a wonderful addition to any menu.
—*Margie Wampler, Butler, PA*

TAKES: 30 min. • **MAKES:** 8 servings

2 lbs. small unpeeled red potatoes, cut into wedges
2 to 3 Tbsp. olive oil
2 garlic cloves, minced
1 Tbsp. minced fresh rosemary or 1 tsp. dried rosemary, crushed
½ tsp. salt
¼ tsp. pepper

1. Place potatoes in a 13x9-in. baking dish. Drizzle with oil. Sprinkle with the garlic, rosemary, salt and pepper; toss gently to coat.

2. Bake at 450° until potatoes are golden brown and tender, 20-30 minutes.

1 CUP 114 cal., 4g fat (0 sat. fat), 0 chol., 155mg sod., 18g carb. (1g sugars, 2g fiber), 2g pro.

Peach Bavarian

Fruit molds are my specialty. This one, with its refreshing peach taste, makes a colorful salad or dessert.
—*Adeline Piscitelli, Sayreville, NJ*

PREP: 15 min. + chilling
MAKES: 8 servings

1   can (15¼ oz.) sliced peaches
2   pkg. (3 oz. each) peach or apricot gelatin
½   cup sugar
2   cups boiling water
1   tsp. almond extract
1   carton (8 oz.) frozen whipped topping, thawed
    Sliced fresh peaches, optional

1. Drain peaches, reserving ⅔ cup juice. Chop peaches into small pieces.

2. In a large bowl, dissolve the gelatin and sugar in the boiling water. Stir in reserved peach juice. Refrigerate until slightly thickened. Stir the extract into whipped topping; gently fold into gelatin mixture. Fold in peaches.

3. Pour mixture into an oiled 6-cup mold. Refrigerate overnight. Unmold onto a serving platter; garnish with additional peaches if desired.

1 SERVING 249 cal., 5g fat (5g sat. fat), 0 chol., 53mg sod., 47g carb. (47g sugars, 0 fiber), 2g pro.

This was super simple to make, and my family loved it. I couldn't find the flavor of gelatin in the recipe, so I used orange—and it was delicious.
—MISSCOFFEEPOT, TASTEOFHOME.COM

Waldorf Salad

Here's an easy take on an all-time classic. Lemon juice gives it quite a zip, and the apples and nuts offer a nice crunch. It's light, refreshing and effortless to assemble.
—*Chuck Hinz, Parma, OH*

TAKES: 30 min. • **MAKES:** 9 servings

2   medium Red Delicious apples, chopped
2   medium Golden Delicious apples, chopped
2   Tbsp. lemon juice
2   celery ribs, chopped
¾   cup chopped walnuts
½   cup raisins
1   cup mayonnaise
    Optional: Ground cinnamon, ground nutmeg and lettuce leaves

In a large bowl, toss apples with lemon juice. Gently stir in the celery, walnuts, raisins and mayonnaise. Refrigerate until serving. If desired, sprinkle with cinnamon and nutmeg, and serve on lettuce leaves.

¾ CUP 284 cal., 24g fat (3g sat. fat), 2mg chol., 133mg sod., 17g carb. (12g sugars, 3g fiber), 2g pro.

Grandma's Potato Salad

This salad is a must for the Fourth of July feast. The red potatoes
hold their shape and texture even after they are boiled.
—*Sue Gronholz, Beaver Dam, WI*

PREP: 1 hour + chilling
MAKES: 24 servings

  6 lbs. medium red potatoes

DRESSING
  1 cup water
 ½ cup butter, cubed
 ¼ cup white vinegar
  2 large eggs
 ½ cup sugar
4½ tsp. cornstarch
 ¾ cup heavy whipping cream
 ¾ cup Miracle Whip

SALAD
  1 small onion, finely chopped
  2 green onions, sliced
  1 tsp. salt
 ½ tsp. pepper
  3 hard-boiled large eggs, sliced
     Paprika

1. Place the potatoes in a stockpot and cover with water. Bring to a boil. Reduce heat; cover and cook until tender, about 20 minutes. Drain. When cool enough to handle, peel and slice potatoes; cool completely.

2. For dressing, in the top of a double boiler or metal bowl over barely simmering water, heat 1 cup water, butter and vinegar until butter is melted. In a small bowl, beat eggs; add sugar and cornstarch. Add to butter mixture; cook and stir until thickened, 5-7 minutes. Transfer to a large bowl; cool completely.

3. In a small bowl, beat cream until stiff peaks form. Stir Miracle Whip into cooled dressing mixture; fold in whipped cream. Stir in onion, green onions, salt and pepper. Add potatoes; toss lightly to combine. Refrigerate, covered, until chilled.

4. To serve, top with hard-boiled eggs; sprinkle with paprika.

¾ CUP 197 cal., 10g fat (5g sat. fat), 58mg chol., 202mg sod., 24g carb. (6g sugars, 2g fiber), 4g pro.

Cheesy Slow-Cooked Corn

Even those who usually don't eat much corn will ask for a second helping of this creamy, cheesy side dish. Folks love the flavor, but I love how easy it is to make with ingredients I usually have on hand.
—*Mary Ann Truitt, Wichita, KS*

PREP: 5 min. • **COOK:** 3 hours
MAKES: 12 servings

- 9½ cups (48 oz.) frozen corn
- 11 oz. cream cheese, softened
- ¼ cup butter, cubed
- 3 Tbsp. water
- 3 Tbsp. 2% milk
- 2 Tbsp. sugar
- 6 slices American cheese, cut into small pieces

In a 4- or 5-qt. slow cooker, combine all ingredients. Cook, covered, on low, until heated through and cheese is melted, 3-4 hours, stirring once.

1 CUP 265 cal., 16g fat (9g sat. fat), 39mg chol., 227mg sod., 27g carb. (6g sugars, 2g fiber), 7g pro.

Classic Macaroni Salad

This retro recipe is a refreshingly light take on an all-time favorite. It's perfect for a fast weeknight dinner or a festive weekend barbecue.
—*Dorothy Bayes, Sardis, OH*

TAKES: 30 min. • **MAKES:** 8 servings

- 2 cups uncooked elbow macaroni
- 1 cup fat-free mayonnaise
- 2 Tbsp. sweet pickle relish
- 2 tsp. sugar
- ¾ tsp. ground mustard
- ¼ tsp. salt
- ⅛ tsp. pepper
- ½ cup chopped celery
- ⅓ cup chopped carrot
- ¼ cup chopped onion
- 1 hard-boiled large egg, chopped
  Dash paprika

1. Cook macaroni according to package directions; drain and rinse with cold water. Cool completely.

2. For dressing, in a small bowl, combine the mayonnaise, pickle relish, sugar, mustard, salt and pepper. In a large bowl, combine the macaroni, celery, carrot and onion. Add dressing and toss gently to coat.

3. Refrigerate until serving. Garnish with egg and paprika.

¾ CUP 115 cal., 2g fat (0 sat. fat), 27mg chol., 362mg sod., 21g carb. (6g sugars, 2g fiber), 4g pro. **DIABETIC EXCHANGES** 1½ starch.

COOL DOWN!
Rinsing the pasta under cold water helps speed up the cooling process and prevents the pasta from overcooking and turning to mush. Ensuring that your pasta is fully cooled before assembling will allow the dressing to adhere to the pasta and coat it evenly.

Strawberry Salad with Poppy Seed Dressing

My family is always happy to see this fruit and veggie salad. If strawberries aren't available, substitute mandarin oranges and dried cranberries.
—*Irene Keller, Kalamazoo, MI*

TAKES: 30 min. • **MAKES:** 10 servings

¼ cup sugar
⅓ cup slivered almonds
1 bunch romaine, torn (about 8 cups)
1 small onion, halved and thinly sliced
2 cups halved fresh strawberries

DRESSING
¼ cup mayonnaise
2 Tbsp. sugar
1 Tbsp. sour cream
1 Tbsp. 2% milk
2¼ tsp. cider vinegar
1½ tsp. poppy seeds

1. Place sugar in a small heavy skillet; cook and stir over medium-low heat until melted and caramel-colored, about 10 minutes. Stir in almonds until coated. Spread on foil to cool.

2. Place romaine, onion and strawberries in a large bowl. Whisk together dressing ingredients; toss with salad. Break the candied almonds into pieces; sprinkle over salad. Serve immediately.

¾ CUP 110 cal., 6g fat (1g sat. fat), 1mg chol., 33mg sod., 13g carb. (10g sugars, 2g fiber), 2g pro. **DIABETIC EXCHANGES** 1 vegetable, 1 fat, ½ starch.

Ambrosia Salad

Because it's so easy to prepare, this tropical medley is great as a last-minute menu addition. Plus, it requires just five ingredients.
—*Judi Bringegar, Liberty, NC*

PREP: 10 min. + chilling
MAKES: 4 servings

1 can (15 oz.) mandarin oranges, drained
1 can (8 oz.) pineapple tidbits, drained
1 cup miniature marshmallows
1 cup sweetened shredded coconut
1 cup sour cream

In a large bowl, combine the oranges, pineapple, marshmallows and coconut. Add sour cream and toss to mix. Cover and refrigerate for several hours.

1 CUP 370 cal., 20g fat (14g sat. fat), 14mg chol., 101mg sod., 48g carb. (43g sugars, 2g fiber), 4g pro.

Easy Old-Fashioned Mashed Potatoes

A pressure cooker makes quick work of mashed potatoes when your stovetop is full with other pans. So easy!
—*Amber Gaines, Colorado Springs, CO*

PREP: 10 min. • **COOK:** 15 min.
MAKES: 6 servings

- 2 lbs. medium russet potatoes, peeled and quartered
- 3 cups water
- ½ tsp. kosher salt
- ⅓ cup 2% milk or buttermilk
- ¼ cup sour cream
- 2 Tbsp. butter
- 1 tsp. kosher salt
- ¼ tsp. pepper
  Optional: Chopped chives or parsley

1. Add potatoes and water to a 6-qt. electric pressure cooker. Lock the lid; close pressure-release valve. Adjust to pressure-cook on high for 10 minutes. Quick-release pressure.

2. Drain, reserving cooking liquid. Add potatoes back to pan. Add milk, sour cream, butter, salt and pepper. Mash until desired consistency, adding the reserved cooking liquid if necessary. If desired, serve with chives or parsley and additional butter.

⅔ CUP 149 cal., 6g fat (4g sat. fat), 18mg chol., 523mg sod., 21g carb. (3g sugars, 1g fiber), 3g pro.

MIX IT UP
Forget the traditional way of mashing potatoes when you use an electric handheld mixer to do the job for you.

Boston Baked Beans

Simmered in molasses, these beans are perfect to take to your next potluck. The sauce is sweet, dark and rich—they complement anything you serve with them.
—*Darlene Duncan, Langhorne, PA*

PREP: 20 min. + soaking • **COOK:** 10 hours
MAKES: 10 servings

- 1 lb. dried navy beans
- ¼ lb. diced salt pork or 6 bacon strips, cooked and crumbled
- 1 large onion, chopped
- ½ cup packed brown sugar
- ½ cup molasses
- ¼ cup sugar
- 1 tsp. ground mustard
- 1 tsp. salt
- ½ tsp. ground cloves
- ½ tsp. pepper
- 2 cups water

1. Rinse and sort beans. Place in a large saucepan; add water to cover by 2 in. Let soak, covered, overnight. Drain and rinse beans, discarding liquid.

2. Return beans to saucepan; add water to cover by 2 in. Bring to a boil. Boil for 15 minutes. Drain and rinse the beans, discarding liquid.

3. Transfer beans to a 3- or 4-qt. slow cooker; add salt pork. In a small bowl, combine onion, brown sugar, molasses, sugar, mustard, salt, cloves, pepper and 2 cups water. Pour mixture over beans; stir to combine. Cook, covered, on low until beans are tender, 10-12 hours.

⅔ CUP 331 cal., 6g fat (2g sat. fat), 12mg chol., 511mg sod., 58g carb. (27g sugars, 7g fiber), 13g pro.

Spiced Cranberry Sauce

While this cranberry sauce is simmering, the wonderful fragrance of the spices brings back happy memories of when my mother made it for the holidays. My husband and three sons are glad I'm carrying on her tradition!
—*Allison Thompson, Lansing, MI*

PREP: 5 min. • **COOK:** 30 min. + chilling
MAKES: 2 cups

- 1 pkg. (12 oz.) fresh or frozen cranberries
- 1¾ cups sugar
- ½ cup water
- ½ tsp. ground cinnamon
- ½ tsp. ground allspice
- ⅛ tsp. salt
- ⅛ tsp. ground ginger
- ⅛ tsp. ground cloves

In a large saucepan, combine all the ingredients. Bring to a boil. Reduce heat; simmer, uncovered, until the berries pop and mixture is thickened, about 30 minutes. Cool. Transfer to a serving bowl; cover and refrigerate until chilled.

¼ CUP 191 cal., 0 fat (0 sat. fat), 0 chol, 38mg sod., 49g carb. (46g sugars, 2g fiber), 0 pro.

Mom's Chopped Coleslaw

For our Friday fish dinners, my mother treated us to her homemade coleslaw on the side. That creamy, tangy flavor is still a family tradition.
—*Cynthia McDowell, Banning, CA*

TAKES: 20 min. • **MAKES:** 6 servings

- ½ medium head cabbage (about 1¼ lbs.)
- ½ cup finely chopped celery
- ½ cup finely chopped sweet red or green pepper
- ⅓ cup finely chopped sweet onion

DRESSING
- ½ cup mayonnaise
- ¼ cup sugar
- ¼ cup 2% milk
- ¼ cup buttermilk
- 2 tsp. white vinegar
- ¼ tsp. hot pepper sauce
  Dash pepper

1. Cut cabbage into 1½- to 2-in. pieces. Place half of the cabbage in a food processor; pulse until chopped. Transfer to a large bowl; repeat with remaining cabbage.

2. Add the remaining vegetables to cabbage. In a small bowl, whisk the dressing ingredients until blended. Pour over coleslaw and toss to coat. Refrigerate until serving.

¾ CUP 203 cal., 15g fat (2g sat. fat), 8mg chol., 147mg sod., 16g carb. (13g sugars, 2g fiber), 2g pro.

Without question, one of the best coleslaws I've ever had! This recipe will be kept with my best potato salad and macaroni salad recipes. I'm set for life!

—KRISTINECHAYES, TASTEOFHOME.COM

Aunt Margaret's Sweet Potato Casserole

My great-aunt made an incredible sweet potato casserole.
I've lightened it up a bit for today, but we love it just the same.
—*Beth Britton, Fairlawn, OH*

PREP: 50 min. • **BAKE:** 40 min. + standing
MAKES: 12 servings

3 lbs. sweet potatoes (about 3 large), peeled and cubed

TOPPING
¾ cup all-purpose flour
¾ cup packed brown sugar
¾ cup old-fashioned oats
⅛ tsp. salt
⅓ cup cold butter, cubed

FILLING
½ cup sugar
½ cup 2% milk
2 large eggs, lightly beaten
¼ cup butter
1 tsp. vanilla extract
2 cups miniature marshmallows

1. Preheat oven to 350°. Place sweet potatoes in a 6-qt. stockpot; add water to cover. Bring to a boil. Reduce heat; cook, uncovered, until tender, 10-12 minutes. Meanwhile, make topping by combining flour, brown sugar, oats and salt; cut in butter until crumbly.

2. Drain potatoes; return to pan. Beat until mashed. Add sugar, milk, eggs, butter and vanilla; mash. Transfer to a broiler-safe 13x9-in. baking dish. Sprinkle topping over potato mixture.

3. Bake, uncovered, until topping is golden brown, 40-45 minutes; let stand 10 minutes. Sprinkle with marshmallows. If desired, broil 4-5 in. from heat until marshmallows are puffed and golden, 30-45 seconds.

½ CUP 373 cal., 11g fat (6g sat. fat), 56mg chol., 134mg sod., 66g carb. (39g sugars, 4g fiber), 5g pro.

Wedge Salad with Blue Cheese Dressing

Wedge salad gets a creamy treatment when topped with blue cheese dressing. The wedges lend a retro feel to menus and help beat the clock too.
—*Jenn Smith, Rumford, RI*

TAKES: 20 min. • **MAKES:** 6 servings

- ⅔ cup crumbled blue cheese
- ⅔ cup mayonnaise
- ⅓ cup reduced-fat sour cream
- 2 tsp. water
- 1½ tsp. red wine vinegar
- ⅛ tsp. Worcestershire sauce
  Dash cayenne pepper
- 1 large head iceberg lettuce
- 2 cups chopped assorted tomatoes
- 6 bacon strips, cooked and crumbled

In a small bowl, mix first 7 ingredients. Cut lettuce into 6 wedges. To serve, top wedges with the dressing, tomatoes and bacon.

1 SERVING 313 cal., 28g fat (7g sat. fat), 33mg chol., 473mg sod., 6g carb. (4g sugars, 2g fiber), 8g pro.

FROM DRESSING TO DIP
Keep this blue cheese dressing in mind. Stir it up the next time you're serving Buffalo wings or chicken tenders.

Grandma's Southern Collard Greens

My grandmother made the best collard greens in the world. Eating them with a slice of buttermilk cornbread is pure bliss.
—*Sherri Williams, Crestview, FL*

PREP: 30 min. • **COOK:** 2 hours
MAKES: 6 servings

- 3 Tbsp. lard or shortening, divided
- 1 large onion, chopped
- 6 garlic cloves, minced
- 1½ lbs. smoked ham hocks
- 6 cups water
- 2 tsp. seasoned salt
- 1 to 3 tsp. crushed red pepper flakes
- ¼ tsp. sugar
- 1 large bunch collard greens (about 2 lbs.), coarsely chopped
- 1½ cups white wine

1. In a 6-qt. stockpot, heat 1 Tbsp. lard over medium heat. Add onion and garlic; cook and stir until tender. Add the ham hocks, water, seasoned salt, pepper flakes and sugar. Bring to a boil. Reduce heat; simmer, uncovered, until meat is tender, 55-60 minutes.

2. Add the collard greens, wine and remaining lard. Return to a boil. Reduce heat; simmer, uncovered, until greens are very tender, 55-60 minutes. Remove meat from bones; finely chop meat and return to pan. Discard bones. Serve with a slotted spoon.

1 CUP 204 cal., 9g fat (3g sat. fat), 19mg chol., 849mg sod., 13g carb. (3g sugars, 7g fiber), 10g pro.

TRADITIONAL
MEAT LOAF, P. 111

Beefy
Entrees

Chili Mac Casserole

This nicely spiced entree comes together in minutes and uses several of my family's favorite ingredients, including macaroni, kidney beans, tomatoes and cheese. Just add a green salad for a complete meal.
—*Marlene Wilson, Rolla, ND*

PREP: 15 min. • **BAKE:** 30 min.
MAKES: 10 servings

- 1   cup uncooked elbow macaroni
- 2   lbs. lean ground beef (90% lean)
- 1   medium onion, chopped
- 2   garlic cloves, minced
- 1   can (28 oz.) diced tomatoes, undrained
- 1   can (16 oz.) kidney beans, rinsed and drained
- 1   can (6 oz.) tomato paste
- 1   can (4 oz.) chopped green chiles
- 1¼ tsp. salt
- 1   tsp. chili powder
- ½   tsp. ground cumin
- ½   tsp. pepper
- 2   cups shredded reduced-fat Mexican cheese blend
     Thinly sliced green onions, optional

1. Cook the macaroni according to package directions. Meanwhile, in a large nonstick skillet, cook the beef, onion and garlic over medium heat until meat is no longer pink, breaking the meat into crumbles; drain. Stir in tomatoes, beans, tomato paste, chiles and seasonings. Drain macaroni; add to beef mixture.

2. Transfer to a 13x9-in. baking dish coated with cooking spray. Cover and bake at 375° until bubbly, 25-30 minutes. Uncover; sprinkle with cheese. Bake until cheese is melted, 5-8 minutes longer. If desired, top with sliced green onions.

1 CUP 313 cal., 13g fat (6g sat. fat), 69mg chol., 758mg sod., 22g carb. (6g sugars, 5g fiber), 30g pro. **DIABETIC EXCHANGES** 3 lean meat, 1½ starch, 1 fat.

Thirty years ago, the hospital where I worked served this in the cafeteria but wouldn't give me the recipe so I made up my own. Awesome recipe; it's quick to throw together and yummy!

—SUSAN006, TASTEOFHOME.COM

Smoky Espresso Steak

This juicy steak rubbed with espresso, cocoa and pumpkin pie spice is one of my husband's favorites. We usually grill it, but broiling works in the chilly months.
—*Deborah Biggs, Omaha, NE*

TAKES: 30 min. • **MAKES:** 4 servings

- 3   tsp. instant espresso powder
- 2   tsp. brown sugar
- 1½   tsp. smoked or regular paprika
- 1   tsp. salt
- 1   tsp. baking cocoa
- ¼   tsp. pumpkin pie spice
- ¼   tsp. pepper
- 1   lb. beef flat iron or top sirloin steak (¾ in. thick)

1. Preheat broiler. Mix first 7 ingredients; rub over both sides of steak. Place steak on a broiler pan; let stand 10 minutes.

2. Broil steak 3-4 in. from heat 4-6 minutes on each side or until meat reaches desired doneness (for medium-rare, a thermometer should read 135°; medium, 140°; medium-well, 145°). Let stand 5 minutes before slicing.

3 OZ. COOKED BEEF 216 cal., 12g fat (5g sat. fat), 73mg chol., 661mg sod., 4g carb. (2g sugars, 0 fiber), 22g pro. **DIABETIC EXCHANGES** 3 lean meat.

Short Rib Poutine

This old-time dish combines the hearty, spicy flavors of my beloved slow-cooker short ribs with my all-time favorite comfort food: fries and gravy. With a little prep in the morning, it's just about ready when I come home from work (plus, the kitchen smells amazing!). If you are sensitive to spice, reduce the amount of sriracha chili sauce.
—*Erin DeWitt, Long Beach, CA*

PREP: 45 min. • **COOK:** 6 hours
MAKES: 4 servings

- 1 lb. well-trimmed boneless beef short ribs
- 3 Tbsp. all-purpose flour
- ½ tsp. pepper
- 2 Tbsp. olive oil
- 1 medium onion, coarsely chopped
- 4 garlic cloves, minced
- 1½ cups beef stock, divided
- ¼ cup Sriracha chili sauce
- 3 Tbsp. ketchup
- 2 Tbsp. Worcestershire sauce
- 1 Tbsp. packed brown sugar
- 3 cups frozen french-fried potatoes (about 11 oz.)
- 1 cup cheese curds or 4 oz. white cheddar cheese, broken into small chunks

1. Toss short ribs with flour and pepper, shaking off excess; reserve remaining flour mixture. In a large skillet, heat oil over medium-high heat; brown ribs on all sides. Transfer to a 3-qt. slow cooker, reserving drippings.

2. In same skillet, saute onion in drippings over medium heat until tender, 2-3 minutes. Add garlic; cook and stir 1 minute. Stir in 1 cup stock; bring to a boil, stirring to loosen browned bits from the pan.

3. In a small bowl, whisk the reserved flour mixture, chili sauce, ketchup, Worcestershire sauce, brown sugar and remaining stock until smooth; stir into onion mixture. Pour over ribs.

4. Cook, covered, on low until ribs are tender, 6-8 hours. Remove ribs; shred with 2 forks and keep warm. Skim fat from onion mixture; puree mixture using an immersion blender. (Or cool slightly and puree in a blender; return to slow cooker to heat through.)

5. Cook potatoes according to package directions. Serve beef over potatoes; top with gravy and cheese curds.

1 SERVING 560 cal., 31g fat (12g sat. fat), 80mg chol., 1453mg sod., 39g carb. (15g sugars, 3g fiber), 28g pro.

Slow-Cooker Sloppy Joes

This easy take on an all-time classic cooks without heating up the kitchen. The recipe is easy to double or triple for crowds, and if there are any leftovers, you can freeze them to enjoy later!
—*Carol Losier, Baldwinsville, NY*

PREP: 20 min. • **COOK:** 3 hours
MAKES: 8 servings

1½ lbs. ground beef
2 celery ribs, chopped
1 small onion, chopped
1 bottle (12 oz.) chili sauce
2 Tbsp. brown sugar
2 Tbsp. sweet pickle relish
1 Tbsp. Worcestershire sauce
1 tsp. salt
⅛ tsp. pepper
8 hamburger buns, split

1. In a large skillet, cook beef, celery and onion over medium-high heat, 8-10 minutes, until beef is no longer pink, breaking beef into crumbles; drain. Transfer to a 3-qt. slow cooker.

2. Stir in chili sauce, brown sugar, pickle relish, Worcestershire sauce, salt and pepper. Cook, covered, on low 3-4 hours or until heated through and flavors are blended. Spoon meat mixture onto bun bottoms. Replace tops.

1 SANDWICH 324 cal., 10g fat (4g sat. fat), 42mg chol., 1313mg sod., 40g carb. (16g sugars, 1g fiber), 19g pro.

Weekday Beef Stew

Beef stew capped with flaky puff pastry adds comfort and joy to the weeknight menu. Make a salad and call your crowd to the table.
—*Daniel Anderson, Kenosha, WI*

TAKES: 30 min. • **MAKES:** 4 servings

1 sheet frozen puff pastry, thawed
1 pkg. (15 oz.) refrigerated beef roast au jus
2 cans (14½ oz. each) diced tomatoes, undrained
1 pkg. (16 oz.) frozen vegetables for stew
¾ tsp. pepper
2 Tbsp. cornstarch
1¼ cups water

1. Preheat oven to 400°. Unfold puff pastry. Using a 4-in. round cookie cutter, cut out 4 circles. Place 2 in. apart on a greased baking sheet. Bake until golden brown, 14-16 minutes.

2. Meanwhile, shred beef with 2 forks; transfer to a large saucepan. Add tomatoes, vegetables and pepper; bring to a boil. In a small bowl, mix cornstarch and water until smooth; stir into beef mixture. Return to a boil, stirring constantly. Cook and stir until thickened, 1-2 minutes.

3. Ladle stew into 4 bowls; top each serving with a pastry round.

1½ CUPS WITH 1 PASTRY ROUND 604 cal., 25g fat (8g sat. fat), 73mg chol., 960mg sod., 65g carb. (10g sugars, 9g fiber), 32g pro.

Beef Short Ribs in Burgundy Sauce

My stepdad—an Army general—got this recipe from his aide, who said it was his mother's best Sunday meal. It's now a mouthwatering favorite in our family too.
—*Judy Batson, Tampa, FL*

PREP: 35 min. • **COOK:** 2¼ hours
MAKES: 6 servings

3   lbs. bone-in beef short ribs
3   Tbsp. butter
1   large sweet onion, halved and sliced
2   celery ribs, thinly sliced
1   medium carrot, thinly sliced
1   garlic clove, minced
    Dash dried thyme
2   Tbsp. all-purpose flour
1   cup water
1   cup dry red wine or beef broth
1   beef bouillon cube or 1 tsp. beef
    bouillon granules
2   Tbsp. minced fresh parsley
½   tsp. Worcestershire sauce
¼   tsp. salt
¼   tsp. browning sauce, optional
⅛   tsp. pepper

1. Preheat oven to 450°. Place short ribs on a rack in a shallow roasting pan. Roast 30-40 minutes or until browned, turning once.

2. Meanwhile, in a Dutch oven, heat butter over medium heat. Add onion, celery and carrot; cook and stir until tender, 10-12 minutes. Add garlic and thyme; cook 1 minute longer. Stir in flour until blended; gradually stir in water and wine. Add bouillon and parsley, stirring to dissolve bouillon.

3. Transfer ribs to Dutch oven; bring to a boil. Reduce heat; simmer, covered, 2-2½ hours or until meat is tender.

4. Remove short ribs; keep warm. Skim fat from sauce; stir in remaining ingredients. Serve with ribs.

1 SERVING 264 cal., 17g fat (8g sat. fat), 70mg chol., 355mg sod., 8g carb. (4g sugars, 1g fiber), 19g pro.

SHORT RIB SECRETS
Are beef short ribs expensive?
Bone-in beef short ribs tend to be a bit more expensive cut of beef because they come from the plate, or front belly, and are much fattier (read: extra delicious!) than a boneless short rib.

How do you thicken short rib sauce?
If your short rib sauce is thin, there are a few ways you can thicken it. We use flour in this recipe, but for a gluten-free option, you can use gluten-free flour or 1 Tbsp. of cornstarch instead.

EASY BEEF
STROGANOFF

Easy Beef Stroganoff

I lightened my mother-in-law's wonderful Stroganoff and came up with this version. In our home, we call it "Special Noodles."
—*Jennifer Riordan, St. Louis, MO*

TAKES: 30 min. • **MAKES:** 6 servings

4½ cups uncooked yolk-free noodles
1 lb. lean ground beef (90% lean)
½ lb. sliced fresh mushrooms
1 large onion, halved and sliced
3 garlic cloves, minced
1 Tbsp. butter
2 Tbsp. all-purpose flour
1 can (14½ oz.) reduced-sodium beef broth
2 Tbsp. tomato paste
1 cup reduced-fat sour cream
¼ tsp. salt
¼ tsp. pepper
   Chopped fresh parsley, optional

1. Cook noodles according to package directions. Meanwhile, in a large saucepan, cook the beef, mushrooms and onion over medium heat until meat is no longer pink, breaking meat into crumbles. Add garlic; cook 1 minute longer. Drain. Remove and keep warm.

2. In the same pan, melt butter. Stir in flour until smooth; gradually add broth and tomato paste. Bring to a boil; cook and stir until thickened, about 2 minutes.

3. Carefully return beef mixture to the pan. Add the sour cream, salt and pepper; cook and stir until heated through (do not boil). Drain noodles; serve with beef mixture. If desired, top with chopped parsley.

⅔ CUP BEEF MIXTURE WITH ¾ CUP NOODLES 333 cal., 11g fat (5g sat. fat), 58mg chol., 329mg sod., 32g carb. (6g sugars, 3g fiber), 25g pro. **DIABETIC EXCHANGES** 2 starch, 2 lean meat, 1 fat.

Slow-Cooked Beef Tips

These slow-cooked beef tips remind me of a childhood favorite. I cook them with mushrooms and serve over brown rice, noodles or mashed potatoes.
—*Amy Lents, Grand Forks, ND*

PREP: 25 min. • **COOK:** 6¼ hours
MAKES: 2 servings

¼ lb. sliced baby portobello mushrooms
½ small onion, sliced
1 beef top sirloin steak (½ lb.), cubed
¼ tsp. salt
⅛ tsp. pepper
1 tsp. olive oil
3 Tbsp. dry red wine or beef broth
1 cup beef broth
1½ tsp. Worcestershire sauce
1 Tbsp. cornstarch
2 Tbsp. water
   Hot cooked mashed potatoes

1. Place mushrooms and onion in a 3-qt. slow cooker. Sprinkle beef with salt and pepper. In a large skillet, heat oil over medium-high heat; brown meat. Transfer meat to slow cooker.

2. Add wine to skillet, stirring to loosen browned bits from pan. Stir in broth and Worcestershire sauce; pour over meat. Cook, covered, on low 6-8 hours or until meat is tender.

3. In a small bowl, mix cornstarch and water until smooth; gradually stir into slow cooker. Cook, covered, on high 15-30 minutes or until gravy is thickened. Serve with mashed potatoes.

1 CUP 213 cal., 7g fat (2g sat. fat), 46mg chol., 836mg sod., 8g carb. (2g sugars, 1g fiber), 27g pro. **DIABETIC EXCHANGES** 3 lean meat, 1½ fat, ½ starch.

Traditional Stuffed Peppers

My husband loves these stuffed peppers because they're so filling. I like how easy they are to prepare and the fact that leftovers don't dominate my refrigerator days after I serve them. They are delightful when coleslaw is served on the side.
—Karen Gentry, Eubank, NY

PREP: 25 min. • **BAKE:** 25 min.
MAKES: 6 servings

- 6 large green peppers
- 1½ lbs. ground beef
- ¾ cup chopped onion
- 3 cans (15 oz. each) tomato sauce, divided
- 3 cups cooked rice
- ½ tsp. salt
- ½ tsp. garlic powder
- ¼ tsp. pepper
  Optional toppings: Shredded cheddar cheese, chopped fresh parsley and sour cream

1. Preheat oven to 350°. Cut and discard tops from peppers; remove seeds. In a Dutch oven, cook peppers in boiling water until crisp-tender, 3-4 minutes; drain and rinse in cold water.

2. In a large skillet, cook beef and onion over medium heat until beef is no longer pink and onion is tender, 8-10 minutes, breaking up beef into crumbles; drain. Remove from the heat. Stir in 3 cups tomato sauce, rice, salt, garlic powder and pepper. Spoon into peppers.

3. Place in an ungreased shallow 3-qt. baking dish. Drizzle with remaining tomato sauce. Bake, covered, until peppers are tender, 25-30 minutes. Serve with toppings as desired.

1 STUFFED PEPPER 430 cal., 15g fat (6g sat. fat), 75mg chol., 1182mg sod., 45g carb. (9g sugars, 5g fiber), 30g pro.

Salisbury Steak Deluxe

This recipe is so good that I truly enjoy sharing it with others. I've always liked Salisbury steak, but I had to search a long time to find a recipe this tasty. It's also handy because it can be prepared ahead, kept in the refrigerator and warmed up later.
—Denise Barteet, Shreveport, LA

TAKES: 30 min. • **MAKES:** 6 servings

- 1 can (10¾ oz.) condensed cream of mushroom soup, undiluted
- 1 Tbsp. prepared mustard
- 2 tsp. Worcestershire sauce
- 1 tsp. prepared horseradish
- 1 large egg
- ¼ cup dry bread crumbs
- ¼ cup finely chopped onion
- ½ tsp. salt
  Dash pepper
- 1½ lb. ground beef
- 1 to 2 Tbsp. canola oil
- ½ cup water
- 2 Tbsp. chopped fresh parsley

1. In a small bowl, combine the soup, mustard, Worcestershire sauce and horseradish. Set aside. In another bowl, lightly beat the egg. Add the bread crumbs, onion, salt, pepper and ¼ cup of the soup mixture. Crumble beef over mixture and mix lightly but thoroughly. Shape into 6 patties.

2. In a large skillet, brown the patties in oil; drain. Combine remaining soup mixture with water; pour over patties. Cover and cook over low heat until meat is no longer pink and a thermometer reads 160°, 10-15 minutes. Remove patties to a serving platter; serve sauce with meat. Sprinkle with parsley.

1 PATTY 319 cal., 20g fat (7g sat. fat), 113mg chol., 706mg sod., 9g carb. (1g sugars, 1g fiber), 25g pro.

Traditional Lasagna

My family tasted this rich lasagna at a friend's home on Christmas Eve, and it became our holiday tradition. My sister's Italian in-laws request it often.
—*Lorri Foockle, Granville, IL*

PREP: 30 min. + simmering
BAKE: 70 min. + standing
MAKES: 12 servings

- 1 lb. ground beef
- ¾ lb. bulk pork sausage
- 3 cans (8 oz. each) tomato sauce
- 2 cans (6 oz. each) tomato paste
- 2 garlic cloves, minced
- 2 tsp. sugar
- 1 tsp. Italian seasoning
- ½ to 1 tsp. salt
- ¼ to ½ tsp. pepper
- 3 large eggs
- 3 Tbsp. minced fresh parsley
- 3 cups 4% small-curd cottage cheese
- 1 cup ricotta cheese
- ½ cup grated Parmesan cheese
- 9 lasagna noodles, cooked and drained
- 6 slices provolone cheese (about 6 oz.)
- 3 cups shredded part-skim mozzarella cheese, divided

1. In a large skillet over medium heat, cook and crumble the beef and sausage until no longer pink; drain. Add next 7 ingredients. Bring to a boil. Reduce heat; simmer, uncovered, 1 hour, stirring occasionally. Adjust seasoning with additional salt and pepper if desired.

2. Meanwhile, in a large bowl, lightly beat eggs. Add parsley; stir in cottage cheese, ricotta and Parmesan cheese.

3. Preheat oven to 375°. Spread 1 cup meat sauce in an ungreased 13x9-in. baking dish. Layer baking dish with 3 noodles, provolone cheese, 2 cups cottage cheese mixture, 1 cup mozzarella, 3 noodles, 2 cups meat sauce, remaining cottage cheese mixture and 1 cup mozzarella. Top with remaining noodles, meat sauce and mozzarella (dish will be full).

4. Cover; bake 50 minutes. Uncover; bake until heated through, about 20 minutes. Let lasagna stand 15 minutes before cutting.

1 PIECE 503 cal., 27g fat (13g sat. fat), 136mg chol., 1208mg sod., 30g carb. (9g sugars, 2g fiber), 36g pro.

FROZEN FEASTS

Lasagna freezes very well. Consider freezing leftovers in individual portions for quick lunches and dinners.

Refrigerate any leftover lasagna. The next day, cut into individual portions. Set the portions on a baking sheet, leaving space around each piece. Cover with foil and set in the freezer overnight.

Remove lasagna servings from sheet. Wrap each serving in heavy-duty foil and refreeze.

Whenever you'd like a serving of lasagna, remove a piece or 2 from the freezer. Remove foil and heat through in the microwave.

Easy Chow Mein

Some years ago, our daughter welcomed me home from a hospital stay with this Asian dish and a copy of the recipe. Now I freeze leftovers for fast future meals.
—*Kay Bade, Mitchell, SD*

PREP: 15 min. • **COOK:** 4 hours
MAKES: 8 servings

1 lb. ground beef
1 medium onion, chopped
1 bunch celery, sliced
2 cans (14 oz. each) Chinese vegetables, drained
2 envelopes brown gravy mix
2 Tbsp. soy sauce
   Hot cooked egg noodles or rice

In a large skillet, cook beef and onion over medium heat until meat is no longer pink, breaking meat into crumbles; drain. Transfer to a 3-qt. slow cooker. Stir in the celery, Chinese vegetables, gravy mix and soy sauce. Cover and cook on low until celery is tender, 4-6 hours, stirring occasionally. Serve with noodles.

1 CUP 361 cal., 6g fat (2g sat. fat), 28mg chol., 897mg sod., 56g carb. (6g sugars, 4g fiber), 18g pro.

Traditional Meat Loaf

Homemade meat loaf is a must-have comfort food and it freezes well, so we double the recipe and stash a loaf for a crazy day.
—*Gail Graham, Maple Ridge, BC*

PREP: 15 min. • **BAKE:** 1 hour + standing
MAKES: 6 servings

3 slices bread
1 large egg, lightly beaten
⅔ cup 2% milk
1 cup shredded cheddar cheese
1 medium onion, finely chopped
½ cup finely shredded carrot
1 tsp. salt
¼ tsp. pepper
1½ lbs. ground beef

GLAZE
¼ cup packed brown sugar
¼ cup ketchup
1 Tbsp. prepared mustard

1. Preheat oven to 350°. Tear bread into 2-in. pieces; place in a blender. Cover and pulse to form coarse crumbs; transfer to a large bowl. Stir in egg, milk, cheese, onion, carrot, salt and pepper. Add beef; mix lightly but thoroughly. Transfer to a greased 9x5-in. loaf pan.

2. In a small bowl, mix glaze ingredients; spread over loaf. Bake 60-75 minutes or until a thermometer reads 160°. Let stand 10 minutes before slicing.

FREEZE OPTION Bake meat loaf without glaze. Securely wrap cooled meat loaf in foil, then freeze. To use, partially thaw meat loaf in refrigerator overnight. Prepare and spread glaze over top; reheat on a greased shallow baking pan in a preheated 350° oven until heated through and a thermometer inserted in center reads 165°.

1 PIECE 394 cal., 21g fat (10g sat. fat), 128mg chol., 843mg sod., 23g carb. (15g sugars, 1g fiber), 28g pro.

Contest-Winning Mushroom Pot Roast

Packed with wholesome veggies and tender beef, this is one company-special entree all ages will like. Serve mashed potatoes alongside to soak up every last drop of the beefy gravy.
—*Angie Stewart, Topeka, KS*

PREP: 25 min. • **COOK:** 6 hours
MAKES: 10 servings

- 1 boneless beef chuck roast (3 to 4 lbs.)
- ½ tsp. salt
- ¼ tsp. pepper
- 1 Tbsp. canola oil
- 1½ lbs. sliced fresh shiitake mushrooms
- 2½ cups thinly sliced onions
- 1½ cups reduced-sodium beef broth
- 1½ cups dry red wine or additional reduced-sodium beef broth
- 1 can (8 oz.) tomato sauce
- ¾ cup chopped peeled parsnips
- ¾ cup chopped celery
- ¾ cup chopped carrots
- 8 garlic cloves, minced
- 2 bay leaves
- 1½ tsp. dried thyme
- 1 tsp. chili powder
- ¼ cup cornstarch
- ¼ cup water
  Mashed potatoes

1. Sprinkle roast with salt and pepper. In a Dutch oven, brown roast in oil on all sides. Transfer to a 6-qt. slow cooker. Add the mushrooms, onions, broth, wine, tomato sauce, parsnips, celery, carrots, garlic, bay leaves, thyme and chili powder. Cover and cook on low for 6-8 hours or until meat is tender.

2. Remove meat and vegetables to a serving platter; keep warm. Discard bay leaves. Skim fat from cooking juices; transfer juices to a small saucepan. Bring liquid to a boil. Combine cornstarch and water until smooth; gradually stir into the pan. Bring to a boil; cook and stir for 2 minutes or until thickened. Serve with mashed potatoes, meat and vegetables.

4 OZ. COOKED BEEF WITH ⅔ CUP VEGETABLES AND ½ CUP GRAVY 310 cal., 14g fat (5g sat. fat), 89mg chol., 363mg sod., 14g carb. (4g sugars, 3g fiber), 30g pro. **DIABETIC EXCHANGES** 4 lean meat, 2 vegetable, 1½ fat.

NOTES

Spaghetti & Meatballs

I've been cooking for 50 years, and this dish is still one that guests request frequently. It is my No. 1 standby recipe and also makes amazing meatball sandwiches. The sauce works for any type of pasta.
—*Jane Whittaker, Pensacola, FL*

PREP: 50 min. • **COOK:** 5 hours
MAKES: 12 servings

1   cup seasoned bread crumbs
2   Tbsp. grated Parmesan and Romano cheese blend
1   tsp. pepper
½   tsp. salt
2   large eggs, lightly beaten
2   lbs. ground beef

SAUCE
1   large onion, finely chopped
1   medium green pepper, finely chopped
3   cans (15 oz. each) tomato sauce
2   cans (14½ oz. each) diced tomatoes, undrained
1   can (6 oz.) tomato paste
6   garlic cloves, minced
2   bay leaves
1   tsp. each dried basil, oregano and parsley flakes
1   tsp. salt
½   tsp. pepper
¼   tsp. crushed red pepper flakes
    Hot cooked spaghetti

1. In a large bowl, mix bread crumbs, cheese, pepper and salt; stir in eggs. Add beef; mix lightly but thoroughly. Shape into 1½-in. balls. In a large skillet, brown the meatballs in batches over medium heat; drain.

2. Place the first 5 sauce ingredients in a 6-qt. slow cooker; stir in garlic and seasonings. Add meatballs, stirring gently to coat. Cook, covered, on low 5-6 hours or until meatballs are cooked through.

3. Remove bay leaves. Serve with spaghetti.

ABOUT 3 MEATBALLS WITH ¾ CUP SAUCE
250 cal., 11g fat (4g sat. fat), 79mg chol., 1116mg sod., 20g carb. (7g sugars, 4g fiber), 20g pro.

TEST KITCHEN TIPS

Can you overcook meatballs in a slow cooker?
Generally, slow cookers cook low and slow, so meatballs are less likely to overcook than if you were to quickly bake them in the oven. The longer you leave meatballs in a slow cooker, however, you do risk them becoming tougher and a bit chewier. For best results, stick to the amount of time suggested in the recipe for perfect, tender meatballs cooked just right.

How do you store this entree?
Store leftover meatballs and sauce in an airtight, lidded container in the refrigerator for 3-5 days. Make a fresh batch of spaghetti when you're ready to reheat and enjoy.

Barbecue Bacon Burger

Every family has a burger of choice, and this is ours. It's stacked tall with bacon and crunchy onion rings.
—*Paula Homer, Nampa, ID*

TAKES: 30 min. • **MAKES:** 6 servings

- 12 frozen onion rings
- 2 lbs. ground beef
- ¼ tsp. garlic salt
- ¼ tsp. pepper
- 6 slices pepper jack cheese
- 6 hamburger buns, split and toasted
- 1 cup barbecue sauce
- 6 cooked bacon strips
  Optional: Lettuce leaves, sliced tomato and dill pickles

1. Bake onion rings according to package directions. Meanwhile, in a large bowl, combine beef, garlic salt and pepper; mix lightly but thoroughly. Shape into six ¾-in.-thick patties.

2. In a large nonstick skillet, cook burgers over medium heat 5-7 minutes on each side or until a thermometer reads 160°, adding cheese during the last minute of cooking. Serve on buns with barbecue sauce, bacon, onion rings and desired toppings.

1 BURGER 768 cal., 39g fat (15g sat. fat), 127mg chol., 1275mg sod., 60g carb. (18g sugars, 2g fiber), 42g pro.

Beef Brisket on Buns

With its slightly smoky flavor, this beef turns out tender and delicious every time. Plus, it slices well so it looks great on a buffet.
—*Debra Waggoner, Grand Island, NE*

PREP: 25 min. + standing • **BAKE:** 5 hours
MAKES: 16 servings

- ½ tsp. ground ginger
- ½ tsp. ground mustard
- 1 fresh beef brisket (4 to 5 lbs.)
- 2 cups water
- 1 cup ketchup
- ½ cup Worcestershire sauce
- 2 Tbsp. brown sugar
- 2 tsp. Liquid Smoke, optional
- 1 tsp. chili powder
- 16 to 20 sandwich buns, split, optional

1. Combine the ginger and mustard; rub over brisket. Place on a rack in a shallow roasting pan. Bake, uncovered, at 325° for 2 hours.

2. Let stand for 20 minutes. Thinly slice meat across the grain. Place in a foil-lined 13x9-in. baking dish. In a bowl, combine the water, ketchup, Worcestershire sauce, brown sugar, Liquid Smoke if desired and chili powder; pour over meat. Cover tightly with foil; bake 3 hours longer or until tender. Serve on buns if desired.

NOTE This is a fresh beef brisket, not corned beef.

3 OZ. COOKED BRISKET 171 cal., 5g fat (2g sat. fat), 48mg chol., 313mg sod., 7g carb. (7g sugars, 0 fiber), 23g pro. **DIABETIC EXCHANGES** 3 lean meat.

Old-Fashioned Cabbage Rolls

It was an abundance of dill in my garden that led me to try this. My family liked the taste so much that from then on, I made my cabbage rolls with dill.
—*Florence Krantz, Bismarck, ND*

PREP: 25 min. • **BAKE:** 1½ hours
MAKES: 6 servings

1   medium head cabbage (3 lbs.)
½   lb. uncooked ground beef
½   lb. uncooked ground pork
1   can (15 oz.) tomato sauce, divided
1   small onion, chopped
½   cup uncooked long grain rice
1   Tbsp. dried parsley flakes
½   tsp. salt
½   tsp. snipped fresh dill or dill weed
⅛   tsp. cayenne pepper
1   can (14½ oz.) diced tomatoes, undrained
½   tsp. sugar

1. Cook cabbage in boiling water just until outer leaves pull away easily from head. Set aside 12 large leaves for rolls. In a small bowl, combine the beef, pork, ½ cup tomato sauce, onion, rice, parsley, salt, dill and cayenne; mix well.

2. Cut out the thick vein from the bottom of each leaf, making a V-shaped cut. Place about ¼ cup meat mixture on a cabbage leaf; overlap cut ends of leaf. Fold in sides. Beginning from the cut end, roll up. Repeat.

3. Slice the remaining cabbage; place in a Dutch oven. Arrange the cabbage rolls seam side down over sliced cabbage. Combine the tomatoes, sugar and remaining tomato sauce; pour over rolls. Cover and bake at 350° until cabbage rolls are tender, about 1½ hours.

2 CABBAGE ROLLS 260 cal., 10g fat (4g sat. fat), 50mg chol., 694mg sod., 23g carb. (5g sugars, 3g fiber), 18g pro.

ETHNIC EATS
Many cultures eat cabbage rolls with a variety of fillings and sauces, but they are especially prevalent in Polish culture and often served for holidays and special occasions.

Golabki is the Polish name for cabbage leaves wrapped around beef or pork with rice or barley. In Eastern Europe, tomato sauce or plain sour cream are the traditional toppings.

Grandma's Swedish Meatballs

My mother made these hearty meatballs when we were growing up, and now my kids love them too. My daughter likes to help toss the meatballs in flour.
—*Karin Ness, Big Lake, MN*

TAKES: 30 min. • **MAKES:** 4 servings

- 1 large egg, lightly beaten
- ½ cup crushed saltines (about 10 crackers)
- ¼ tsp. seasoned salt
- ¼ tsp. pepper
- ¼ tsp. ground nutmeg, optional
- ½ lb. ground beef
- ½ lb. bulk pork sausage
- ¼ cup plus 2 Tbsp. all-purpose flour, divided
- 2½ cups reduced-sodium beef broth, divided
  - Hot mashed potatoes
  - Minced fresh parsley, optional

1. Mix first 4 ingredients and nutmeg if desired. Add beef and sausage; mix lightly but thoroughly. Shape into 1-in. balls; toss with ¼ cup flour, coating lightly.

2. In a large skillet, brown meatballs over medium-high heat. Add 2 cups broth; bring to a boil. Reduce heat; simmer, covered, until meatballs are cooked through, 5-6 minutes.

3. Remove meatballs with a slotted spoon. Mix the remaining flour and broth until smooth; add to pan. Bring to a boil; cook and stir until thickened, 1-2 minutes. Return meatballs to pan; heat through. Serve with mashed potatoes. If desired, sprinkle with parsley.

1 SERVING 348 cal., 21g fat (7g sat. fat), 115mg chol., 846mg sod., 17g carb. (1g sugars, 1g fiber), 21g pro.

Easy Goulash

With this slow-cooker recipe, you can put in a full day's work, run some errands and still get dinner on the table in hardly any time. Make it extra special by serving the meat sauce over spaetzle.
—*Cyndy Gerken, Naples, FL*

PREP: 25 min. • **COOK:** 8½ hours
MAKES: 2 servings

- 1 lb. beef stew meat
- 1 Tbsp. olive oil
- 1 cup beef broth
- 1 small onion, chopped
- ¼ cup ketchup
- 1 Tbsp. Worcestershire sauce
- 1½ tsp. brown sugar
- 1½ tsp. paprika
- ¼ tsp. ground mustard
- 1 Tbsp. all-purpose flour
- 2 Tbsp. water
  - Hot cooked egg noodles or spaetzle
  - Chopped fresh parsley, optional

1. In a large skillet, brown beef in oil; drain. Transfer to a 1½-qt. slow cooker. Combine the broth, onion, ketchup, Worcestershire sauce, brown sugar, paprika and mustard. Pour over beef. Cover and cook on low 8-10 hours or until meat is tender.

2. In a small bowl, combine flour and water until smooth. Gradually stir into beef mixture. Cover and cook on high until thickened, about 30 minutes longer. Serve with noodles. If desired, sprinkle with parsley.

1 CUP 478 cal., 23g fat (7g sat. fat), 141mg chol., 1005mg sod., 20g carb. (14g sugars, 1g fiber), 45g pro.

Aberdeen Beef Pie

Set in the middle of the table, this hearty beef pie will be the center of attention. With chunks of tender beef and tasty vegetables under a flaky pastry crust, this is pure comfort food to welcome your family home.
—*Peggy Goodrich, Enid, OK*

PREP: 1½ hours
BAKE: 35 min. + standing
MAKES: 12 servings

- ¼ lb. sliced bacon, diced
- 3 lbs. beef stew meat, cut into 1-in. cubes
- 1 cup chopped onion
- 1½ cups halved fresh baby carrots
- 6 Tbsp. all-purpose flour
- 1 cup beef broth
- 1 Tbsp. Worcestershire sauce
- 1 pkg. (10 oz.) frozen peas
- ½ tsp. salt
- ½ tsp. pepper
- 1 sheet refrigerated pie crust
- 1 large egg, lightly beaten, optional

1. Preheat oven to 375°. In a Dutch oven, cook bacon over medium heat until crisp. Remove to paper towels to drain. Brown the beef in drippings in batches; drain and set beef aside. Add onion to the pan; saute until crisp-tender. Add carrots, bacon and beef.

2. Meanwhile, in a small bowl, combine the flour, broth and Worcestershire sauce until smooth; add to beef mixture. Bring to a boil. Reduce heat; cover and simmer until meat is tender, 1-1½ hours. Stir in peas, salt and pepper. Transfer to an ungreased 11x7-in. baking dish.

3. On a lightly floured surface, roll out crust into a 12x8-in. rectangle. Cut slits in crust. Place over filling; trim and seal edges. If desired, brush with beaten egg. Bake until crust is golden and filling is bubbly, 35-40 minutes. Let stand for 15 minutes before serving. Refrigerate leftovers.

1 SERVING 308 cal., 14g fat (6g sat. fat), 76mg chol., 389mg sod., 18g carb. (3g sugars, 2g fiber), 25g pro.

Guinness Corned Beef & Cabbage

A dear friend of my mother's shared this recipe with her years ago. My husband and kids request it for special occasions such as birthdays and, of course, St. Patrick's Day.
—*Karin Brodbeck, Red Hook, NY*

PREP: 20 min. • **COOK:** 8 hours
MAKES: 9 servings

- 2 lbs. red potatoes, quartered
- 1 lb. carrots, cut into 3-in. pieces
- 2 celery ribs, cut into 3-in. pieces
- 1 small onion, quartered
- 1 corned beef brisket with spice packet (3 to 3½ lbs.)
- 8 whole cloves
- 6 whole peppercorns
- 1 bay leaf
- 1 bottle (12 oz.) Guinness stout or reduced-sodium beef broth
- ½ small head cabbage, thinly sliced
   Prepared horseradish

1. In a 6-qt. slow cooker, combine potatoes, carrots, celery and onion. Add corned beef (discard spice packet or save for another use).

2. Place cloves, peppercorns and bay leaf on a double thickness of cheesecloth. Gather corners of cloth to enclose seasonings; tie securely with string. Place in slow cooker. Pour stout over top.

3. Cook, covered, on low 8-10 hours or until meat and vegetables are tender, adding cabbage during the last hour of cooking. Discard spice bag.

4. Cut beef diagonally across the grain into thin slices. Serve beef with vegetables and horseradish.

3 OZ. COOKED BEEF WITH ¾ CUP VEGETABLES 374 cal., 20 g fat (7 g sat. fat), 104 mg chol., 1256 mg sod., 25 g carb. (5 g sugars, 4 g fiber), 22 g pro.

ABERDEEN
BEEF PIE

CITRUS—MUSTARD
ROASTED CHICKEN, P. 145

Poultry
Mains

Old-Fashioned Chicken Potpie

Although this uses leftover chicken, I serve it sometimes as a special company dinner. Actually, my husband may enjoy it more than the original roasted bird with all the fixings!
—*Marilyn Hockey, Lisle, ON*

PREP: 30 min. • **BAKE:** 30 min.
MAKES: 6 servings

- ⅓ cup butter
- ⅓ cup all-purpose flour
- 1 garlic clove, minced
- ½ tsp. salt
- ¼ tsp. pepper
- 1½ cups water
- ⅔ cup 2% milk
- 2 tsp. chicken bouillon granules
- 2 cups cubed cooked chicken
- 1 cup frozen mixed vegetables

CRUST
- 1⅔ cups all-purpose flour
- 2 tsp. celery seeds
- 1 pkg. (8 oz.) cream cheese, cubed
- ⅓ cup cold butter

1. Preheat oven to 425°. In a saucepan, melt butter over medium heat. Stir in flour, garlic, salt and pepper until blended. Gradually stir in water, milk and bouillon. Bring to a boil; cook and stir until thickened, 1-2 minutes. Remove from the heat. Stir in chicken and vegetables; set aside.

2. For crust, in a large bowl, combine flour and celery seed. Cut in cream cheese and butter until crumbly. Work mixture by hand until dough forms a ball. On a lightly floured surface, roll two-thirds dough into a 12-in. square. Transfer to an 8-in. square baking dish; press crust up sides of the dish. Pour filling into crust. Roll remaining dough into a 9-in. square; place over filling. Trim, seal and flute edges. Cut slits in crust.

3. Bake until crust is golden brown and filling is bubbly, 30-35 minutes.

1 SERVING 592 cal., 38g fat (22g sat. fat), 136mg chol., 823mg sod., 40g carb. (4g sugars, 3g fiber), 22g pro.

Roasted Chicken & Red Potatoes

Pop this homey dinner in the oven for about an hour, then enjoy! It has so much flavor—the meat juices help cook the veggies just perfectly.
—*Sherri Melotik, Oak Creek, WI*

PREP: 15 min. • **BAKE:** 55 min.
MAKES: 6 servings

- 2 lbs. red potatoes, cut into 1-in. pieces
- 1 pkg. (9 oz.) fresh spinach
- 1 large onion, cut into 1-in. pieces
- 2 Tbsp. olive oil
- 4 garlic cloves, minced
- 1 tsp. salt, divided
- 1 tsp. dried thyme
- ¾ tsp. pepper, divided
- 6 chicken leg quarters
- ¾ tsp. paprika

1. Preheat oven to 375°. Place potatoes, spinach and onion in a greased shallow roasting pan. Add oil, garlic, ¾ tsp. salt, thyme and ½ tsp. pepper; toss to combine.

2. Arrange chicken over vegetables; sprinkle with paprika and remaining salt and pepper. Roast on an upper oven rack 55-60 minutes or until a thermometer inserted in chicken reads 170°-175° and potatoes are tender.

1 CHICKEN LEG QUARTER WITH 1 CUP VEGETABLE MIXTURE 449 cal., 21g fat (5g sat. fat), 105mg chol., 529mg sod., 29g carb. (3g sugars, 4g fiber), 35g pro.

Chicken & Dumpling Casserole

This classic, savory casserole is one of my husband's favorites. He loves the fluffy dumplings with plenty of gravy. The basil adds just the right flavor and makes the whole house smell so good while this dish bakes.
—*Sue Mackey, Jackson, WI*

PREP: 30 min. • **BAKE:** 40 min.
MAKES: 8 servings

- ½ cup chopped onion
- ½ cup chopped celery
- ¼ cup butter, cubed
- 2 garlic cloves, minced
- ½ cup all-purpose flour
- 2 tsp. sugar
- 1 tsp. salt
- 1 tsp. dried basil
- ½ tsp. pepper
- 4 cups chicken broth
- 1 pkg. (10 oz.) frozen green peas
- 4 cups cubed cooked chicken

DUMPLINGS
- 2 cups biscuit/baking mix
- 2 tsp. dried basil
- ⅔ cup 2% milk

1. Preheat oven to 350°. In a large saucepan, saute onion and celery in butter until tender. Add garlic; cook 1 minute longer. Stir in flour, sugar, salt, basil and pepper until blended. Gradually add broth; bring to a boil. Cook and stir 1 minute or until thickened; reduce heat. Add peas and cook 5 minutes, stirring constantly. Stir in the chicken. Pour into a greased 13x9-in. baking dish.

2. For dumplings, in a small bowl, combine baking mix and basil. Stir in milk with a fork until moistened. Drop by tablespoonfuls into mounds over chicken mixture.

3. Bake, uncovered, 30 minutes. Cover and bake 10 minutes longer or until a toothpick inserted in a dumpling comes out clean.

1 SERVING 393 cal., 17g fat (7g sat. fat), 80mg chol., 1313mg sod., 33g carb. (6g sugars, 3g fiber), 27g pro.

NOTES

Cranberry-Orange Roast Ducklings

I came up with this recipe a few years ago. The first time I served it, there wasn't a speck of food left on the platter and I knew I had a winning recipe.
—*Gloria Warczak, Cedarburg, WI*

PREP: 20 min. • **BAKE:** 3 hours + standing
MAKES: 10 servings

  2   domestic ducklings (4 to 5 lbs. each)
  2   medium navel oranges, quartered
  2   sprigs fresh rosemary
1½   cups fresh or frozen cranberries,
        divided
  4   cups orange juice
  1   cup chicken broth
  ¼   cup soy sauce
  2   tsp. sugar
  2   garlic cloves, minced
  1   tsp. grated fresh gingerroot
  ⅔   cup orange marmalade

1. Preheat oven to 350°. Pierce duckling skin all over with a fork. Place 4 orange quarters, 1 sprig of rosemary and ¼ cup cranberries in each duckling cavity; tie drumsticks together. Place on a rack in a roasting pan, breast side up.

2. In a bowl, mix orange juice, broth, soy sauce, sugar, garlic and ginger. Refrigerate ½ cup for glaze. Pour 1 cup over ducklings; sprinkle with remaining cranberries. Cover and bake 1 hour. Uncover and bake 1½ hours longer, basting frequently with remaining orange juice mixture. (Drain fat from pan as it accumulates.)

3. Mix marmalade and reserved orange juice mixture; spread over ducklings. Bake, uncovered, until a thermometer inserted in thigh reads 180°, 30-40 minutes. Discard oranges, rosemary and cranberries from cavities. Let ducklings stand 10 minutes before carving.

8 OZ. COOKED DUCK 373 cal., 21g fat (7g sat. fat), 61mg chol., 517mg sod., 31g carb. (27g sugars, 1g fiber), 16g pro.

Creamy Turkey Casserole

I sometimes make turkey just so I have the extras for this casserole!
—Mary Jo O'Brien, Hastings, MN

PREP: 15 min. • **BAKE:** 40 min.
MAKES: 12 servings

- 1 can (10¾ oz.) condensed cream of celery soup, undiluted
- 1 can (10¾ oz.) condensed cream of mushroom soup, undiluted
- 1 can (10¾ oz.) condensed cream of onion soup, undiluted
- 5 oz. cubed Velveeta
- ⅓ cup mayonnaise
- 3½ to 4 cups shredded cooked turkey
- 1 pkg. (16 oz.) frozen broccoli florets or cuts, thawed
- 1½ cups cooked white rice
- 1½ cups cooked wild rice
- 1 can (8 oz.) sliced water chestnuts, drained
- 1 jar (4 oz.) sliced mushrooms, drained
- 1½ to 2 cups salad croutons

1. In a large bowl, combine the soups, cheese and mayonnaise. Stir in the turkey, broccoli, rice, water chestnuts and mushrooms.

2. Transfer to a greased 13x9-in. baking dish. Bake, uncovered, at 350° for 30 minutes; stir. Sprinkle with croutons. Bake until bubbly, 8-12 minutes longer.

¾ CUP 311 cal., 14g fat (4g sat. fat), 52mg chol., 846mg sod., 25g carb. (3g sugars, 3g fiber), 20g pro.

Seasoned Roast Turkey

Rubbing the skin with melted butter keeps this simply seasoned turkey moist and tender.
—Nancy Reichert, Thomasville, GA

PREP: 15 min.
BAKE: 2¾ hours + standing
MAKES: 15 servings

- ¼ cup butter, melted
- 2 tsp. salt
- 2 tsp. garlic powder
- 2 tsp. seasoned salt
- 1½ tsp. paprika
- 1 tsp. ground ginger
- ¾ tsp. pepper
- ½ tsp. dried basil
- ¼ tsp. cayenne pepper
- 1 turkey (13 to 15 lbs.)
- 2 medium lemons, halved, optional

1. Preheat oven to 325°. In a small bowl, combine the first 9 ingredients. Place turkey, breast side up, on a rack in a roasting pan; pat dry. Brush with butter mixture. If desired, place lemons in cavity; tie legs with kitchen twine.

2. Bake, uncovered, 2¾-3¼ hours or until a thermometer inserted in thickest part of thigh reads 170°-175°. Cover loosely with foil if turkey browns too quickly. Cover and let stand 20 minutes before carving.

9 OZ. COOKED TURKEY 488 cal., 24g fat (8g sat. fat), 221mg chol., 698mg sod., 1g carb. (0 sugars, 0 fiber), 63g pro.

NO PEEKING!
Resist the urge to baste your turkey, as every time you open the oven door, you let heat escape. This can increase the cook time, which can lead to drier meat.

Chicken & Chiles Casserole

This casserole is easy to prepare and can be made ahead if you have a busy day coming up. It makes good use of leftover meat and is very filling.
—*Lois Keel, Alburquerque, NM*

PREP: 15 min. • **BAKE:** 1¼ hours
MAKES: 8 servings

 1 cup sour cream
 1 cup half-and-half cream
 1 cup chopped onion
 1 can (4 oz.) chopped green chiles
 1 tsp. salt
 ½ tsp. pepper
 1 pkg. (2 lbs.) frozen shredded hash brown potatoes
 2½ cups cubed cooked chicken
 2½ cups shredded cheddar cheese, divided
   Chopped fresh cilantro, optional

1. Preheat oven to 350°. In a large bowl, combine the sour cream, half-and-half cream, onion, chiles, salt and pepper. Stir in potatoes, chicken and 2 cups cheese.

2. Pour the mixture into a greased 13x9-in. or 3-qt. baking dish. Bake, uncovered, until golden brown, about 1¼ hours. Sprinkle with remaining cheese before serving. If desired, sprinkle with chopped cilantro.

1½ CUPS 410 cal., 21g fat (14g sat. fat), 111mg chol., 647mg sod., 25g carb. (4g sugars, 2g fiber), 26g pro.

Turkey Bundles

This recipe is definitely a must-try—just bundle up creamy turkey filling in crescent dough. Double the recipe if you hope to have some left over for lunch the next day.
—*Lydia Garrod, Tacoma, WA*

TAKES: 30 min. • **MAKES:** 6 servings

 4 oz. cream cheese, softened
 2 Tbsp. 2% milk
 ½ tsp. dill weed
 ¼ tsp. celery salt
 ¼ tsp. pepper
 2 cups cubed cooked turkey
 ¼ cup chopped water chestnuts
 1 green onion, chopped
 2 tubes (one 8 oz., one 4 oz.) refrigerated crescent rolls
 2 Tbsp. butter, melted
 2 Tbsp. seasoned bread crumbs

1. Preheat oven to 375°. In a large bowl, beat the first 5 ingredients until smooth. Stir in the turkey, water chestnuts and green onion.

2. Unroll both tubes of crescent dough and separate dough into 6 rectangles; press perforations to seal. Place ⅓ cup turkey mixture in center of each rectangle. Bring 4 corners of dough together above filling; twist and pinch seams to seal.

3. Place on an ungreased baking sheet. Brush tops with butter; sprinkle with bread crumbs. Bake 15-20 minutes or until golden brown.

1 BUNDLE 418 cal., 25g fat (10g sat. fat), 67mg chol., 674mg sod., 26g carb. (5g sugars, 0 fiber), 20g pro.

The Best Chicken & Dumplings

Chicken and dumplings harken back to my childhood and chilly days when we devoured those cute little balls of dough swimming in hot, rich broth.
—*Erika Monroe-Williams, Scottsdale, AZ*

PREP: 25 min. • **COOK:** 1 hour 10 min.
MAKES: 8 servings (3 qt.)

- ¾ cup all-purpose flour, divided
- ½ tsp. salt
- ½ tsp. freshly ground pepper
- 1 broiler/fryer chicken (about 3 lbs.), cut up
- 2 Tbsp. canola oil
- 1 large onion, chopped
- 2 medium carrots, chopped
- 2 celery ribs, chopped
- 3 garlic cloves, minced
- 6 cups chicken stock
- ½ cup white wine or apple cider
- 2 tsp. sugar
- 2 bay leaves
- 5 whole peppercorns

DUMPLINGS
- 1⅓ cups all-purpose flour
- 2 tsp. baking powder
- ¾ tsp. salt
- ⅔ cup 2% milk
- 1 Tbsp. butter, melted

SOUP
- ½ cup heavy whipping cream
- 2 tsp. minced fresh parsley
- 2 tsp. minced fresh thyme
  Additional salt and pepper to taste

1. In a shallow bowl, mix ½ cup flour, salt and pepper. Add chicken, 1 piece at a time, and toss to coat; shake off excess. In a 6-qt. stockpot, heat oil over medium-high heat. Brown chicken in batches on all sides; remove from pan.

2. Add onion, carrots and celery to same pan; cook and stir 6-8 minutes or until onion is tender. Add garlic; cook and stir 1 minute longer. Stir in ¼ cup flour until blended. Gradually add stock, stirring constantly. Stir in wine, sugar, bay leaves and peppercorns. Return chicken to pan; bring to a boil. Reduce heat; simmer, covered, 20-25 minutes or until chicken juices run clear.

3. For dumplings, in a bowl, whisk flour, baking powder and salt. In another bowl, whisk milk and melted butter until blended. Add to flour mixture; stir just until moistened (do not overmix). Drop by rounded tablespoonfuls onto a parchment-lined baking sheet; set aside.

4. Remove chicken from stockpot; cool slightly. Discard bay leaves and skim fat from soup. Remove skin and bones from chicken and discard. Using 2 forks, coarsely shred meat into 1- to 1½-in. pieces; return to soup. Cook, covered, on high until mixture reaches a simmer.

5. Drop dumplings on top of simmering soup, a few at a time. Reduce heat to low; cook, covered, 15-18 minutes or until a toothpick inserted in center of dumplings comes out clean (do not lift cover while simmering). Gently stir in cream, parsley and thyme. Season with additional salt and pepper to taste.

1½ CUPS 470 cal., 24g fat (8g sat. fat), 104mg chol., 892mg sod., 29g carb. (5g sugars, 2g fiber), 32g pro.

THE SECRET TO FULL-FLAVORED SOUP

If the butcher includes a backbone with your chicken, don't throw it away. Use it to bolster the flavor of the soup by tossing it into the pot to simmer with the chicken and vegetables. Discard before adding dumplings.

Favorite Barbecued Chicken

Is there a better place than Texas to find a fantastic barbecue sauce? That's where the one in this recipe is from—it's my father-in-law's own creation. We have served it at many family reunions and think it's the best!
—*Bobbie Morgan, Woodstock, GA*

PREP: 15 min. • **GRILL:** 35 min.
MAKES: 12 servings

2   broiler/fryer chickens (3 to 4 lbs. each), cut into 8 pieces each
    Salt and pepper

BARBECUE SAUCE
2   Tbsp. canola oil
2   small onions, finely chopped
2   cups ketchup
¼   cup lemon juice
2   Tbsp. brown sugar
2   Tbsp. water
1   tsp. ground mustard
½   tsp. garlic powder
¼   tsp. pepper
⅛   tsp. salt
⅛   tsp. hot pepper sauce

1. Sprinkle chicken pieces with salt and pepper. Grill, skin side down, uncovered, on a greased rack over medium heat for 20 minutes.

2. Meanwhile, in a small saucepan, make barbecue sauce by heating oil over medium heat. Add onion; saute until tender. Stir in remaining sauce ingredients and bring to a boil. Reduce heat; simmer, uncovered, for 10 minutes.

3. Turn chicken; brush with barbecue sauce. Grill 15-25 minutes longer, brushing frequently with sauce, until a thermometer reads 165° when inserted in the breast and 170°-175° in the thigh.

4 OZ. COOKED CHICKEN 370 cal., 19g fat (5g sat. fat), 104mg chol., 622mg sod., 15g carb. (14g sugars, 0 fiber), 33g pro.

NOTES

Roast Chicken with Vegetables

Love a moist and tender chicken but not the mess of actual roasting? Use an oven cooking bag to keep chicken and veggies easily under control.
—Taste of Home *Test Kitchen*

PREP: 15 min. • **BAKE:** 1¼ hours + standing
MAKES: 6 servings

- 1 Tbsp. all-purpose flour
- 1 large oven roasting bag
- 8 small red potatoes, halved
- 6 medium carrots, cut into 2-in. pieces
- 6 half-ears frozen corn on the cob, thawed
- 1 tsp. salt, divided
- ½ tsp. pepper, divided
- ¼ tsp. paprika, divided
- 1 medium onion, quartered
- 3 fresh rosemary sprigs or 1 Tbsp. dried rosemary, crushed
- 1 roasting chicken (6 to 7 lbs.)
- 2 Tbsp. olive oil
- 2 tsp. minced fresh rosemary or ½ tsp. dried rosemary, crushed

1. Preheat oven to 350°. Sprinkle flour into oven bag; shake to coat. Add the potatoes, carrots, corn, ½ tsp. salt, ¼ tsp. pepper and ⅛ tsp. paprika. Shake bag to coat vegetables; place in a 13x9-in. baking pan.

2. Place onion and rosemary sprigs in cavity of chicken. Rub skin with oil; sprinkle with minced rosemary and remaining salt, pepper and paprika. Skewer chicken openings; tie drumsticks together. Place chicken in center of bag, breast side up; place vegetables around chicken.

3. Cut six ½-in. slits in top of bag; close with tie provided. Bake 1¼-1½ hours or until a thermometer inserted in thickest part of thigh reads 170°-175°. Let stand in oven bag 15 minutes before carving. Discard onion and rosemary sprigs.

1 SERVING 711 cal., 37g fat (10g sat. fat), 179mg chol., 615mg sod., 34g carb. (6g sugars, 5g fiber), 61g pro.

Turkey Lattice Pie

With its pretty lattice crust, this cheesy old-time entree is as appealing as it is tasty. It's easy to make too, since it uses ready-to-go crescent roll dough.
—Lorraine Naig, Emmetsburg, IA

PREP: 20 min. • **BAKE:** 25 min.
MAKES: 12 servings

- 3 tubes (8 oz. each) refrigerated crescent rolls, divided
- 4 cups cubed cooked turkey
- 1½ cups shredded cheddar or Swiss cheese
- 3 cups frozen chopped broccoli, thawed and drained
- 1 can (10¾ oz.) condensed cream of chicken soup, undiluted
- 1⅓ cups 2% milk
- 2 Tbsp. Dijon mustard
- 1 Tbsp. dried minced onion
- ½ tsp. salt
  Dash pepper
- 1 large egg, lightly beaten

1. Preheat oven to 375°. Unroll 2 tubes of crescent roll dough; separate into rectangles. Place rectangles in an ungreased 15x10x1-in. baking pan; press onto the bottom and ¼ in. up sides of the pan to form a crust, sealing seams and perforations. Bake 5-7 minutes or until light golden brown.

2. Meanwhile, in a large bowl, combine turkey, cheese, broccoli, soup, milk, mustard, onion, salt and pepper. Spoon over crust.

3. Unroll remaining dough; divide into 2 rectangles. Seal perforations. Cut each rectangle lengthwise into 1-in. strips. Using strips, make a lattice design on top of turkey mixture. Brush with egg. Bake 17-22 minutes longer or until top crust is golden brown and filling is bubbly.

1 SERVING 396 cal., 20g fat (4g sat. fat), 81mg chol., 934mg sod., 30g carb. (8g sugars, 2g fiber), 24g pro.

Mom's Turkey Tetrazzini

If you're looking for old-fashioned, stick-to-your-ribs comfort food, this hearty dish will meet your needs.
—Judy Batson, Tampa, FL

PREP: 25 min. • **BAKE:** 25 min. + standing
MAKES: 6 servings

- 1 pkg. (12 oz.) fettuccine
- ½ lb. sliced fresh mushrooms
- 1 medium onion, chopped
- ¼ cup butter, cubed
- 3 Tbsp. all-purpose flour
- 1 cup white wine or chicken broth
- 3 cups 2% milk
- 3 cups cubed cooked turkey
- ¾ tsp. salt
- ½ tsp. pepper
- ½ tsp. hot pepper sauce
- ½ cup shredded Parmesan cheese
  Paprika, optional

1. Preheat oven to 375°. Cook fettuccine according to package directions.

2. Meanwhile, in a large skillet, saute mushrooms and onion in butter until tender. Stir in flour until blended; whisk in wine until smooth, about 2 minutes. Slowly whisk in milk. Bring to a boil; cook and stir until thickened. Stir in turkey, salt, pepper and pepper sauce.

3. Drain fettuccine. Layer half of the fettuccine, turkey mixture and cheese in a greased 13x9-in. baking dish. Repeat layers. Sprinkle with paprika if desired.

4. Cover and bake 25-30 minutes or until heated through. Let stand 10 minutes before serving.

1 CUP 516 cal., 17g fat (9g sat. fat), 87mg chol., 596mg sod., 53g carb. (10g sugars, 4g fiber), 37g pro.

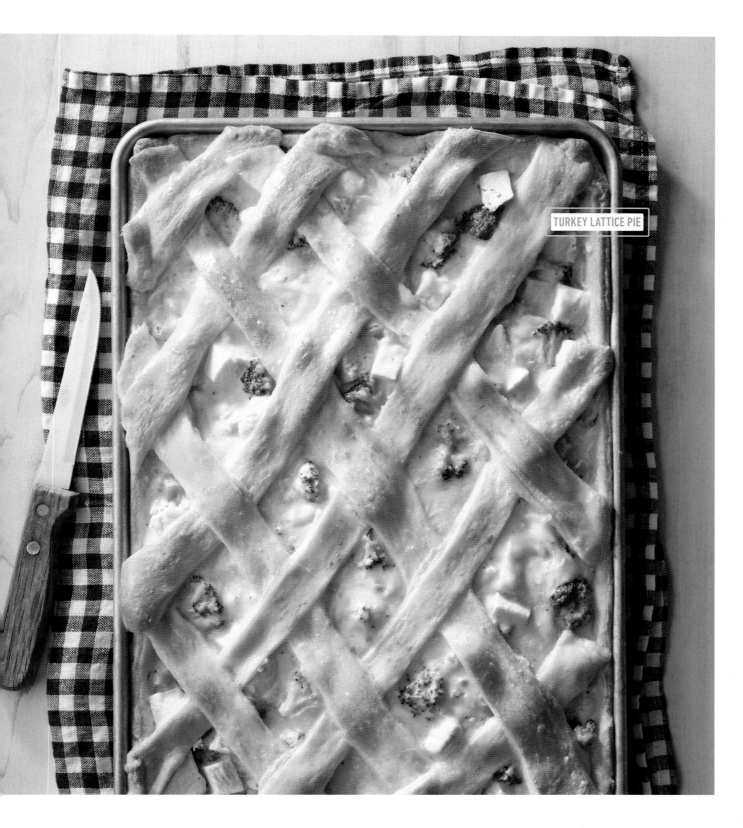

TURKEY LATTICE PIE

CHICKEN DIVAN

Chicken Divan

This tasty recipe was given to me by a friend years ago, and it's been a family favorite ever since. My daughters enjoy making this dish in their own homes now and get the same enthusiastic compliments I have always received!
—Mary Pat Lucia, North East, PA

PREP: 20 min. • **BAKE:** 35 min.
MAKES: 10 servings

¼ cup plus 1 Tbsp. butter, divided
¼ cup all-purpose flour
1½ cups half-and-half cream
½ cup cooking sherry or water
2 cans (10¾ oz. each) condensed cream of chicken soup, undiluted
2 pkg. (10 oz. each) frozen cut or chopped broccoli, thawed
1 cup cooked rice
3 to 4 cups cubed cooked chicken
2 cups shredded cheddar cheese
1 cup soft bread crumbs
Minced fresh parsley, optional

1. In a small saucepan, melt ¼ cup butter. Add flour, stirring until blended. Stir in the cream and cooking sherry or water; cook and stir until thickened and bubbly. Cook and stir 2 more minutes. Blend in soup until smooth; remove from the heat and set aside.

2. Place broccoli in an ungreased 13x9-in. baking dish. Cover with rice and then half of the sauce. Top with chicken. Stir shredded cheese into remaining sauce; pour over the chicken.

3. Melt the remaining butter and toss with bread crumbs. Sprinkle over the casserole. Bake, uncovered, at 350° for 35-45 minutes or until heated through. If desired, sprinkle with parsley before serving.

NOTE To make soft bread crumbs, tear bread into pieces and place in a food processor or blender. Cover and pulse until crumbs form. One slice of bread yields ½ to ¾ cup crumbs.

1 CUP 412 cal., 24g fat (12g sat. fat), 98mg chol., 798mg sod., 20g carb. (3g sugars, 3g fiber), 22g pro.

Slow-Cooked Chicken a la King

When I know I'll be having a busy day with little time to prepare a meal,
I use my slow cooker to make chicken a la king. It smells so good while it's cooking.
—Eleanor Mielke, Snohomish, WA

PREP: 10 min. • **COOK:** 7½ hours
MAKES: 6 servings

1 can (10¾ oz.) reduced-fat reduced-sodium condensed cream of chicken soup, undiluted
3 Tbsp. all-purpose flour
¼ tsp. pepper
Dash cayenne pepper
1 lb. boneless skinless chicken breasts, cubed
1 celery rib, chopped
½ cup chopped green pepper
¼ cup chopped onion
1 pkg. (10 oz.) frozen peas, thawed
2 Tbsp. diced pimientos, drained
Hot cooked rice

1. In a 3-qt. slow cooker, combine soup, flour, pepper and cayenne until smooth. Stir in the chicken, celery, green pepper and onion.

2. Cover and cook on low for 7-8 hours or until meat is no longer pink. Stir in peas and pimientos. Cook 30 minutes longer or until heated through. Serve with rice.

1 CUP CHICKEN MIXTURE 174 cal., 3g fat (1g sat. fat), 44mg chol., 268mg sod., 16g carb. (6g sugars, 3g fiber), 19g pro. **DIABETIC EXCHANGES** 2 lean meat, 1 starch.

This was really good! The family loved it! So easy and great for a weeknight meal. I will definitely make again. Thanks for sharing!
—KATECRID47, TASTEOFHOME.COM

Four-Cheese Chicken Fettuccine

As a cattle rancher, my husband's a big fan of beef. For him to comment on a poultry dish is rare. But he always tells me, "I love this casserole!" I first tasted it at a potluck; now, I fix it for my family (we have a 3-year-old daughter) once or twice a month, and I'm asked to take it to most every get-together.
—*Rochelle Brownlee, Big Timber, MT*

PREP: 20 min. • **BAKE:** 30 min.
MAKES: 8 servings

- 8 oz. uncooked fettuccine
- 1 can (10¾ oz.) condensed cream of mushroom soup, undiluted
- 1 pkg. (8 oz.) cream cheese, cubed
- 1 jar (4½ oz.) sliced mushrooms, drained
- 1 cup heavy whipping cream
- ½ cup butter
- ¼ tsp. garlic powder
- ¾ cup grated Parmesan cheese
- ½ cup shredded part-skim mozzarella cheese
- ½ cup shredded Swiss cheese
- 2½ cups cubed cooked chicken

TOPPING
- ⅓ cup seasoned bread crumbs
- 2 Tbsp. butter, melted
- 1 to 2 Tbsp. grated Parmesan cheese

1. Cook fettuccine according to package directions.

2. Meanwhile, in a large kettle, combine the soup, cream cheese, mushrooms, cream, butter and garlic powder. Stir in cheeses; cook and stir until melted. Add chicken; heat through. Drain fettuccine; add to the sauce.

3. Transfer to a shallow greased 2½-qt. baking dish. Combine topping ingredients; sprinkle over chicken mixture. Cover and bake at 350° for 25 minutes. Uncover; bake 5-10 minutes longer or until golden brown.

1 SERVING 641 cal., 47g fat (27g sat. fat), 167mg chol., 895mg sod., 29g carb. (3g sugars, 2g fiber), 28g pro.

Chicken & Rice Casserole

Everyone loves this casserole because it's a tasty combination of hearty and crunchy ingredients in a creamy sauce. It's a time-tested classic. You can assemble the casserole ahead of time and keep it in the fridge; just wait to add the chips until you're ready to bake it.
—*Myrtle Matthews, Marietta, GA*

PREP: 15 min. • **BAKE:** 1 hour
MAKES: 12 servings

- 4 cups cooked white rice or a combination of wild and white rice
- 4 cups diced cooked chicken
- ½ cup slivered almonds
- 1 small onion, chopped
- 1 can (8 oz.) sliced water chestnuts, drained
- 1 pkg. (10 oz.) frozen peas, thawed
- ¾ cup chopped celery
- 1 can (10¾ oz.) condensed cream of celery soup, undiluted
- 1 can (10¾ oz.) condensed cream of chicken soup, undiluted
- 1 cup mayonnaise
- 2 tsp. lemon juice
- 1 tsp. salt
- 2 cups crushed potato chips
  Paprika

1. Preheat oven to 350°. In a greased 13x9-in. baking dish, combine first 7 ingredients. In a large bowl, combine soups, mayonnaise, lemon juice and salt. Pour over the chicken mixture and toss to coat.

2. Sprinkle with potato chips and paprika. Bake until heated through, about 1 hour.

1 CUP 439 cal., 26g fat (5g sat. fat), 51mg chol., 804mg sod., 31g carb. (3g sugars, 3g fiber), 19g pro.

NOTES

Chicken Amandine

With colorful green beans and pimientos, this attractive casserole is terrific for family dinners. This is true comfort food at its finest.
—Kat Woolbright, Wichita Falls, TX

PREP: 35 min. • **BAKE:** 30 min.
MAKES: 8 servings

- ¼ cup chopped onion
- 1 Tbsp. butter
- 1 pkg. (6 oz.) long grain and wild rice
- 2¼ cups chicken broth
- 3 cups cubed cooked chicken
- 2 cups frozen french-style green beans, thawed
- 1 can (10¾ oz.) condensed cream of chicken soup, undiluted
- ¾ cup sliced almonds, divided
- 1 jar (4 oz.) diced pimientos, drained
- 1 tsp. pepper
- ½ tsp. garlic powder
- 1 bacon strip, cooked and crumbled

1. In a large saucepan, saute onion in butter until tender. Add rice with contents of seasoning packet and broth. Bring to a boil. Reduce heat; cover and simmer until liquid is absorbed, about 25 minutes. Uncover; set aside to cool.

2. In a large bowl, combine chicken, green beans, soup, ½ cup almonds, pimientos, pepper and garlic powder. Stir in rice.

3. Transfer to a greased 2½-qt. baking dish. Sprinkle with bacon and remaining ¼ cup almonds. Cover and bake at 350° until heated through, 30-35 minutes.

1 CUP 297 cal., 13g fat (3g sat. fat), 54mg chol., 912mg sod., 24g carb. (3g sugars, 3g fiber), 22g pro.

SPEED IT UP
This classic entree is made easy with frozen vegetables, canned soup and other convenience items. You can speed up prep further by using a bacon strip left over from breakfast and chopped onion sold in your grocer's produce area.

Cornbread Chicken Bake

To make the most of leftover cornbread, try this hearty main-dish casserole. It's moist, delicious and good on any occasion.
—Madge Britton, Afton, TN

PREP: 20 min. • **BAKE:** 45 min.
MAKES: 10 servings

- 1¼ lbs. boneless skinless chicken breasts
- 6 cups cubed cornbread
- 8 bread slices, cubed
- 1 medium onion, chopped
- 2 cans (10¾ oz. each) condensed cream of chicken soup, undiluted
- 1 cup chicken broth
- 2 Tbsp. butter, melted
- 1½ to 2 tsp. rubbed sage
- 1 tsp. salt
- ½ to 1 tsp. pepper

1. Preheat oven to 350°. Place chicken in a large skillet and cover with water; bring to a boil. Reduce heat; cover and simmer until a thermometer reads 165°, 12-14 minutes. Drain and cut into cubes.

2. In a large bowl, combine the remaining ingredients. Add chicken. Transfer to a greased 13x9-in. baking dish.

3. Bake, uncovered, until heated through, 45 minutes.

FREEZE OPTION Cover and freeze unbaked casserole. To use, partially thaw in refrigerator overnight. Remove from refrigerator 30 minutes before baking. Bake casserole as directed, increasing time as necessary to heat through and for a thermometer inserted in center to read 165°.

1 CUP 392 cal., 9g fat (3g sat. fat), 40mg chol., 1307mg sod., 57g carb. (3g sugars, 4g fiber), 20g pro.

CHICKEN AMANDINE

Citrus-Mustard Roasted Chicken

Tender roast chicken is a snap to make and elegant to serve. We love the tang of orange and lemon slices and subtle heat from mustard.
—*Debra Keil, Owasso, OK*

PREP: 20 min. + chilling
BAKE: 1¼ hours + standing
MAKES: 4 servings

- 3   Tbsp. mustard seed
- ¼   cup olive oil
- 1   Tbsp. minced fresh chervil or 1 tsp. dried chervil
- 1   Tbsp. champagne vinegar
- 1   Tbsp. Worcestershire sauce
- ½   tsp. pepper
- 1   broiler/fryer chicken (3 to 4 lbs.)
- 2   orange slices
- 2   lemon slices
- 2   onion slices
- 3   sprigs fresh parsley, stems removed

1. Using a spice grinder or a mortar and pestle, grind mustard seed to a powder; transfer to a small bowl. Stir in oil, chervil, vinegar, Worcestershire sauce and pepper. Rub over outside and inside of chicken; place on a large plate. Refrigerate, covered, overnight.

2. Preheat oven to 350°. Place chicken in a shallow roasting pan, breast side up. Loosely stuff chicken with orange, lemon, onion and parsley. Tuck wings under chicken; tie drumsticks together.

3. Roast 1¼-1¾ hours or until a thermometer inserted in thickest part of thigh reads 170°-175°. (Cover loosely with foil if chicken browns too quickly.) Remove chicken from oven; tent with foil. Let stand 15 minutes before carving.

1 SERVING 537 cal., 37g fat (8g sat. fat), 131mg chol., 156mg sod., 6g carb. (2g sugars, 2g fiber), 44g pro.

Turkey Biscuit Stew

This chunky stew makes a hearty supper, especially in the fall and winter. It's also a great way to use extra turkey during the holidays.
—*Lori Schlecht, Wimbledon, ND*

PREP: 15 min. • **BAKE:** 20 min.
MAKES: 8 servings

- ⅓   cup chopped onion
- ¼   cup butter, cubed
- ⅓   cup all-purpose flour
- ½   tsp. salt
- ⅛   tsp. pepper
- 1   can (10½ oz.) condensed chicken broth, undiluted
- ¾   cup 2% milk
- 2   cups cubed cooked turkey
- 1   cup cooked peas
- 1   cup cooked whole baby carrots
- 1   tube (16.3 oz.) large refrigerated buttermilk biscuits

1. Preheat oven to 375°. In a 10-in. cast-iron or other ovenproof skillet, saute onion in butter until tender. Stir in the flour, salt and pepper until blended. Gradually add broth and milk. Bring to a boil. Cook and stir until thickened and bubbly, about 2 minutes. Add the turkey, peas and carrots; heat through. Separate biscuits and arrange over the stew.

2. Bake until biscuits are golden brown, 20-25 minutes.

¾ CUP STEW WITH 1 BISCUIT 345 cal., 15g fat (7g sat. fat), 53mg chol., 960mg sod., 36g carb. (7g sugars, 2g fiber), 18g pro.

CREAMY TUNA-NOODLE
CASSEROLE, P. 163

Fish & Seafood Dinners

Breaded Sea Scallops

I never liked seafood until my husband urged me to try scallops, and now I love them. He says my crispy breaded version is the best he's ever had.
—Martina Preston, Willow Grove, PA

TAKES: 15 min. • **MAKES:** 2 servings

- 1 large egg
- 1/3 cup mashed potato flakes
- 1/3 cup seasoned bread crumbs
- 1/8 tsp. salt
- 1/8 tsp. pepper
- 6 sea scallops (about 3/4 lb.)
- 2 Tbsp. all-purpose flour
- 2 Tbsp. butter
- 1 Tbsp. canola oil

1. In a shallow bowl, lightly beat egg. In another bowl, toss potato flakes and bread crumbs with salt and pepper. In a third bowl, toss scallops with flour to coat lightly. Dip in egg, then in potato mixture, patting to adhere.

2. In a large skillet, heat butter and oil over medium heat. Add scallops; cook until golden brown and scallops are firm and opaque, 2-3 minutes per side.

3 SCALLOPS 454 cal., 23g fat (9g sat. fat), 164mg chol., 1262mg sod., 33g carb. (2g sugars, 2g fiber), 28g pro.

ALMOND-CRUSTED SEA SCALLOPS Substitute 1/3 cup ground almonds for the potato flakes. Add 1/2 tsp. grated lemon peel to the bread crumb mixture. Proceed as directed.

Slow-Cooker Tuna Hot Dish

We tweaked this family-friendly classic to work for the slow cooker. It's easy, wholesome and totally homemade!
—Taste of Home *Test Kitchen*

PREP: 25 min. • **COOK:** 4 hours + standing
MAKES: 10 servings

- 1/4 cup butter, cubed
- 1/2 lb. sliced fresh mushrooms
- 1 medium onion, chopped
- 1 medium sweet pepper, chopped
- 1 tsp. salt, divided
- 1 tsp. pepper, divided
- 2 garlic cloves, minced
- 1/4 cup all-purpose flour
- 2 cups reduced-sodium chicken broth
- 2 cups half-and-half cream
- 4 cups uncooked egg noodles (about 6 oz.)
- 3 cans (5 oz. each) light tuna in water, drained
- 2 Tbsp. lemon juice
- 2 cups shredded Monterey Jack cheese
- 2 cups frozen peas, thawed
- 2 cups crushed potato chips

1. In a large skillet, melt butter over medium-high heat. Add mushrooms, onion, sweet pepper, 1/2 tsp. salt and 1/2 tsp. pepper; cook and stir until tender, 6-8 minutes. Add garlic; cook 1 minute longer. Stir in flour until blended. Gradually whisk in broth. Bring to a boil, stirring constantly; cook and stir until thickened, 1-2 minutes.

2. Transfer to a 5-qt. slow cooker. Stir in cream and noodles. Cook, covered, on low until noodles are tender, 4-5 hours. Meanwhile, in a small bowl, combine tuna, lemon juice and remaining salt and pepper.

3. Remove insert from slow cooker. Stir cheese, tuna mixture and peas into noodle mixture. Let stand, uncovered, 20 minutes. Just before serving, sprinkle with potato chips.

1 CUP 393 cal., 21g fat (12g sat. fat), 84mg chol., 752mg sod., 28g carb. (5g sugars, 3g fiber), 22g pro.

This was great! Total throwback to childhood. I did cut back on the salt, cheese and potato chips a bit but it still worked out just fine.
—POLS005, TASTEOFHOME.COM

BREADED
SEA SCALLOPS

SALMON QUICHE

Salmon Quiche

Cooking is something that I've always liked doing. I pore over cookbooks the way other people read novels. This recipe came to me from my mother—it's the kind you request after just one bite. And unlike some other quiches, it's very hearty!
—Deanna Baldwin, Bermuda Dunes, CA

PREP: 15 min. • **BAKE:** 1 hour
MAKES: 8 servings

- 1 sheet refrigerated pie crust
- 1 medium onion, chopped
- 1 Tbsp. butter
- 2 cups shredded Swiss cheese
- 1 can (14¾ oz.) salmon, drained, flaked and cartilage removed
- 5 large eggs
- 2 cups half-and-half cream
- ¼ tsp. salt
  Minced fresh parsley, optional

1. Unroll the crust into a 9-in. pie plate. Line unpricked pie crust with a double thickness of heavy-duty foil. Bake at 450° for 8 minutes. Remove foil; bake 5 minutes longer. Cool on a wire rack.

2. In a small skillet, saute onion in butter until tender. Sprinkle cheese in the crust; top with salmon and onion.

3. In a small bowl, whisk the eggs, cream and salt; pour over salmon mixture. Bake at 350° for 45-50 minutes or until a knife inserted in the center comes out clean. Sprinkle with parsley if desired. Let stand 5 minutes before cutting.

1 PIECE 456 cal., 30g fat (15g sat. fat), 221mg chol., 524mg sod., 17g carb. (4g sugars, 0 fiber), 27g pro.

Pretzel-Crusted Catfish

I'm not a big fish lover, so any concoction that has me enjoying fish is a keeper in my book. This combination of flavors works for me. It's awesome served with corn muffins, butter and honey!
—Kelly Williams, Forked River, NJ

TAKES: 30 min. • **MAKES:** 4 servings

- 4 catfish fillets (6 oz. each)
- ½ tsp. salt
- ½ tsp. pepper
- 2 large eggs
- ⅓ cup Dijon mustard
- 2 Tbsp. 2% milk
- ½ cup all-purpose flour
- 4 cups honey mustard miniature pretzels, coarsely crushed
  Oil for frying
  Lemon slices, optional

1. Sprinkle catfish with salt and pepper. Whisk the eggs, mustard and milk in a shallow bowl. Place flour and pretzels in separate shallow bowls. Coat fillets with flour, then dip in egg mixture and coat with pretzels.

2. Heat ¼ in. oil to 375° in an electric skillet. Fry fillets, a few at a time, until fish flakes easily with a fork, 3-4 minutes on each side. Drain on paper towels. Serve with lemon slices if desired.

1 FILLET 610 cal., 31g fat (4g sat. fat), 164mg chol., 1579mg sod., 44g carb. (2g sugars, 2g fiber), 33g pro.

Blend of the Bayou

My sister-in-law shared this recipe with me when I first moved here.
It's been handed down in my husband's family for generations. It's quick
to prepare, nutritious and flavorful. I've passed it on to my children too.
—*Ruby Williams, Bogalusa, LA*

PREP: 20 min. • **BAKE:** 25 min.
MAKES: 8 servings

- 1 pkg. (8 oz.) cream cheese, cubed
- 4 Tbsp. butter, divided
- 1 large onion, chopped
- 2 celery ribs, chopped
- 1 large green pepper, chopped
- 1 lb. cooked shrimp (31-40 per lb.),
  peeled and deveined
- 2 cans (6 oz. each) crabmeat, drained,
  flaked and cartilage removed
- 1 can (10¾ oz.) condensed cream of
  mushroom soup, undiluted
- ¾ cup cooked rice
- 1 jar (4½ oz.) sliced mushrooms,
  drained
- 1 tsp. garlic salt
- ¾ tsp. hot pepper sauce
- ½ tsp. cayenne pepper
- ¾ cup shredded cheddar cheese
- ½ cup crushed butter-flavored
  crackers (about 12 crackers)

1. Preheat oven to 350°. In a saucepan, cook and stir cream cheese and 2 Tbsp. butter over low heat until melted and smooth.

2. In a large cast-iron or other ovenproof skillet, saute onion, celery and green pepper in remaining butter until tender. Stir in shrimp, crab, soup, rice, mushrooms, garlic salt, pepper sauce, cayenne and cream cheese mixture.

3. Combine the cheddar cheese and cracker crumbs; sprinkle over top. Bake, uncovered, for 25-30 minutes or until bubbly.

1 CUP 366 cal., 23g fat (13g sat. fat), 164mg chol., 981mg sod., 17g carb. (3g sugars, 2g fiber), 23g pro.

NOTES

Carolina Shrimp & Cheddar Grits

Shrimp and grits are a house favorite—if only we could agree on a recipe.
I stirred things up with cheddar and Cajun seasoning to find a winner.
—*Charlotte Price, Raleigh, NC*

PREP: 15 min. • **COOK:** 2¾ hours
MAKES: 6 servings

1 cup uncooked stone-ground grits
1 large garlic clove, minced
½ tsp. salt
¼ tsp. pepper
4 cups water
2 cups shredded cheddar cheese
¼ cup butter, cubed
1 lb. peeled and deveined cooked shrimp (31-40 per lb.)
2 medium tomatoes, seeded and finely chopped
4 green onions, finely chopped
2 Tbsp. chopped fresh parsley
4 tsp. lemon juice
2 to 3 tsp. Cajun seasoning

1. Place first 5 ingredients in a 3-qt. slow cooker; stir to combine. Cook, covered, on high until water is absorbed and grits are tender, 2½-3 hours, stirring every 45 minutes.

2. Stir in cheese and butter until melted. Stir in remaining ingredients; cook, covered, on high until heated through, 15-30 minutes.

1⅓ CUPS 417 cal., 22g fat (13g sat. fat), 175mg chol., 788mg sod., 27g carb. (2g sugars, 2g fiber), 27g pro.

Speedy Salmon Patties

When I was a girl growing up on the farm, my mom often fixed these nicely seasoned patties when we were working late in the field. They're also tasty with chopped green peppers added to the mixture.
—*Bonnie Evans, Cameron, NC*

TAKES: 25 min. • **MAKES:** 3 servings

⅓ cup finely chopped onion
1 large egg, beaten
5 saltines, crushed
½ tsp. Worcestershire sauce
¼ tsp. salt
⅛ tsp. pepper
1 can (14¾ oz.) salmon, drained, bones and skin removed
2 tsp. butter

1. In a large bowl, combine the first 6 ingredients. Crumble salmon over mixture and gently fold in. Shape into 6 patties.

2. In a large skillet over medium heat, fry patties in butter for 3-4 minutes on each side or until set and golden brown.

2 PATTIES 307 cal., 15g fat (4g sat. fat), 179mg chol., 896mg sod., 6g carb. (1g sugars, 0 fiber), 36g pro.

KEEP IT TOGETHER
To keep salmon patties from falling apart, shape the patties gently but firmly to help all of the ingredients adhere. Some people like to refrigerate the uncooked patties prior to cooking to help them hold together. Also, be sure to gently flip the patties in the pan when cooking them.

Slow-Cooked Jambalaya

During chilly times of the year, I fix this jambalaya at least once a month. It's so easy—just chop the vegetables, dump everything in the slow cooker and forget it! Even my sons, who are picky about spicy things, like this dish.
—*Cindi Coss, Coppell, TX*

PREP: 35 min. • **COOK:** 4¼ hours
MAKES: 11 servings

 1 can (14½ oz.) diced tomatoes, undrained
 1 can (14½ oz.) beef or chicken broth
 1 can (6 oz.) tomato paste
 3 celery ribs, chopped
 2 medium green peppers, chopped
 1 medium onion, chopped
 5 garlic cloves, minced
 3 tsp. dried parsley flakes
 2 tsp. dried basil
1½ tsp. dried oregano
1¼ tsp. salt
 ½ tsp. cayenne pepper
 ½ tsp. hot pepper sauce
 1 lb. boneless skinless chicken breasts, cut into 1-in. cubes
 1 lb. smoked sausage, halved and cut into ¼-in. slices
 ½ lb. uncooked shrimp (31-40 per lb.), peeled and deveined
    Hot cooked rice

1. In a 5-qt. slow cooker, combine tomatoes, broth and tomato paste. Stir in celery, green peppers, onion, garlic, seasonings and pepper sauce. Stir in chicken and sausage.

2. Cover and cook on low for 4-6 hours or until chicken is no longer pink. Stir in shrimp. Cover and cook 15-30 minutes longer or until shrimp turn pink. Serve with rice.

FREEZE OPTION Place individual portions of cooled stew in freezer containers and freeze. To use, partially thaw stew in refrigerator overnight. Heat through in a saucepan, stirring occasionally and adding broth or water if necessary.

1 CUP JAMBALAYA 230 cal., 13g fat (5g sat. fat), 75mg chol., 1016mg sod., 9g carb. (5g sugars, 2g fiber), 20g pro.

QUICK TIP
To make a fresh garlic clove easy to peel, gently crush it with the flat side of a large knife blade to loosen the peel. If you don't have a large knife, you can crush the garlic with a small can. The peel will come right off.

Cod with Hearty Tomato Sauce

My father made up this sweet, flavorful recipe for my mother when he took over the cooking.
—*Ann Marie Eberhart, Gig Harbor, WA*

TAKES: 30 min. • **MAKES:** 4 servings

- 2 cans (14½ oz. each) diced tomatoes with basil, oregano and garlic, undrained
- 4 cod fillets (6 oz. each)
- 2 Tbsp. olive oil, divided
- 2 medium onions, halved and thinly sliced (about 1½ cups)
- ½ tsp. dried oregano
- ¼ tsp. pepper
- ¼ tsp. crushed red pepper flakes
  Hot cooked whole wheat pasta
  Minced fresh parsley, optional

1. Place tomatoes in a blender. Cover and process until pureed.

2. Pat fish dry with paper towels. In a large skillet, heat 1 Tbsp. oil over medium-high heat. Add cod fillets; cook until surface of fish begins to color, 2-4 minutes on each side. Remove from pan.

3. In same skillet, heat remaining oil over medium-high heat. Add onions; cook and stir until tender, 2-4 minutes. Stir in seasonings and pureed tomatoes; bring to a boil. Add cod; return just to a boil, spooning sauce over tops. Reduce heat; simmer, uncovered, until fish just begins to flake easily with a fork, 5-7 minutes. Serve with pasta. If desired, sprinkle with parsley.

1 FILLET WITH ¾ CUP SAUCE 271 cal., 8g fat (1g sat. fat), 65mg chol., 746mg sod., 17g carb. (9g sugars, 4g fiber), 29g pro. **DIABETIC EXCHANGES** 3 lean meat, 2 vegetable, 1½ fat.

Breaded Baked Tilapia

So much flavor yet so few ingredients! A quick and easy crumb coating makes this yummy tilapia recipe ideal for busy weeknights. Try the breading on cod for a change of pace.
—*Brandi Castillo, Santa Maria, CA*

TAKES: 20 min. • **MAKES:** 4 servings

- ¾ cup soft bread crumbs
- ⅓ cup grated Parmesan cheese
- 1 tsp. garlic salt
- 1 tsp. dried oregano
- 4 tilapia fillets (5 oz. each)

1. Preheat oven to 425°. In a shallow bowl, combine bread crumbs, cheese, garlic salt and oregano. Coat fillets in crumb mixture. Place on a baking sheet coated with cooking spray.

2. Bake 8-12 minutes or until fish flakes easily with a fork.

NOTE To make soft bread crumbs, tear bread into pieces and place in a food processor or blender. Cover and pulse until crumbs form. One slice of bread yields ½ to ¾ cup crumbs.

1 FILLET 143 cal., 2g fat (1g sat. fat), 72mg chol., 356mg sod., 2g carb. (0 sugars, 0 fiber), 28g pro. **DIABETIC EXCHANGES** 4 lean meat.

Caesar Orange Roughy

I'm so thankful that my mother, a fantastic cook, taught me the ropes in the kitchen when I was fairly young. Mom won several cooking contests over the years, and this is one of my favorite recipes of hers.
—Mary Lou Boyce, Wilmington, DE

TAKES: 25 min. • **MAKES:** 8 servings

- 8 orange roughy fillets (4 oz. each)
- 1 cup creamy Caesar salad dressing
- 2 cups crushed butter-flavored crackers (about 50 crackers)
- 1 cup shredded cheddar cheese

1. Preheat oven to 400°. Place fillets in an ungreased 13x9-in. baking dish. Drizzle with salad dressing; sprinkle with crushed crackers.

2. Bake, uncovered, 10 minutes. Sprinkle with cheese. Bake until fish flakes easily with a fork and cheese is melted, 3-5 minutes longer.

1 SERVING 421 cal., 28g fat (6g sat. fat), 93mg chol., 716mg sod., 17g carb. (3g sugars, 1g fiber), 24g pro.

Homemade Fish Sticks

I am a nutritionist and needed a healthier breaded fish fix. Moist inside and crunchy outside, these are amazing with oven fries or roasted veggies and low-fat homemade tartar sauce.
—Jennifer Rowland, Elizabethtown, KY

TAKES: 25 min. • **MAKES:** 2 servings

- ½ cup dry bread crumbs
- ½ tsp. salt
- ½ tsp. paprika
- ½ tsp. lemon-pepper seasoning
- ½ cup all-purpose flour
- 1 large egg, beaten
- ¾ lb. cod fillets, cut into 1-in. strips
  Butter-flavored cooking spray

1. Preheat oven to 400°. In a shallow bowl, mix bread crumbs and seasonings. Place flour and egg in separate shallow bowls. Dip fish in flour to coat both sides; shake off excess. Dip in egg, then in the crumb mixture, patting to help coating adhere.

2. Place on a baking sheet coated with cooking spray; spritz fish with butter-flavored cooking spray. Bake 10-12 minutes or until fish just begins to flake easily with a fork, turning once.

1 SERVING 278 cal., 4g fat (1g sat. fat), 129mg chol., 718mg sod., 25g carb. (2g sugars, 1g fiber), 33g pro. **DIABETIC EXCHANGES** 4 lean meat, 1½ starch.

Oyster Fricassee

I work at Colonial Williamsburg near the Chesapeake Bay, where there is a ready source of oysters. This special casserole comes from its holiday recipe collection.
—*Susan Dippre, Williamsburg, VA*

PREP: 20 min. • **BAKE:** 25 min. + standing
MAKES: 6 servings

- 1 qt. shucked oysters
- ¾ cup butter, divided
- 2 medium onions, chopped
- 1½ cups chopped celery
- ½ cup all-purpose flour
- 2 cups half-and-half cream
- 2 tsp. minced fresh parsley
- 1 tsp. salt
- 1 tsp. minced fresh thyme or ½ tsp. dried thyme
- ¼ tsp. pepper
- ⅛ tsp. cayenne pepper
- 4 large egg yolks, lightly beaten
- 2 cups crushed Ritz crackers (about 50 crackers)
    Lemon wedges
    Fresh thyme sprigs

1. Preheat oven to 400°. Drain oysters, reserving oyster liquor. In a large saucepan, heat ½ cup butter over medium heat. Add onions and celery; cook and stir until tender, 4-6 minutes. Stir in flour until blended; gradually whisk in cream. Bring to a boil, whisking constantly; cook until thickened, about 2 minutes.

2. Reduce heat; add next 5 ingredients and reserved oyster liquor. Cook and stir until smooth, about 2 minutes. Remove from heat. Stir a small amount of hot liquid into egg yolks; return all to pan, stirring constantly.

3. Pour half the sauce into a greased 13x9-in. baking dish. Top with half the oysters; sprinkle with half the cracker crumbs. Repeat layers. Melt remaining butter; drizzle over top.

4. Bake, uncovered, until golden brown, for 23-28 minutes. Let stand 10 minutes. Serve with lemon wedges and thyme sprigs.

1 SERVING 639 cal., 44g fat (23g sat. fat), 297mg chol., 1024mg sod., 42g carb. (9g sugars, 2g fiber), 17g pro.

Sweet & Tangy Salmon with Green Beans

I'm always up for new ways to cook salmon. In this dish, a sweet sauce gives the fish and green beans some down-home barbecue tang. Even our kids love it.
—Aliesha Caldwell, Robersonville, NC

PREP: 20 min. • **BAKE:** 15 min.
MAKES: 4 servings

- 4   salmon fillets (6 oz. each)
- 1   Tbsp. butter
- 2   Tbsp. brown sugar
- 2   Tbsp. reduced-sodium soy sauce
- 2   Tbsp. Dijon mustard
- 1   Tbsp. olive oil
- ½   tsp. pepper
- ⅛   tsp. salt
- 1   lb. fresh green beans, trimmed

1. Preheat oven to 425°. Place fillets in a 15x10x1-in. baking pan coated with cooking spray. In a small skillet, melt butter; stir in brown sugar, soy sauce, mustard, oil, pepper and salt. Brush half of the mixture over the salmon.

2. Place green beans in a large bowl; drizzle with remaining brown sugar mixture and toss to coat. Arrange green beans around fillets. Roast until fish just begins to flake easily with a fork and green beans are crisp-tender, 14-16 minutes.

1 FILLET WITH ¾ CUP GREEN BEANS 394 cal., 22g fat (5g sat. fat), 93mg chol., 661mg sod., 17g carb. (10g sugars, 4g fiber), 31g pro. **DIABETIC EXCHANGES** 5 lean meat, 1½ fat, 1 vegetable, ½ starch.

Honey Walleye

My state is known as the Land of 10,000 Lakes, so fishing is a favorite recreational activity here. This recipe is a quick way to prepare all the fresh walleye hooked by the anglers in my family.
—Kitty McCue, St. Louis Park, MN

TAKES: 20 min. • **MAKES:** 6 servings

- 1   large egg
- 2   tsp. honey
- 2   cups crushed Ritz crackers (about 45 to 50)
- ½   tsp. salt
- 1½ lbs. walleye fillets
- ⅓   to ½ cup canola oil
     Optional: Minced fresh parsley and lemon wedges

1. In a shallow bowl, beat egg; add honey. In a shallow dish, combine crackers and salt. Dip fish in egg mixture, then in cracker mixture; turn until coated.

2. In a cast-iron or other heavy skillet, cook fillets in oil over medium heat until golden and fish flakes easily with a fork, 3-5 minutes on each side. If desired, top with parsley and serve with lemon wedges.

3 OZ. COOKED FISH 389 cal., 22g fat (3g sat. fat), 133mg chol., 514mg sod., 23g carb. (5g sugars, 1g fiber), 25g pro.

Creamy Tuna-Noodle Casserole

When you need supper fast, this tuna casserole with peas, peppers and onions makes a super one-dish meal. Cooked chicken breast works well in place of the tuna.
—*Edie DeSpain, Logan, UT*

PREP: 20 min. • **BAKE:** 25 min.
MAKES: 6 servings

- 5 cups uncooked egg noodles
- 1 cup frozen peas
- 1 can (10¾ oz.) reduced-fat reduced-sodium condensed cream of mushroom soup, undiluted
- 1 cup fat-free sour cream
- ⅔ cup grated Parmesan cheese
- ⅓ cup 2% milk
- ¼ tsp. salt
- 2 cans (5 oz. each) light tuna in water, drained and flaked
- ¼ cup finely chopped onion
- ¼ cup finely chopped green pepper

TOPPING
- ½ cup soft bread crumbs
- 1 Tbsp. butter, melted

1. Preheat oven to 350°. Cook noodles according to package directions for al dente, adding peas during the last minute of cooking; drain.

2. Meanwhile, in a large bowl, combine soup, sour cream, cheese, milk and salt; stir in tuna, onion and pepper. Add noodles and peas; toss to combine.

3. Transfer to an 11x7-in. baking dish coated with cooking spray. In a small bowl, toss bread crumbs with melted butter; sprinkle over top. Bake, uncovered, 25-30 minutes or until bubbly.

NOTE To make soft bread crumbs, tear bread into pieces and place in a food processor or blender. Cover and pulse until crumbs form. One slice of bread yields ½ to ¾ cup crumbs.

1⅓ CUPS 340 cal., 8g fat (4g sat. fat), 63mg chol., 699mg sod., 41g carb. (7g sugars, 3g fiber), 25g pro. **DIABETIC EXCHANGES** 3 starch, 2 lean meat, ½ fat.

CASSEROLE CLUES

What can I substitute for peas in this recipe?
If peas aren't a favorite, you can substitute a cup of frozen mixed vegetables or frozen chopped broccoli in this tuna casserole recipe.

Does tuna noodle casserole freeze well?
An unbaked tuna noodle casserole freezes nicely, so consider doubling this recipe and saving the second for another time. To enjoy later, remove the casserole from the freezer and place it in the refrigerator 24 hours before baking. Bring it up to room temp before putting it in the oven, baking as directed.

How do you thicken tuna casserole?
To thicken your tuna casserole, keep it in the oven longer. This should thicken it right up.

How do you fix a dry casserole?
Warm up ½ cup of chicken or vegetable broth and drizzle it over the baked dish. Cover with foil and let it stand for 10 minutes before serving.

Shrimp Puttanesca

I quickly throw together these bold ingredients for a feisty seafood pasta.
—*Lynda Balslev, Sausalito, CA*

TAKES: 30 min. • **MAKES:** 4 servings

2 Tbsp. olive oil, divided
1 lb. uncooked shrimp (31-40 per lb.), peeled and deveined
¾ to 1 tsp. crushed red pepper flakes, divided
¼ tsp. salt
1 small onion, chopped
2 to 3 anchovy fillets, finely chopped
3 garlic cloves, minced
2 cups grape tomatoes or small cherry tomatoes
½ cup dry white wine or vegetable broth
⅓ cup pitted Greek olives, coarsely chopped
2 tsp. drained capers
Sugar to taste
Chopped fresh Italian parsley
Hot cooked spaghetti, optional

1. In a large skillet, heat 1 Tbsp. oil; saute shrimp with ½ tsp. pepper flakes until shrimp turn pink, 2-3 minutes. Stir in salt; remove from pan.

2. In same pan, heat remaining oil over medium heat; saute onion until tender, about 2 minutes. Add anchovies, garlic and remaining pepper flakes; cook and stir until fragrant, about 1 minute. Stir in the tomatoes, wine, olives and capers; bring to a boil. Reduce heat; simmer, uncovered, until tomatoes are softened and mixture is thickened, 8-10 minutes.

3. Stir in shrimp. Add sugar to taste; sprinkle with parsley. If desired, serve with spaghetti.

1 CUP SHRIMP MIXTURE 228 cal., 12g fat (2g sat. fat), 140mg chol., 579mg sod., 8g carb. (3g sugars, 1g fiber), 20g pro.

NOTES

Classic Crab Cakes

Our region is known for good seafood, and crab cakes are a traditional favorite. I learned to make them from a chef in a restaurant where they were a bestseller. The crabmeat's sweet and mild flavor is sparked by the blend of other ingredients.
—Debbie Terenzini, Lusby, MD

TAKES: 20 min. • **MAKES:** 8 servings

- 1 lb. fresh or canned crabmeat, drained, flaked and cartilage removed
- 2 to 2½ cups soft bread crumbs
- 1 large egg, beaten
- ¾ cup mayonnaise
- ⅓ cup each chopped celery, green pepper and onion
- 2 tsp. lemon juice
- 1 Tbsp. seafood seasoning
- 1 Tbsp. minced fresh parsley
- 1 tsp. Worcestershire sauce
- 1 tsp. prepared mustard
- ¼ tsp. pepper
- ⅛ tsp. hot pepper sauce
  Optional: 2 to 4 Tbsp. canola oil and lemon wedges

In a large bowl, combine the crab, bread crumbs, egg, mayonnaise, vegetables, juice and seasonings. Shape mixture into 8 patties. Broil the patties in a cast-iron or other broiler-safe skillet or, if desired, cook the patties in a skillet on the stovetop in oil; cook for 4 minutes on each side or until golden brown. If desired, serve with lemon.

FREEZE OPTION Freeze cooled crab cakes in freezer containers, separating layers with waxed paper. To use, place crab cakes on a baking sheet in a preheated 325° oven until heated through.

1 CRAB CAKE 282 cal., 22g fat (3g sat. fat), 85mg chol., 638mg sod., 7g carb. (1g sugars, 1g fiber), 14g pro.

Parmesan Baked Cod

This is a goof-proof way to keep oven-baked cod moist and flavorful. My mom shared this recipe with me years ago and I've loved it ever since.
—Mary Jo Hoppe, Pewaukee, WI

TAKES: 25 min. • **MAKES:** 4 servings

- 4 cod fillets (4 oz. each)
- ⅔ cup mayonnaise
- 4 green onions, chopped
- ¼ cup grated Parmesan cheese
- 1 tsp. Worcestershire sauce

1. Preheat oven to 400°. Place cod in an 8-in. square baking dish coated with cooking spray. Mix remaining ingredients; spread over fillets.

2. Bake, uncovered, until fish just begins to flake easily with a fork, 15-20 minutes.

1 FILLET 247 cal., 15g fat (2g sat. fat), 57mg chol., 500mg sod., 7g carb. (2g sugars, 0 fiber), 20g pro. **DIABETIC EXCHANGES** 3 lean meat, 3 fat.

SAUCY SUGGESTION

Worcestershire is a thin sauce used to season meats, gravies, sauces and salad dressing, or to use as a condiment. It's made of soy sauce, vinegar, garlic, onions, tamarind, molasses and various seasonings. It is widely available in supermarkets.

COUNTRY HAM
& POTATOES, P. 176

Pork, Ham
& More

Sunday Pork Roast

Mom would prepare pork roast for our family, friends and customers at the three restaurants she and Dad owned. The herb rub and vegetables give it a remarkable flavor. It's one of my favorite pork roast recipes.
—*Sandi Pichon, Memphis, TN*

PREP: 20 min.
BAKE: 1¾ hours + standing
MAKES: 12 servings

2 medium onions, chopped
2 medium carrots, chopped
1 celery rib, chopped
4 Tbsp. all-purpose flour, divided
1 bay leaf, finely crushed
½ tsp. dried thyme
1¼ tsp. salt, divided
1¼ tsp. pepper, divided
1 boneless pork loin roast (3 to 4 lbs.)
⅓ cup packed brown sugar

1. Preheat oven to 325°. Place vegetables on bottom of a shallow roasting pan. Mix 2 Tbsp. flour, bay leaf, thyme, and 1 tsp. each salt and pepper; rub over roast. Place roast on top of vegetables, fat side up. Add 2 cups water to pan.

2. Roast, uncovered, 1½ hours. Sprinkle brown sugar over roast. Roast 15-20 minutes longer or until a thermometer reads 140°. (Temperature of roast will continue to rise another 5-10° upon standing.)

3. Remove roast to a platter. Tent with foil; let stand 15 minutes before slicing.

4. Strain drippings from roasting pan into a measuring cup; skim fat. Add enough water to the drippings to measure 1½ cups.

5. In a small saucepan over medium heat, whisk remaining 2 Tbsp. flour and ⅓ cup water until smooth. Gradually whisk in drippings mixture and the remaining salt and pepper. Bring to a boil over medium-high heat, stirring constantly; cook and stir 2 minutes or until thickened. Serve roast with gravy.

FREEZE OPTION Freeze cooled sliced pork and gravy in freezer containers. To use, partially thaw in refrigerator overnight. Heat through in a covered saucepan, gently stirring and adding a little broth or water if necessary.

3 OZ. COOKED PORK WITH ABOUT 2 TBSP. GRAVY 174 cal., 5g fat (2g sat. fat), 57mg chol., 280mg sod., 8g carb. (6g sugars, 0 fiber), 22g pro. **DIABETIC EXCHANGES** 3 lean meat, ½ starch.

Ham & Bean Stew

You need only five ingredients to fix this thick and flavorful stew. It's so easy to make and always a favorite with my family. I top each bowl with a sprinkling of shredded cheese.
—*Teresa D'Amato, East Granby, CT*

PREP: 5 min. • **COOK:** 7 hours
MAKES: 6 servings

2 cans (16 oz. each) baked beans
2 medium potatoes, peeled and cubed
2 cups cubed fully cooked ham
1 celery rib, chopped
½ cup water

In a 3-qt. slow cooker, combine all ingredients; mix well. Cover and cook on low for 7 hours or until the potatoes are tender.

1 CUP 213 cal., 5g fat (2g sat. fat), 30mg chol., 919mg sod., 29g carb. (6g sugars, 5g fiber), 14g pro.

Country Pork & Sauerkraut

The secret ingredient in this recipe is the applesauce. When everything is cooked, you wouldn't know it's in there—yet the taste is just a bit sweeter. My mother and grandmother once ran a beanery for a train crew. That inspired a lot of my cooking. In fact, I adapted this recipe from one of theirs. Luckily for me, my husband likes to eat what I fix as much as I like to cook it!
—Donna Hellendrung, Minneapolis, MN

PREP: 15 min. • **BAKE:** 1½ hours
MAKES: 4 servings

- 2 lbs. bone-in country-style pork ribs
- 1 medium onion, chopped
- 1 Tbsp. canola oil
- 1 can (14 oz.) sauerkraut, undrained
- 1 cup unsweetened applesauce
- 2 Tbsp. brown sugar
- 2 tsp. caraway seeds
- 1 tsp. garlic powder
- ½ tsp. pepper

1. In a Dutch oven, cook ribs and onion in oil until ribs are browned and onion is tender. Remove from the heat. Combine remaining ingredients and pour over ribs.

2. Cover and bake at 350° until ribs are tender, 1½-2 hours.

1 SERVING 477 cal., 24g fat (8g sat. fat), 130mg chol., 757mg sod., 23g carb. (15g sugars, 5g fiber), 41g pro.

Great recipe! I made it tonight and the family loved it. Pork was tender, juicy and flavorful. Will definitely be making this again!
—KRISTINECHAYES, TASTEOFHOME.COM

Five-Spice Glazed Smoked Chops

I started out fixing another recipe but didn't have all the ingredients, so I came up with this one! The spice gives it a flavorful kick. You can make your own five-spice powder by combining cloves, cinnamon, anise and nutmeg. I love that you can prepare this dish on the stovetop or the grill.
—Jill Thomas, Washington, IN

TAKES: 25 min. • **MAKES:** 4 servings

- ¼ cup unsweetened apple juice
- ¼ cup grape jelly
- 2 Tbsp. cider vinegar
- ½ tsp. Chinese five-spice powder
- ½ tsp. minced fresh gingerroot
- ¼ tsp. crushed red pepper flakes
- 1 Tbsp. butter
- 4 smoked bone-in pork chops (7½ oz. each)

1. Place the first 6 ingredients in a small saucepan; bring just to a boil. Reduce heat; simmer, uncovered, 10 minutes.

2. In a 12-in. skillet, heat butter over medium-high heat. Add pork chops; cook until bottoms are browned, 4-5 minutes. Turn chops; spoon glaze over top. Cook, uncovered, until chops are glazed and heated through, 3-4 minutes.

1 PORK CHOP 363 cal., 22g fat (10g sat. fat), 77mg chol., 1345mg sod., 16g carb. (15g sugars, 0 fiber), 27g pro.

Lamb with Figs

I've been making rack of lamb for years. My grandma gave me this recipe because she knew how much I love figs. And the toasted walnuts sprinkled on top give it just the right finishing touch.
—Sylvia Castanon, Long Beach, CA

PREP: 30 min. • **BAKE:** 45 min.
MAKES: 8 servings

- 2 racks of lamb (2 lbs. each)
- 1 tsp. salt, divided
- 1 cup water
- 1 small onion, finely chopped
- 1 Tbsp. canola oil
- 1 garlic clove, minced
- 2 Tbsp. cornstarch
- 1 cup port wine, or ½ cup grape juice plus ½ cup reduced-sodium beef broth
- 10 dried figs, halved
- ¼ tsp. pepper
- ½ cup coarsely chopped walnuts, toasted
  Chopped fresh parsley, optional

1. Rub lamb with ½ tsp. salt. Place meat side up on a rack in a greased roasting pan. Bake, uncovered, at 375° for 45-60 minutes or until meat reaches desired doneness (for medium-rare, a thermometer should read 135°; medium, 140°; medium-well, 145°).

2. Remove to a serving platter; cover loosely with foil. Add 1 cup water to pan; stir to loosen browned bits from pan. Using a fine sieve, strain mixture; set drippings aside. Discard solids in sieve.

3. In a small saucepan, saute onion in oil until tender. Add garlic; cook 1 minute longer. Stir in cornstarch until blended; gradually add wine, drippings, figs, pepper and remaining salt. Bring to a boil. Reduce heat to medium-low; cook, uncovered, until figs are tender and sauce is thickened, about 10 minutes, stirring occasionally.

4. Sprinkle walnuts over lamb; serve with fig sauce. If desired, top with chopped parsley.

2 LAMB CHOPS 363 cal., 16g fat (4g sat. fat), 66mg chol., 362mg sod., 23g carb. (14g sugars, 3g fiber), 23g pro.

Sweet Barbecued Pork Chops

I often prepare a double batch of these tangy chops, then freeze half to keep on hand for fast family dinners. They are so easy and taste so fresh, no one ever guesses that my quick entree was frozen!
—Susan Holderman, Fostoria, OH

TAKES: 25 min. • **MAKES:** 8 servings

- 2 Tbsp. canola oil
- 8 boneless pork loin chops (¾ in. thick and 8 oz. each)
- ½ cup packed brown sugar
- ½ cup chopped sweet onion
- ½ cup each ketchup, barbecue sauce, French salad dressing and honey

1. In a large skillet, heat oil over medium heat. In batches, brown pork chops 2-3 minutes on each side. Return all to pan.

2. In a small bowl, mix the remaining ingredients; pour over chops. Bring to a boil. Reduce heat; simmer, covered, 4-5 minutes or until a thermometer inserted in pork reads 145°. Let stand 5 minutes before serving.

FREEZE OPTION Place pork chops in freezer containers; top with sauce. Cool and freeze. To use, partially thaw in refrigerator overnight. Heat through in a covered saucepan, gently stirring sauce; add water if necessary.

1 PORK CHOP 282 cal., 12g fat (3g sat. fat), 14mg chol., 533mg sod., 41g carb. (37g sugars, 1g fiber), 6g pro.

Pasta Fagioli al Forno

The name of this Italian-inspired dish means baked pasta with beans. But my busy family translates it as a super satisfying dinner.
—*Cindy Preller, Grayslake, IL*

PREP: 35 min. • **BAKE:** 30 min.
MAKES: 8 servings

- 3 cups uncooked penne pasta (about 12 oz.)
- 1 can (28 oz.) whole plum tomatoes
- 1 lb. bulk Italian sausage
- 1 medium onion, chopped
- 1 medium carrot, chopped
- 1 celery rib, chopped
- 4 garlic cloves, minced
- 2 Tbsp. tomato paste
- 1 tsp. dried oregano
- ½ tsp. salt
- ½ tsp. dried basil
- ¼ tsp. crushed red pepper flakes
- ¼ tsp. pepper
- 1 can (15 oz.) cannellini beans, rinsed and drained
- ½ cup grated Parmesan cheese, divided
- ½ cup minced fresh parsley, divided
- 2 cups shredded fontina or provolone cheese

1. Preheat oven to 350°. Cook pasta according to package directions for al dente; drain.

2. Meanwhile, drain tomatoes, reserving juices; coarsely chop tomatoes. In a 6-qt. stockpot, cook and crumble sausage with onion, carrot, celery and garlic over medium-high heat until no longer pink, 6-8 minutes; drain. Stir in tomato paste, seasonings, chopped tomatoes and reserved juices; bring to a boil. Reduce heat; simmer, uncovered, 10 minutes.

3. Stir in beans and ¼ cup each Parmesan cheese and parsley. Stir in pasta. Transfer to a greased 13x9-in. baking dish; sprinkle with fontina cheese and remaining Parmesan cheese.

4. Bake, covered, 20 minutes. Uncover; bake until cheese is melted, 10-15 minutes. Sprinkle with remaining parsley.

FREEZE OPTION Cool unbaked casserole; cover and freeze. To use, partially thaw in refrigerator overnight. Remove from refrigerator 30 minutes before baking. Preheat oven to 350°. Bake casserole as directed, increasing time as necessary to heat through and for a thermometer inserted in center to read 165°.

1 SERVING 440 cal., 23g fat (10g sat. fat), 66mg chol., 1029mg sod., 37g carb. (5g sugars, 6g fiber), 22g pro.

Mom's Molasses Ham & Beans

This is a recipe my mom made frequently while I was growing up. It's perfect for a cold day when you don't want to bother with lots of cooking. My mother actually used lima beans, but because not many people are into those, I tweaked this dish to make it more enjoyable for my own family.
—*Nancy Heishman, Las Vegas, NV*

PREP: 15 min. • **COOK:** 7 hours
MAKES: 8 servings

- 4 cans (15½ oz. each) navy or cannellini beans, rinsed and drained
- 2 smoked ham hocks (about 1 lb.)
- 1 can (15 oz.) tomato sauce
- 1 large onion, chopped
- ¾ cup packed brown sugar
- ¾ cup molasses
- ¼ cup cider vinegar
- 1 Tbsp. Worcestershire sauce
- 2½ tsp. ground mustard
- 1 tsp. salt
- ½ tsp. pepper
- 12 bacon strips, cooked and crumbled
  Optional: Pickled jalapeno peppers and pickled red onions

1. In a greased 5-qt. slow cooker, combine the first 11 ingredients. Cook, covered, on low 7-9 hours.

2. Remove ham hocks. When cool enough to handle, remove meat from bones; discard bones. Cut meat into small cubes; return to slow cooker. Stir in crumbled bacon. If desired, serve with pickled jalapeno peppers and pickled red onions.

FREEZE OPTION Freeze cooled beans in freezer containers. To use, partially thaw in refrigerator overnight. Heat through in a saucepan, stirring occasionally; add water or broth if necessary.

¾ CUP 521 cal., 7g fat (2g sat. fat), 19mg chol., 1543mg sod., 93g carb. (45g sugars, 13g fiber), 24g pro.

NO SLOW COOKER?
The slow cooker makes this dish easy to prepare, but if you don't have a slow cooker, don't worry! Simply bake the ham and beans in a 325° oven for 1½-2½ hours. If you feel the sauce is too thick after baking, add a bit more tomato sauce.

NOTES

Asparagus Ham Dinner

I've been making this light meal for my family for years now, and it's always well received. With asparagus, tomato, pasta and chunks of ham, it's a tempting blend of tastes and textures.
—Rhonda Zavodny, David City, NE

TAKES: 25 min. • **MAKES:** 6 servings

- 2 cups uncooked corkscrew or spiral pasta
- ¾ lb. fresh asparagus, cut into 1-in. pieces
- 1 medium sweet yellow pepper, julienned
- 1 Tbsp. olive oil
- 6 medium tomatoes, diced
- 6 oz. boneless fully cooked ham, cubed
- ¼ cup minced fresh parsley
- ½ tsp. salt
- ½ tsp. dried oregano
- ½ tsp. dried basil
- ⅛ to ¼ tsp. cayenne pepper
- ¼ cup shredded Parmesan cheese

Cook pasta according to package directions. Meanwhile, in a large cast-iron or other heavy skillet, saute asparagus and yellow pepper in oil until crisp-tender. Add tomatoes and ham; heat through. Drain the pasta; add to mixture. Stir in parsley and seasonings. Sprinkle with cheese.

1⅓ CUPS 204 cal., 5g fat (1g sat. fat), 17mg chol., 561mg sod., 29g carb. (5g sugars, 3g fiber), 12g pro. **DIABETIC EXCHANGES** 1½ starch, 1 vegetable, 1 lean meat, ½ fat.

STREAMLINED SUPPER
Keep this quick recipe handy. It's a smart way to use up leftover chicken, beef or pork in place of the ham originally called for. Toss in last night's taco meat for a spicy twist, or add bacon strips left from breakfast!

Country Ham & Potatoes

Browned potatoes are a simple but perfect side for country ham. Not only do the potatoes pick up the flavor of the ham, but they also look beautiful! Just add veggies or a salad and dinner's done.
—Helen Bridges, Washington, VA

TAKES: 30 min. • **MAKES:** 6 servings

- 2 lbs. fully cooked sliced ham (about ½ in. thick)
- 2 to 3 Tbsp. butter
- 1½ lbs. potatoes, peeled, quartered and cooked
  Snipped fresh parsley

In a large heavy skillet, brown ham over medium-high heat in butter on both sides until heated through. Move ham to 1 side of the skillet; brown potatoes in drippings until tender. Sprinkle potatoes with parsley.

1 SERVING 261 cal., 9g fat (5g sat. fat), 64mg chol., 1337mg sod., 21g carb. (1g sugars, 1g fiber), 28g pro.

Roast Pork Loin with Rosemary Applesauce

I made this for a family get-together on my husband's birthday. The homemade rosemary applesauce adds an extra layer of comfort to the tender pork.
—*Angela Lemoine, Howell, NJ*

PREP: 15 min. + marinating
BAKE: 55 min. + standing
MAKES: 8 servings (3 cups applesauce)

- ¼ cup olive oil
- 2 tsp. salt
- 4 tsp. garlic powder
- 4 tsp. minced fresh rosemary or 1½ tsp. dried rosemary, crushed
- 2 tsp. pepper
- 1 boneless pork loin roast (2 to 3 lbs.), halved

APPLESAUCE
- ¼ cup butter, cubed
- 6 medium Golden Delicious apples, peeled and chopped (about 5 cups)
- 1 to 2 tsp. ground cinnamon
- 2 tsp. brown sugar
- 1½ tsp. minced fresh rosemary or ½ tsp. dried rosemary, crushed
- ½ tsp. salt
- 1 cup water

1. In a large shallow dish, combine the first 5 ingredients. Add pork; turn to coat. Cover; refrigerate 8 hours or overnight.

2. Preheat oven to 350°. Place pork roast on a rack in a shallow roasting pan, fat side up. Roast until a thermometer reads 145°, 55-65 minutes.

3. Meanwhile, in a large skillet, heat butter over medium heat. Add apples, cinnamon, brown sugar, rosemary and salt; cook until apples are tender, 8-10 minutes, stirring occasionally.

4. Stir in water; bring to a boil. Reduce heat; simmer, uncovered, until apples are very soft, about 10 minutes. Remove from heat; mash apples to desired consistency.

5. Remove roast from oven; tent with foil. Let stand 10 minutes before slicing. Serve with warm applesauce.

3 OZ. COOKED PORK WITH ⅓ CUP APPLESAUCE 287 cal., 16g fat (6g sat. fat), 72mg chol., 581mg sod., 15g carb. (11g sugars, 2g fiber), 22g pro.

NOTES

Authentic Pasta Carbonara

I learned on my culinary internship in Tuscany that real Italian cuisine is simpler than you think!
This carbonara is quick, simple and delicious, just the way they like it in Italy.
—*Lauren Brien-Wooster, South Lake Tahoe, CA*

PREP: 20 min. • **COOK:** 15 min.
MAKES: 8 servings

- 1 pkg. (1 lb.) spaghetti or linguine
- 6 bacon strips, chopped
- 1 cup fresh or frozen peas
- 2 Tbsp. lemon juice
- 1½ tsp. grated lemon zest
- 2 large eggs, lightly beaten
- 2 Tbsp. minced fresh parsley
- ½ cup grated Parmigiano-Reggiano cheese
- ¼ tsp. salt
- ¼ tsp. pepper
  Additional grated Parmigiano-Reggiano cheese, optional

1. In a large saucepan, cook pasta according to package directions for al dente. Drain pasta, reserving pasta water; keep pasta warm. In same pot, cook bacon over medium heat until crisp, stirring occasionally. Add peas; cook until just heated through.

2. Add pasta to pot; toss to combine. Stir in remaining ingredients, adding enough reserved pasta water for sauce to reach desired consistency. If desired, serve with additional cheese.

1 CUP 353 cal., 12g fat (4g sat. fat), 65mg chol., 326mg sod., 46g carb. (3g sugars, 3g fiber), 14g pro.

Breaded Pork Chops

These traditional pork chops have a wonderful home-cooked flavor like the ones Mom used to make.
The breading makes them crispy outside and tender and juicy inside. Why not treat your family to them tonight?
—*Deborah Amrine, Fort Myers, FL*

TAKES: 20 min. • **MAKES:** 6 servings

- 1 large egg, lightly beaten
- ½ cup 2% milk
- 1½ cups crushed saltine crackers
- 6 boneless pork loin chops (1 in. thick)
- ¼ cup canola oil

1. In a shallow bowl, combine egg and milk. Place cracker crumbs in another shallow bowl. Dip each pork chop into egg mixture, then coat with cracker crumbs, patting to make a thick coating.

2. In a large skillet, cook chops in oil for 4-5 minutes on each side or until a thermometer reads 145°. Let meat stand for 5 minutes before serving.

1 PORK CHOP 405 cal., 22g fat (5g sat. fat), 115mg chol., 233mg sod., 14g carb. (1g sugars, 0 fiber), 36g pro.

Sausage, Pear & Sweet Potato Sheet-Pan Dinner

This old-time weeknight dinner is naturally gluten free and is on your table in no time! You can easily adapt the recipe to use seasonal fruits or veggies.
—Melissa Erdelac, Valparaiso, IN

PREP: 15 min. • **BAKE:** 45 min.
MAKES: 5 servings

- 2   large sweet potatoes, peeled and cut into ½-in. cubes
- 1   large sweet onion, cut into wedges
- 2   Tbsp. olive oil
- 1   Tbsp. brown sugar
- ½   tsp. salt
- ½   tsp. ground allspice
- ¼   tsp. ground cinnamon
- ⅛   tsp. pepper
- 3   small pears, quartered
- 1   pkg. (19 oz.) Italian sausage links

1. Preheat oven to 425°. Place sweet potatoes and onion in a 15x10x1-in. baking pan; drizzle with oil. Sprinkle with brown sugar and seasonings; toss to coat. Bake for 15 minutes.

2. Gently stir in pears; top with sausages. Bake 20 minutes longer, stirring once. Increase oven temperature to 450°. Bake for 8-10 minutes or until sausages are golden brown and a thermometer inserted into sausage reads at least 160°, turning once.

1 SERVING 533 cal., 29g fat (8g sat. fat), 58mg chol., 912mg sod., 56g carb. (28g sugars, 8g fiber), 15g pro.

KEEP IT SIMPLE
The trick with sheet-pan suppers is the timing. Ingredients are cut in specific ways and added at the right time so everything gets done at the same time. That said, keep the sausages whole while cooking. Cutting the sausages means they'd cook much faster than whole links, so they'd be fully cooked long before the veggies.

Honey-Glazed Ham

Here's an easy solution for feeding a large group. The simple ham is perfect for family dinners where time in the kitchen is as valuable as space in the oven.
—Jacquie Stolz, Little Sioux, IA

PREP: 10 min. • **COOK:** 4½ hours
MAKES: 14 servings

- 1   boneless fully cooked ham (4 lbs.)
- 1½ cups ginger ale
- ¼   cup honey
- ½   tsp. ground mustard
- ½   tsp. ground cloves
- ¼   tsp. ground cinnamon

1. Cut ham in half; place in a 5-qt. slow cooker. Pour ginger ale over ham. Cook, covered, on low until heated through, 4-5 hours.

2. Combine the honey, mustard, cloves and cinnamon; stir until smooth. Spread over ham; cook 30 minutes longer.

3 OZ. COOKED HAM 165 cal., 5g fat (2g sat. fat), 66mg chol., 1348mg sod., 8g carb. (7g sugars, 0 fiber), 24g pro.

Au Gratin Ham Potpie

We first had Aunt Dolly's potpie at a family get-together. We loved it and were so happy she shared the recipe. Now we make it almost every time we bake a ham.
—Mary Zinsmeister, Slinger, WI

PREP: 15 min. • **BAKE:** 40 min.
MAKES: 6 servings

- 1 pkg. (4.9 oz.) au gratin potatoes
- 1½ cups boiling water
- 2 cups frozen peas and carrots
- 1½ cups cubed fully cooked ham
- 1 can (10¾ oz.) condensed cream of chicken soup, undiluted
- 1 can (4 oz.) mushroom stems and pieces, drained
- ½ cup 2% milk
- ½ cup sour cream
- 1 jar (2 oz.) diced pimientos, drained
- 1 sheet refrigerated pie crust

1. Preheat oven to 400°. In a large bowl, combine the potatoes, contents of sauce mix and water. Stir in the peas and carrots, ham, soup, mushrooms, milk, sour cream, and pimientos. Transfer to an ungreased 2-qt. round baking dish.

2. Unroll crust; roll out to fit top of dish. Place over potato mixture; flute edges and cut slits in crust. Bake until golden brown, 40-45 minutes. Let stand for 5 minutes before serving.

1 PIECE 434 cal., 20g fat (9g sat. fat), 45mg chol., 1548mg sod., 47g carb. (7g sugars, 3g fiber), 14g pro.

KITCHEN CREATIVITY
Try a few swaps to make this dish more fitting to your personal taste. If you don't have ham, the same amount of cooked chicken, turkey or even leftover pot roast works well. If you don't like peas and carrots, swap in your favorite veggie mix. You can also use any kind of cream soup, such as cream of mushroom.

Ham & Swiss Casserole

When I prepare this noodle casserole for church gatherings, it's always a hit. It can easily be doubled or tripled for a crowd.
—Doris Barb, El Dorado, KS

PREP: 15 min. • **BAKE:** 40 min.
MAKES: 8 servings

- 1 pkg. (8 oz.) egg noodles, cooked and drained
- 2 cups cubed fully cooked ham
- 2 cups shredded Swiss cheese
- 1 can (10¾ oz.) condensed cream of celery soup, undiluted
- 1 cup sour cream
- ½ cup chopped green pepper
- ½ cup chopped onion

1. In a greased 13x9-in. baking dish, layer half each of the noodles, ham and cheese.

2. In a large bowl, combine the soup, sour cream, green pepper and onion; spread half over the top. Repeat layers. Bake, uncovered, at 350° for 40-45 minutes or until heated through.

1 SERVING 360 cal., 18g fat (10g sat. fat), 92mg chol., 815mg sod., 27g carb. (4g sugars, 1g fiber), 20g pro.

Pork Chops with Apples & Stuffing

The heartwarming taste of cinnamon and apples is the perfect accompaniment for these tender pork chops. The dish is always a winner with my family. Because it calls for only a few ingredients, it's a main course I can serve with little preparation.
—*Joan Hamilton, Worcester, MA*

PREP: 15 min. • **BAKE:** 45 min.
MAKES: 6 servings

- 6   boneless pork loin chops (6 oz. each)
- 1   Tbsp. canola oil
- 1   pkg. (6 oz.) crushed stuffing mix
- 1   can (21 oz.) apple pie filling with cinnamon
     Minced fresh parsley, optional

1. In a large skillet, brown pork chops in oil over medium-high heat. Meanwhile, prepare stuffing according to package directions. Spread pie filling into a greased 13x9-in. baking dish. Place the pork chops on top; spoon stuffing over the chops.

2. Cover and bake at 350° for 35 minutes. Uncover; bake until a thermometer inserted in the pork reads 145°, about 10 minutes longer. If desired, sprinkle with parsley.

1 SERVING 527 cal., 21g fat (9g sat. fat), 102mg chol., 550mg sod., 48g carb. (15g sugars, 3g fiber), 36g pro.

Sweet Ham Steak

You need just three ingredients to fix this sweetly seasoned ham slice. It's a quick and easy addition to brunch—or any meal for that matter.
—*Nancy Smits, Markesan, WI*

TAKES: 15 min. • **MAKES:** 6 servings

- 1   bone-in fully cooked ham steak (2 lbs.)
- 5   Tbsp. butter, cubed
- 5   Tbsp. brown sugar

1. In a large skillet over medium heat, brown ham steak on both sides; drain. Remove ham.

2. In the same skillet, melt the butter; stir in brown sugar. Return ham to skillet; cook until a thermometer reads 140°, turning often.

3 OZ. COOKED HAM 269 cal., 17g fat (8g sat. fat), 84mg chol., 1157mg sod., 13g carb. (12g sugars, 0 fiber), 18g pro.

DONE AND DONE
Ham's doneness can be a little difficult to determine. That's why you need to know the food-safe cooking temperatures. Since ham steak is already fully cooked when you purchase it, you should heat it only to 140°. If you cook it longer than that, it will start to get tough and chewy.

Louisiana Jambalaya

My husband helped add a little spice to my life. He grew up on Cajun cooking, while I ate mostly meat-and-potato meals. We both love this recipe.
—*Sandi Pichon, Memphis, TN*

PREP: 20 min. • **COOK:** 30 min.
MAKES: 12 servings

- ¼ cup canola oil
- ½ lb. smoked sausage, halved and sliced
- 2 cups cubed fully cooked ham
- 2 celery ribs, chopped
- 1 large onion, chopped
- 1 medium green pepper, chopped
- 5 green onions, thinly sliced
- 2 garlic cloves, minced
- 1 can (14½ oz.) diced tomatoes, undrained
- 1 tsp. dried thyme
- 1 tsp. salt
- ½ tsp. pepper
- ¼ tsp. cayenne pepper
- 2 cans (14½ oz. each) chicken broth
- 1 cup uncooked long grain rice
- ⅓ cup water
- 4½ tsp. Worcestershire sauce
- 2 lbs. peeled and deveined cooked shrimp (31-40 per lb.)

1. In a Dutch oven, heat oil over medium-high heat. Add sausage and ham; cook and stir until lightly browned. Remove and keep warm. In drippings, saute celery, onion, green pepper and green onions until tender. Add garlic; cook and stir 1 minute longer. Stir in tomatoes, thyme, salt, pepper and cayenne; cook 5 minutes longer.

2. Stir in broth, rice, water and Worcestershire sauce. Bring to a boil. Reduce heat; simmer, covered, until rice is tender, about 20 minutes. Stir in sausage mixture and shrimp; heat through.

FREEZE OPTION Prepare jambalaya as directed, omitting rice and shrimp. Freeze shrimp and cooled jambalaya in separate freezer containers. Store uncooked rice in an airtight container at room temperature. To use, partially thaw jambalaya in refrigerator overnight. Place jambalaya in a 6-qt. stockpot. Bring to a boil; add rice. Reduce heat; simmer, covered, 10 minutes. Add frozen shrimp. Continue cooking until shrimp are heated through and rice is tender, 10-15 minutes.

1 CUP 295 cal., 12g fat (3g sat. fat), 143mg chol., 1183mg sod., 20g carb. (3g sugars, 1g fiber), 25g pro.

Moussaka

Moussaka is traditionally made with lamb, but I often use ground beef to make things easier.
The recipe looks a bit daunting, but if you prepare one step while working on another, it will save time.
—*Kim Powell, Knoxville, TN*

PREP: 45 min. • **BAKE:** 30 min. + standing
MAKES: 8 servings

- 3 medium potatoes, peeled and cut into ¼-in. slices
- 1 medium eggplant, cut into ½-in. slices
- 1½ lbs. ground lamb or ground beef
- 1 small onion, chopped
- 2 garlic cloves, minced
- 2 plum tomatoes, chopped
- 1¼ cups hot water
- 1 can (6 oz.) tomato paste
- 1¼ tsp. salt, divided
- ½ tsp. dried oregano
- ½ tsp. paprika
- ½ tsp. ground cinnamon
- ½ tsp. ground nutmeg, divided
- 3 Tbsp. butter
- ¼ cup all-purpose flour
- 4 cups 2% milk
- 2 cups shredded mozzarella cheese

1. Preheat oven to 450°. Arrange the potato slices and eggplant slices separately in 2 greased 15x10x1-in. baking pans, overlapping as needed. Bake until cooked through, about 20 minutes. Set aside. Reduce oven setting to 400°.

2. In a large skillet, cook lamb, onion and garlic over medium heat until meat is no longer pink, 7-9 minutes, breaking into crumbles; drain. Stir in tomatoes, water, tomato paste, ¼ tsp. salt, oregano, paprika, cinnamon and ¼ tsp. nutmeg. Bring to a boil. Reduce heat; simmer, uncovered, 5 minutes.

3. In a large saucepan, melt butter over medium heat. Stir in flour until smooth; gradually whisk in milk. Bring to a boil, stirring constantly; cook and stir until thickened, 2-3 minutes. Stir in remaining 1 tsp. salt and ¼ tsp. nutmeg.

4. Arrange parcooked potatoes in a greased 13x9-in. baking dish, overlapping as needed. Top with lamb mixture. Arrange eggplant over top, overlapping as needed.

5. Top with bechamel sauce. Sprinkle with mozzarella cheese. Bake, uncovered, until bubbly and golden brown, about 30 minutes. Let stand 20 minutes before serving.

1 SERVING 453 cal., 25g fat (13g sat. fat), 99mg chol., 700mg sod., 30g carb. (12g sugars, 4g fiber), 28g pro.

SERVING SUGGESTIONS

This classic dish is a fine meal-in-one option, but you may want to round it out with some quick menu additions. Swing by the grocery store and pick up a bottle of Greek salad dressing and greens of your choice for a no-fuss salad, and add a loaf of crusty bread from the bakery for a crowd-pleasing dinner.

Country-Style Pork Loin

This pork roast is so moist and tender, it melts in your mouth. My son puts it at the top of his list of favorite foods. We like it with mashed potatoes.
—*Corina Flansberg, Carson City, NV*

PREP: 20 min. • **COOK:** 5 hours + standing
MAKES: 8 servings

- 1 boneless pork loin roast (3 lbs.)
- ½ cup all-purpose flour
- 1 tsp. onion powder
- 1 tsp. ground mustard
- 2 Tbsp. canola oil
- 2 cups reduced-sodium chicken broth
- ¼ cup cornstarch
- ¼ cup cold water
  Hot mashed potatoes, optional

1. Cut roast in half. In a large shallow dish, combine the flour, onion powder and mustard. Add pork, 1 portion at a time, and turn to coat. In a large skillet, brown pork in oil on all sides.

2. Transfer to a 5-qt. slow cooker. Pour broth over pork. Cook, covered, on low for 5-6 hours or until tender. Remove pork and keep warm. Let pork stand for 10-15 minutes before slicing.

3. Strain cooking juices, reserving 2½ cups juices; skim fat from reserved juices. Transfer liquid to a small saucepan. Bring to a boil. Combine cornstarch and water until smooth; gradually stir into the pan. Bring to a boil; cook and stir for 2 minutes or until thickened. Serve pork and gravy with mashed potatoes if desired.

FREEZE OPTION Cool pork and gravy. Freeze sliced pork and gravy in freezer containers. To use, partially thaw in refrigerator overnight. Heat through slowly in a covered skillet, stirring occasionally; add broth or water if necessary. Serve as directed.

5 OZ. COOKED MEAT WITH ¼ CUP GRAVY 291 cal., 11g fat (3g sat. fat), 85mg chol., 204mg sod., 10g carb. (0 sugars, 0 fiber), 34g pro. **DIABETIC EXCHANGES** 5 lean meat, ½ starch, ½ fat.

Slow-Cooked Scalloped Potatoes & Ham

Mom's friend gave her this recipe years ago, and she shared it with me. When we have leftover ham to use up, it's the most-requested recipe at my house.
—*Kelly Graham, St. Thomas, ON*

PREP: 20 min. • **COOK:** 8 hours
MAKES: 9 servings

- 10 medium potatoes (about 3 lbs.), peeled and thinly sliced
- 3 cups cubed fully cooked ham
- 2 large onions, thinly sliced
- 2 cups shredded cheddar cheese
- 1 can (10¾ oz.) condensed cream of mushroom soup, undiluted
- ½ tsp. paprika
- ¼ tsp. pepper

1. In a greased 6-qt. slow cooker, layer half of the potatoes, ham, onions and cheese. Repeat layers. Pour soup over top. Sprinkle with paprika and pepper.

2. Cover and cook on low for 8-10 hours or until potatoes are tender.

1½ CUPS 344 cal., 13g fat (7g sat. fat), 53mg chol., 995mg sod., 40g carb. (4g sugars, 3g fiber), 17g pro.

I made the recipe as is and it was absolutely delicious. It tasted just as good as when Mom made it when I was growing up. Thank you!
—AMANDA694, TASTEOFHOME.COM

COUNTRY-STYLE
PORK LOIN

FLUFFY WAFFLES, P. 196

Old-Fashioned Breakfasts

The Best French Toast

There's no question that this is the best French toast recipe. The caramelized exterior meets a soft, custardlike center that practically melts in your mouth. Not only that, but it's quick and easy, too!
—Audrey Rompon, Milwaukee, WI

TAKES: 15 min. • **MAKES:** 4 servings

1½ cups half-and-half cream
3 large egg yolks
3 Tbsp. brown sugar
2 tsp. vanilla extract
¾ tsp. ground cinnamon
½ tsp. salt
¼ tsp. ground nutmeg
8 slices day-old brioche bread
(1 in. thick)
Optional toppings: Butter, maple syrup, fresh berries and confectioners' sugar

1. In a shallow dish, whisk together the first 7 ingredients. Preheat a greased griddle over medium heat.

2. Dip bread into egg mixture, letting it soak 5 seconds on each side. Cook on griddle until golden brown on both sides. Serve with toppings as desired.

2 PIECES 546 cal., 24g fat (15g sat. fat), 263mg chol., 786mg sod., 64g carb. (25g sugars, 2g fiber), 13g pro.

THE OLDIES ARE GOODIES
Using day-old bread from a bakery helps the French toast to keep its shape. If you're using commercially produced brioche, be sure to allow the bread to become slightly stale for the best results.

Baked Cheddar Eggs & Potatoes

I love having breakfast for dinner, especially this combo of eggs, potatoes and cheese. It starts in a skillet on the stovetop and then I pop it into the oven to bake.
—Nadine Merheb, Tucson, AZ

TAKES: 30 min. • **MAKES:** 4 servings

3 Tbsp. butter
1½ lbs. red potatoes, chopped
¼ cup minced fresh parsley
2 garlic cloves, minced
¾ tsp. kosher salt
⅛ tsp. pepper
8 large eggs
½ cup shredded extra-sharp cheddar cheese

1. Preheat oven to 400°. In a 10-in. cast-iron or other ovenproof skillet, heat butter over medium-high heat. Add potatoes; cook and stir until golden brown and tender. Stir in parsley, garlic, salt and pepper. With the back of a spoon, make 4 wells in the potato mixture; break 2 eggs into each well.

2. Bake until egg whites are completely set and yolks begin to thicken but are not hard, 9-11 minutes. Sprinkle with cheese; bake until cheese is melted, about 1 minute.

1 SERVING 395 cal., 23g fat (12g sat. fat), 461mg chol., 651mg sod., 29g carb. (3g sugars, 3g fiber), 19g pro.

Old-Fashioned Buttermilk Doughnuts

Guests will have a touch of nostalgia when they bite into one of these old-fashioned doughnuts. Accents of nutmeg and cinnamon, along with a subtle burst of lemon, make them hard to resist.
—*June Jones, Harveyville, KS*

PREP: 20 min. • **COOK:** 5 min./batch
MAKES: 2½ dozen

- 2 cups mashed potatoes (without added milk and butter)
- 2 large eggs, room temperature
- 1¼ cups sugar
- ⅔ cup buttermilk
- ¼ cup butter, melted
- 1 Tbsp. grated lemon zest
- 4 cups all-purpose flour
- 3 tsp. baking powder
- 2 tsp. salt
- 2 tsp. ground nutmeg
- ¼ tsp. baking soda
  Oil for deep-fat frying

TOPPING
- ½ cup sugar
- 1½ tsp. ground cinnamon

1. In a large bowl, beat the potatoes, eggs, sugar, buttermilk, butter and lemon zest until blended. Combine the flour, baking powder, salt, nutmeg and baking soda; gradually beat into potato mixture and mix well.

2. Turn out onto a lightly floured surface; roll out to ½-in. thickness. Cut with a floured 2½-in. doughnut cutter. In a deep cast-iron or electric skillet, heat oil to 375°. Fry doughnuts and doughnut holes, a few at a time, until golden brown on both sides. Drain on paper towels. Combine sugar and cinnamon; roll warm doughnuts in mixture.

NOTE To substitute for each cup of buttermilk, use 1 Tbsp. white vinegar or lemon juice plus enough milk to measure 1 cup. Stir, then let stand 5 min. Or, use 1 cup plain yogurt or 1¾ tsp. cream of tartar plus 1 cup milk.

1 DOUGHNUT WITH 1 DOUGHNUT HOLE 184 cal., 7g fat (2g sat. fat), 18mg chol., 232mg sod., 27g carb. (12g sugars, 1g fiber), 3g pro.

Cheesy Hash Brown Bake

Prepare this cheesy dish ahead of time for less stress on brunch day. You'll love it!
—*Karen Burns, Chandler, TX*

PREP: 10 min. • **BAKE:** 40 min.
MAKES: 10 servings

- 1 pkg. (30 oz.) frozen shredded hash brown potatoes, thawed
- 2 cans (10¾ oz. each) condensed cream of potato soup, undiluted
- 2 cups sour cream
- 2 cups shredded cheddar cheese, divided
- 1 cup grated Parmesan cheese
  Sliced green onions, optional

1. Preheat oven to 350°. In a large bowl, combine potatoes, soup, sour cream, 1¾ cups cheddar cheese and the Parmesan cheese. Place in a greased 3-qt. baking dish. Sprinkle with the remaining ¼ cup cheddar cheese.

2. Bake, uncovered, until casserole is bubbly and cheese is melted, 40-45 minutes. Let stand 5 minutes before serving. If desired, sprinkle with onions.

½ CUP 305 cal., 18g fat (12g sat. fat), 65mg chol., 554mg sod., 21g carb. (3g sugars, 1g fiber), 12g pro.

Savory Apple-Chicken Sausage

These easy, healthy sausages taste incredible, and they make an elegant brunch dish. The recipe is also very versatile. It can be doubled or tripled for a crowd, and the sausage freezes well either cooked or raw.
—*Angela Buchanan, Longmont, CO*

TAKES: 25 min. • **MAKES:** 8 patties

- 1   large tart apple, peeled and diced
- 2   tsp. poultry seasoning
- 1   tsp. salt
- ¼   tsp. pepper
- 1   lb. ground chicken

1. In a large bowl, combine the first 4 ingredients. Crumble chicken over the mixture and mix lightly but thoroughly. Shape into eight 3-in. patties.

2. In a large, greased cast-iron or other heavy skillet, cook patties over medium heat until no longer pink, 5-6 minutes on each side. Drain if necessary.

1 SAUSAGE PATTY 92 cal., 5g fat (1g sat. fat), 38mg chol., 328mg sod., 4g carb. (3g sugars, 1g fiber), 9g pro. **DIABETIC EXCHANGES** 1 medium-fat meat.

Fluffy Waffles

A friend shared the recipe for these light and delicious waffles. The cinnamon cream syrup is a nice change from maple syrup, and it keeps quite well in the fridge. Our two children also like it on toast.
—*Amy Gilles, Ellsworth, WI*

PREP: 25 min. • **COOK:** 20 min.
MAKES: 10 waffles (6½ in.) and 1⅔ cups syrup

- 2   cups all-purpose flour
- 1   Tbsp. sugar
- 2   tsp. baking powder
- ½   tsp. salt
- 3   large eggs, separated
- 2   cups 2% milk
- ¼   cup canola oil

CINNAMON CREAM SYRUP
- 1   cup sugar
- ½   cup light corn syrup
- ¼   cup water
- 1   can (5 oz.) evaporated milk
- 1   tsp. vanilla extract
- ½   tsp. ground cinnamon
     Mixed fresh berries, optional

1. In a bowl, combine the flour, sugar, baking powder and salt. Combine the egg yolks, milk and oil; stir into dry ingredients just until moistened. In a small bowl, beat egg whites until stiff peaks form; fold into batter. Bake in a preheated waffle maker according to manufacturer's directions.

2. Meanwhile, for syrup, combine sugar, corn syrup and water in a saucepan. Bring to a boil over medium heat; cook and stir for 2 minutes or until thickened. Remove from heat; stir in milk, vanilla and cinnamon. Serve with waffles, with fresh berries if desired.

FREEZE OPTION Cool waffles on wire racks. Freeze between layers of waxed paper in a freezer container. Reheat waffles in a toaster on medium setting. Or, microwave each waffle on high for 30-60 seconds or until heated through.

1 WAFFLE WITH 2½ TBSP. SYRUP 424 cal., 12g fat (4g sat. fat), 94mg chol., 344mg sod., 71g carb. (41g sugars, 1g fiber), 9g pro.

Old-Fashioned Stack Cakes

My grandmother has always fixed these at Christmas and they are the first thing everyone asks about. "Where is the stack cake?" The thin layers are what make this recipe stand out ... delicious!
—*Stephanie Gilbert, Whitesburg, KY*

PREP: 35 min.
BAKE: 5 min./batch + cooling
MAKES: 3 stack cakes (6 pieces each)

½ cup butter, softened
1 cup sugar
2 large eggs, room temperature
2 tsp. vanilla extract
4 cups all-purpose flour
4 tsp. baking powder
1½ tsp. ground ginger
½ tsp. baking soda
1 tsp. salt
½ cup molasses
½ cup buttermilk
2 cups apple butter
    Additional apple butter, optional

1. Preheat oven to 450°. In a large bowl, cream butter and sugar until light and fluffy, 5-7 minutes. Beat in eggs and vanilla. In another bowl, whisk flour, baking powder, ginger, baking soda and salt; add to creamed mixture alternately with molasses and buttermilk, beating well after each addition.

2. Drop 2 scant ¼ cupfuls of batter, at least 7 in. apart, onto a parchment-lined baking sheet. With well-floured fingers, pat each into a 5- to 6-in. circle. Bake 2-3 minutes or until golden brown. Remove from pans to wire racks to cool completely. Repeat with remaining batter.

3. To assemble, place 1 cake layer on a serving plate; spread with 2 Tbsp. apple butter. Repeat layers 4 times; top with a sixth layer. Repeat to make 2 more stack cakes. Refrigerate, covered, until serving. If desired, serve with additional apple butter.

1 PIECE 280 cal., 6g fat (4g sat. fat), 35mg chol., 343mg sod., 52g carb. (29g sugars, 1g fiber), 4g pro.

A SOUTHERN SPECIALTY
While stack cake is typically enjoyed as a dessert, it can also be served as a special-occasion brunch dish. Enjoy the central Appalachian staple alongside grits, country ham, fried apples, bacon, biscuits and gravy or scrambled eggs.

Eggs Benedict with Homemade Hollandaise

Legend has it that poached eggs on an English muffin started at Delmonico's in New York. Here's my take on this brunch classic, and don't spare the hollandaise.
—*Barbara Pletzke, Herndon, VA*

TAKES: 30 min. • **MAKES:** 8 servings

4 large egg yolks
2 Tbsp. water
2 Tbsp. lemon juice
¾ cup butter, melted
   Dash white pepper

ASSEMBLY
8 large eggs
4 English muffins, split and toasted
8 slices Canadian bacon, warmed
   Paprika

1. For hollandaise sauce, in top of a double boiler or in a metal bowl over simmering water, whisk egg yolks, water and lemon juice until blended; cook until mixture is just thick enough to coat a metal spoon and temperature reaches 160°, whisking constantly. Remove from heat. Very slowly drizzle in warm melted butter, whisking constantly. Whisk in pepper. Transfer to a small bowl if necessary. Place bowl in a larger bowl of warm water. Keep warm, stirring occasionally, until ready to serve, up to 30 minutes.

2. Place 2-3 in. water in a large saucepan or skillet with high sides. Bring to a boil; adjust heat to maintain a gentle simmer.

Break 1 egg into a small bowl; holding bowl close to surface of water, slip egg into water. Repeat with 3 more eggs.

3. Cook, uncovered, 2-4 minutes or until whites are completely set and yolks begin to thicken but are not hard. Using a slotted spoon, lift eggs out of water. Repeat with remaining 4 eggs.

4. Top each muffin half with a slice of Canadian bacon, a poached egg and 2 Tbsp. sauce; sprinkle with paprika. Serve immediately.

1 SERVING 345 cal., 26g fat (14g sat. fat), 331mg chol., 522mg sod., 15g carb. (1g sugars, 1g fiber), 13g pro.

Biscuits & Sausage Gravy

This is an old southern recipe that I've adapted. It's the kind of hearty breakfast that will warm you right up.
—*Sue Baker, Jonesboro, AR*

TAKES: 15 min. • **MAKES:** 2 servings

¼ lb. bulk pork sausage
2 Tbsp. butter
2 to 3 Tbsp. all-purpose flour
¼ tsp. salt
⅛ tsp. pepper
1¼ to 1⅓ cups whole milk
   Warm biscuits

In a small skillet, cook sausage over medium heat until no longer pink, 3-5 minutes, breaking into crumbles; drain. Add butter and heat until melted. Add the flour, salt and pepper; cook and stir until blended. Gradually add the milk, stirring constantly. Bring to a boil; cook and stir until thickened, about 2 minutes. Serve with biscuits.

¾ CUP 337 cal., 27g fat (14g sat. fat), 72mg chol., 718mg sod., 14g carb. (8g sugars, 0 fiber), 10g pro.

Cream-Filled Cinnamon Coffee Cake

When guests stay over, they ask that I make this old-time cinnamon coffee cake for breakfast. You can prepare it in advance to make the morning super easy.
—Arlene Wengerd, Millersburg, OH

PREP: 25 min. + chilling
BAKE: 20 min. + cooling
MAKES: 12 servings

½ cup butter, softened
1 cup sugar
2 large eggs, room temperature
1 tsp. vanilla extract
1½ cups all-purpose flour
½ tsp. baking soda
½ tsp. salt
1 cup sour cream

TOPPING
½ cup sugar
½ cup chopped pecans
2 tsp. ground cinnamon

FILLING
1 Tbsp. cornstarch
¾ cup 2% milk
¼ cup butter, softened
¼ cup shortening
½ cup sugar
½ tsp. vanilla extract
Caramel ice cream topping, optional

1. In a large bowl, cream butter and sugar until light and fluffy, 5-7 minutes. Add eggs, 1 at a time, beating well after each addition. Beat in vanilla. Combine the flour, baking soda and salt; add to creamed mixture alternately with sour cream, beating just until combined.

2. Pour into 2 greased and waxed paper-lined 9-in. round baking pans. Combine topping ingredients; sprinkle over batter. Lightly cut through with a knife to swirl.

3. Bake at 350° until a toothpick inserted in the center comes out clean, 20-25 minutes. Cool for 10 minutes; remove from the pans to wire racks to cool completely.

4. For filling, in a small saucepan, combine cornstarch and milk until smooth. Bring to a boil; cook and stir for 1-2 minutes or until thickened. Cover and refrigerate until chilled. In a small bowl, cream the butter, shortening and sugar until light and fluffy, 5-7 minutes. Add vanilla and chilled milk mixture; beat on medium speed until smooth and creamy, about 10 minutes.

5. Place 1 cake on a serving plate and spread with filling. Top with remaining cake. Store in the refrigerator. If desired, serve with caramel topping.

1 PIECE 419 cal., 24g fat (11g sat. fat), 67mg chol., 268mg sod., 49g carb. (35g sugars, 1g fiber), 4g pro.

NOTES

Sunday Brunch Casserole

My father was a chef, and this was one of his favorite recipes. He served it in the hotels where he worked as well as at home. Whenever it's served today in my home, it never fails to bring back fond memories of a table laden with food and encircled with family and friends enjoying the aromas, tastes and laughter.
—*Roy Lyon, Coupeville, WA*

PREP: 15 min. + chilling • **BAKE:** 45 min.
MAKES: 10 servings

- 6   slices sourdough bread
- 3   to 4 Tbsp. butter, softened
- 2   cups shredded cheddar cheese
- 1   lb. bulk pork sausage, cooked and drained
- ½   medium sweet red pepper, cut into thin strips
- ¼   cup sliced green onion tops
- 3   large eggs
- 1   can (10¾ oz.) condensed cream of asparagus soup, undiluted
- 2   cups whole milk
- ¼   cup white wine or chicken broth
- ½   tsp. Dijon mustard
- ¼   tsp. pepper

1. Remove and discard crust from bread if desired. Butter bread; cube and place in a greased 13x9-in. baking dish. Sprinkle with the cheese, sausage, red pepper and onions in order given.

2. In a large bowl, beat eggs. Add the soup, milk, wine, mustard and pepper. Pour over bread mixture; cover and refrigerate overnight.

3. Remove from refrigerator 30 minutes before baking. Bake, uncovered, at 350° for 45-55 minutes or until a knife inserted in the center comes out clean. Let stand for 5 minutes before cutting.

1 CUP 331 cal., 23g fat (12g sat. fat), 121mg chol., 708mg sod., 17g carb. (4g sugars, 1g fiber), 14g pro.

NOTES

Rise-and-Shine Fruit Biscuits

Because these sweet treats are so easy, I'm almost embarrassed when people ask me for the recipe.
They're a snap to make with refrigerated buttermilk biscuits, sugar, cinnamon and your favorite fruit preserves.
—Ione Burham, WA, IA

PREP: 15 min. • **BAKE:** 15 min. + cooling
MAKES: 10 servings

½   cup sugar
½   tsp. ground cinnamon
1   tube (12 oz.) refrigerated buttermilk
    biscuits, separated into 10 biscuits
¼   cup butter, melted
10 tsp. strawberry preserves

1. In a small bowl, combine sugar and cinnamon. Dip top and sides of biscuits in butter, then in cinnamon sugar.

2. Place on ungreased baking sheets. With the end of a wooden spoon handle, make a deep indentation in the center of each biscuit; fill with 1 tsp. preserves.

3. Bake at 375° for 15-18 minutes or until golden brown. Cool for 15 minutes before serving (preserves will be hot).

1 BISCUIT 178 cal., 5g fat (3g sat. fat), 12mg chol., 323mg sod., 31g carb. (14g sugars, 0 fiber), 3g pro.

Quiche Lorraine

Ideal for a brunch or luncheon, this classic recipe highlights a delicious meal. Try serving a wedge with fresh fruit of the season and homemade muffins for a plate that will look as good as the food tastes!
—Marcy Cella, L'Anse, MI

PREP: 20 min. • **BAKE:** 45 min. + cooling
MAKES: 8 servings

1   cup sifted all-purpose flour
¼   tsp. salt
6   Tbsp. butter-flavored shortening
2   to 3 Tbsp. ice water

FILLING
12   bacon strips, cooked and crumbled
4   large eggs
2   cups half-and-half cream
¼   tsp. salt
⅛   tsp. ground nutmeg
1¼   cups shredded Swiss cheese

1. Combine flour and salt; cut in the shortening until crumbly. Gradually add ice water, tossing with a fork until dough holds together when pressed. Shape into a disk; wrap and refrigerate 1 hour or overnight.

2. Preheat oven to 425°. On a lightly floured surface, roll out dough to a ⅛-in.-thick circle; transfer to a 9-in. pie plate. Trim pastry to ½ in. beyond rim of plate; flute edge.

3. For filling, sprinkle pastry with bacon. Whisk eggs, cream, salt and nutmeg until blended; stir in cheese. Pour over the top.

4. Bake on a lower oven rack for 15 minutes. Reduce temperature to 325°; continue to bake until a knife inserted in center comes out clean, 30-40 minutes. Let stand 10 minutes before cutting.

1 PIECE 618 cal., 44g fat (18g sat. fat), 71mg chol., 596mg sod., 32g carb. (4g sugars, 1g fiber), 17g pro.

CORNED BEEF
HASH & EGGS

Corned Beef Hash & Eggs

Sunday breakfasts have always been special in our house. It's fun to get in the kitchen and cook with the kids. No matter how many new recipes we try, the kids always rate this No. 1.
—*Rick Skildum, Maple Grove, MN*

PREP: 15 min. • **BAKE:** 20 min.
MAKES: 8 servings

- 1 pkg. (32 oz.) frozen cubed hash browns
- 1½ cups chopped onion
- ½ cup canola oil
- 4 to 5 cups chopped cooked corned beef
- ½ tsp. salt
- 8 large eggs
    Salt and pepper to taste
- 2 Tbsp. minced fresh parsley

1. In a large ovenproof skillet, cook hash browns and onion in oil until tender and potatoes are browned. Remove from heat; stir in corned beef and salt.

2. Make 8 wells in the hash browns. Break 1 egg into each well. Sprinkle with salt and pepper. Cover and bake at 325° until eggs reach desired doneness, 20-25 minutes. Garnish with parsley.

1 SERVING 442 cal., 30g fat (6g sat. fat), 242mg chol., 895mg sod., 24g carb. (3g sugars, 2g fiber), 20g pro.

Excellent! I had turnips and potatoes left over from my boiled dinner, so I incorporated them into the dish. This is an excellent use of leftovers and eggs— I would definitely make it again.
—RAE777, TASTEOFHOME.COM

Country-Style Scrambled Eggs

I added extra colors and flavors to ordinary scrambled eggs with green pepper, onion and red potatoes.
—*Joyce Platfoot, Wapakoneta, OH*

TAKES: 30 min. • **MAKES:** 4 servings

- 8 bacon strips, diced
- 2 cups diced red potatoes
- ½ cup chopped onion
- ½ cup chopped green pepper
- 8 large eggs
- ¼ cup 2% milk
- 1 tsp. salt
- ¼ tsp. pepper
- 1 cup shredded cheddar cheese

1. In a 9-in. cast-iron or other ovenproof skillet, cook bacon over medium heat until crisp. Using a slotted spoon, remove to paper towels to drain. Cook and stir potatoes in drippings over medium heat for 12 minutes or until tender. Add onion and green pepper. Cook and stir for 3-4 minutes or until crisp-tender; drain. Stir in bacon.

2. In a large bowl, whisk the eggs, milk, salt and pepper; add to skillet. Cook and stir until eggs are completely set. Sprinkle with cheese; stir it in or let stand until melted.

1 SERVING 577 cal., 45g fat (19g sat. fat), 487mg chol., 1230mg sod., 18g carb. (4g sugars, 2g fiber), 25g pro.

Aunt Edith's Baked Pancake

My aunt made a mighty breakfast that revolved around "The Big Pancake." I always enjoyed watching as she poured the batter into her huge iron skillet, then baked the confection to perfection in the oven.
—*Marion Kirst, Troy, MI*

PREP: 15 min. • **BAKE:** 20 min. • **MAKES:** 4 servings

- 3 large eggs, room temperature
- ½ tsp. salt
- ½ cup all-purpose flour
- ½ cup 2% milk
- 2 Tbsp. butter, softened
  Confectioners' sugar
  Lemon wedges

1. In a bowl, beat eggs until very light. Add salt, flour and milk; beat well. Thoroughly rub bottom and side of a 10-in. cast-iron or other heavy ovenproof skillet with butter. Pour batter into skillet.

2. Bake at 450° for 15 minutes. Reduce heat to 350° and bake until set, about 5 minutes longer. If desired, remove pancake from the skillet and place on a large hot platter. Dust with confectioners' sugar and serve immediately, with lemon wedges on the side.

1 PIECE 180 cal., 10g fat (5g sat. fat), 158mg chol., 407mg sod., 14g carb. (2g sugars, 0 fiber), 7g pro.

Old-Fashioned Fruit Compote

This warm and fruity side dish can simmer while you prepare the rest of your menu, or make it a day ahead and reheat it before serving.
—*Shirley Glaab, Hattiesburg, MS*

PREP: 15 min. • **COOK:** 1 hour
MAKES: 8 cups

- 1 can (20 oz.) pineapple chunks, undrained
- 1 can (15¼ oz.) sliced peaches, undrained
- 1 can (11 oz.) mandarin oranges, undrained
- 1 pkg. (18 oz.) pitted dried plums (prunes)
- 2 pkg. (3½ oz. each) dried blueberries
- 1 pkg. (6 oz.) dried apricots
- ½ cup golden raisins
- 4 lemon zest strips
- 1 cinnamon stick (3 in.)
- 1 jar (10 oz.) maraschino cherries, drained

Drain pineapple, peaches and oranges, reserving the juices; set drained fruit aside. In a Dutch oven, combine fruit juice, dried fruits, lemon zest strips and cinnamon stick. Bring to a boil. Reduce heat; cover and simmer until dried fruit is tender, about 30 minutes. Add reserved canned fruit and cherries; heat just until warmed through. Serve warm or at room temperature.

¼ CUP 126 cal., 0 fat (0 sat. fat), 0 chol., 4mg sod., 31g carb. (22g sugars, 2g fiber), 1g pro.

7-LAYER GELATIN
SALAD, P. 217

Grandma's Odds & Ends

Old-Fashioned Lemonade

A sweet-tart lemonade is a traditional part of my Memorial Day and Fourth of July parties. Folks can't get enough of the fresh-squeezed flavor in this old-time recipe.
—*Tammi Simpson, Greensburg, KY*

PREP: 10 min. • **COOK:** 5 min. + chilling
MAKES: 7 servings

- 1⅓ cups sugar
- 5 cups water, divided
- 1 Tbsp. grated lemon zest
- 1¾ cups lemon juice (about 10 large lemons)

In a large saucepan, combine sugar, 1 cup water and lemon zest. Cook and stir over medium heat until sugar is dissolved, about 4 minutes. Remove from heat. Stir in lemon juice and remaining water; refrigerate until cold. Serve over ice.

1 CUP 142 cal., 0 fat (0 sat. fat), 0 chol., 1mg sod., 37g carb. (35g sugars, 0 fiber), 0 pro.

TO MAKE LIMEADE, substitute lime zest for lemon zest and limes for lemons.

TO MAKE LAVENDER LEMONADE, add 2 Tbsp. dried lavender to the sugar and lemon zest mixture before simmering. If desired, strain before serving.

TO MAKE GINGER-MINT LEMONADE, add 1-2 Tbsp. grated fresh gingerroot and 1-2 mint sprigs to the sugar and lemon zest mixture before simmering. If desired, strain before serving.

Jazzy Gelatin

This colorful gelatin is a tasty toss back to simpler times. Loaded with mandarin oranges and crushed pineapple, it's so refreshing that guests won't be able to refrain from seconds.
—*Taste of Home Test Kitchen*

PREP: 10 min. + chilling
MAKES: 12 servings

- 1 pkg. (6 oz.) orange gelatin
- 2 cups boiling water
- 1 cup ice cubes
- 1 can (15 oz.) mandarin oranges, drained
- 1 can (8 oz.) unsweetened crushed pineapple, undrained
- 1 can (6 oz.) frozen orange juice concentrate, thawed
  Green grapes and fresh mint, optional

1. In a large bowl, dissolve gelatin in boiling water. Add ice cubes, oranges, pineapple and orange juice concentrate. Pour into a 6-cup ring mold coated with cooking spray. Refrigerate overnight or until firm.

2. Just before serving, unmold onto a serving plate. Fill center with grapes and garnish with mint if desired.

1 PIECE 107 cal., 0 fat (0 sat. fat), 0 chol., 35mg sod., 26g carb. (25g sugars, 1g fiber), 2g pro.

GRANDMA'S MOLASSES
FRUITCAKE

Grandma's Molasses Fruitcake

This dense, dark, moist fruitcake was my grandmother's recipe. The flavor just gets better and better as it sits in the fridge, so be sure to make it ahead!
—*Debbie Harmon, Lavina, MT*

PREP: 25 min. + chilling
BAKE: 1¼ hours + cooling
MAKES: 3 loaves (16 pieces each)

3¼ cups dried currants
2⅔ cups raisins
1 cup chopped walnuts
⅔ cup chopped candied citron or candied lemon peel
4 cups all-purpose flour, divided
1 cup butter, softened
2 cups packed brown sugar
4 large eggs, room temperature
1 cup molasses
1 tsp. baking soda
1 tsp. each ground cinnamon, nutmeg and cloves
1 cup strong brewed coffee

1. Preheat oven to 300°. Grease and flour three 9x5-in. loaf pans. Line bottoms with waxed paper; grease and flour the paper. Combine currants, raisins, walnuts, candied citron and ¼ cup flour. Toss to coat.

2. Cream butter and brown sugar until light and fluffy, 5-7 minutes. Add the eggs, 1 at a time, beating well after each addition. Beat in molasses. In another bowl, whisk baking soda, cinnamon, nutmeg, cloves and remaining 3 ¾ cups flour; add to creamed mixture alternately with coffee. Stir into currant mixture and mix well.

3. Transfer to prepared pans. Bake until a toothpick inserted in the center comes out clean, 1¼ to 1½ hours. Cool in pans 10 minutes before removing to wire racks to cool completely. Wrap tightly and store in the refrigerator for at least 2 days to blend flavors. Slice and bring to room temperature before serving. Refrigerate leftovers.

1 PIECE 210 cal., 6g fat (3g sat. fat), 26mg chol., 79mg sod., 39g carb. (28g sugars, 2g fiber), 3g pro.

Chocolate-Strawberry Milk Shake

I don't crave sweets that often, but one thing I can't resist is a creamy milkshake. This slimmed-down version tastes just like one straight off a Steak 'n Shake menu. One taste and you'll be slurping it down!
—Taste of Home *Test Kitchen*

TAKES: 10 min. • **MAKES:** 1 serving

⅔ cup fat-free milk
⅔ cup reduced-fat strawberry ice cream
⅔ cup frozen unsweetened sliced strawberries
1 Tbsp. fat-free hot fudge ice cream topping
2 Tbsp. whipped cream in a can
1 maraschino cherry

In a blender, combine the milk, ice cream and strawberries; cover and process until smooth. Drizzle the inside of a chilled glass with fudge topping. Add ice cream mixture. Garnish with whipped cream and a cherry. Serve immediately.

1 SERVING 302 cal., 6g fat (4g sat. fat), 29mg chol., 173mg sod., 56g carb. (42g sugars, 3g fiber), 11g pro.

I made this for my daughter. She thought it was great. I had to take just a little taste. Yum, it was good.
—QUEENLALISA, TASTEOFHOME.COM

Pickled Eggs with Beets

Red beets act as a natural dye for these pickled eggs and beets. They look gorgeous on salads and make the most vibrant deviled eggs for Easter appetizers or snacks.
—*Mary Banker, Fort Worth, TX*

PREP: 10 min. + chilling
MAKES: 12 servings

2 cans (15 oz. each) whole beets
12 hard-boiled large eggs, peeled
1 cup sugar
1 cup water
1 cup cider vinegar

1. Drain beets, reserving 1 cup juice (discard remaining juice or save for another use). Place beets and eggs in a 2-qt. glass jar.

2. In a small saucepan, bring the sugar, water, vinegar and reserved beet juice to a boil. Pour over beets and eggs; cool.

3. Cover tightly and refrigerate for at least 24 hours before serving.

1 SERVING 168 cal., 5g fat (2g sat. fat), 212mg chol., 200mg sod., 23g carb. (21g sugars, 1g fiber), 7g pro.

Aunt Rose's Fantastic Butter Toffee

I don't live in the country, but I love everything about it—especially good old-fashioned home cooking!
Every year, you'll find me at our county fair, entering a different recipe contest. This toffee is a family favorite!
—*Kathy Dorman, Snover, MI*

PREP: 25 min. • **COOK:** 15 min. + chilling
MAKES: 32 pieces

2 cups unblanched whole almonds
11 oz. milk chocolate, chopped
1 cup butter, cubed
1 cup sugar
3 Tbsp. cold water

1. Preheat oven to 350°. In a shallow baking pan, toast the almonds until golden brown, 5-10 minutes, stirring occasionally. Cool. Pulse chocolate in a food processor until finely ground (do not overprocess); transfer to a bowl. Pulse almonds in food processor until coarsely chopped. Sprinkle 1 cup almonds over bottom of a greased 15x10x1-in. pan. Sprinkle with 1 cup chocolate.

2. In a heavy saucepan, combine butter, sugar and water. Cook over medium heat until a candy thermometer reads 290° (soft-crack stage), stirring occasionally.

3. Immediately pour mixture over almonds and chocolate in pan. Sprinkle with remaining chocolate and almonds. Refrigerate until set; break into pieces.

NOTE We recommend that you always test your candy thermometer before each use by bringing water to a boil; the thermometer should read 212°. Adjust your recipe temperature up or down based on your test.

1 OZ. 177 cal., 13g fat (6g sat. fat), 17mg chol., 51mg sod., 14g carb. (12g sugars, 1g fiber), 3g pro.

Old-Time Custard Ice Cream

I think my most memorable summertime dessert for get-togethers has always been homemade ice cream. This recipe is so rich and creamy and is the perfect splurge on a hot summer afternoon.
—*Martha Self, Montgomery, TX*

PREP: 55 min. + chilling
PROCESS: 55 min./batch + freezing
MAKES: 2¾ qt.

1½ cups sugar
¼ cup all-purpose flour
½ tsp. salt
4 cups whole milk
4 large eggs, lightly beaten
2 pints heavy whipping cream
3 Tbsp. vanilla extract

1. In a large heavy saucepan, combine sugar, flour and salt. Gradually add milk until smooth. Cook and stir over medium heat until thickened and bubbly. Reduce heat to low; cook and stir 2 minutes longer. Remove from heat.

2. In a small bowl, whisk a small amount of hot mixture into eggs; return all to pan, whisking constantly. Bring to a gentle boil; cook and stir 2 minutes. Remove from heat immediately.

3. Quickly transfer to a large bowl; place bowl in a pan of ice water. Stir gently and occasionally for 2 minutes. Press plastic wrap onto the surface of the custard. Refrigerate several hours or overnight.

4. Stir cream and vanilla into custard. Fill cylinder of an ice cream maker two-thirds full; freeze according to manufacturer's directions. (Refrigerate remaining mixture until ready to freeze.) Transfer ice cream to freezer containers, allowing headspace for expansion. Freeze 2-4 hours or until firm. Repeat with remaining ice cream mixture.

½ CUP 252 cal., 18g fat (11g sat. fat), 88mg chol., 98mg sod., 18g carb. (17g sugars, 0 fiber), 4g pro.

NOTES

7-Layer Gelatin Salad

My mother makes this colorful gelatin salad to accompany our Christmas dinner each year. Choose different flavors to create special color combinations for particular holidays or gatherings.
—Jan Hemness, Stockton, MO

PREP: 30 min. + chilling
MAKES: 20 servings

4½ cups boiling water, divided
7 pkg. (3 oz. each) assorted flavored gelatin
4½ cups cold water, divided
1 can (12 oz.) evaporated milk, divided
1 carton (8 oz.) frozen whipped topping, thawed
Optional: Sliced strawberries and kiwifruit

1. In a small bowl, add ¾ cup boiling water to 1 gelatin package; stir 2 minutes to completely dissolve. Stir in ¾ cup cold water. Pour into a 3-qt. trifle or glass bowl. Refrigerate until set but not firm, about 40 minutes.

2. In a clean bowl, dissolve another gelatin package into ½ cup boiling water. Stir in ½ cup cold water and ½ cup milk. Spoon over the first layer. Refrigerate until set but not firm.

3. Repeat 5 times, alternating plain and creamy gelatin layers. Refrigerate each layer until set but not firm before adding the next layer. Refrigerate, covered, overnight. Serve with whipped topping and, if desired, fruit.

1 SERVING 163 cal., 3g fat (3g sat. fat), 6mg chol., 85mg sod., 30g carb. (30g sugars, 0 fiber), 4g pro.

Homemade Applesauce

We had all kinds of apple trees in the yard when I was growing up, so I don't know for sure which ones Mother liked best for applesauce. (Today I use Cortlands.) The secret, she said, was to keep the apples in salt water while she peeled them so that they wouldn't darken.
—Doris Natvig, Jesup, IA

TAKES: 30 min. • **MAKES:** 6 cups

4 lbs. tart apples
1 cup water
1 cinnamon stick or ½ tsp. cinnamon extract
½ to 1 cup sugar

Peel, core and quarter the apples. In a Dutch oven, bring apples, water and cinnamon to a boil. Reduce heat; cover and simmer 10-15 minutes or until apples are tender. Remove from the heat. Add sugar to taste and stir until dissolved. If you used a cinnamon stick, remove and discard. Mash apples with a potato masher until desired texture is reached. Serve warm or chilled.

½ CUP 122 cal., 1g fat (0 sat. fat), 0 chol., 0 sod., 31g carb. (26g sugars, 4g fiber), 0 pro.

Dime-Store Whoopie Pies

Who can resist soft chocolate sandwich cookies filled with a layer of fluffy white frosting? Mom has made these for years. They're a classic treat that never lasted very long with my two brothers and me around.
—*Maria Costello, Monroe, NC*

PREP: 35 min. + chilling
BAKE: 10 min./batch + cooling
MAKES: 2 dozen

½ cup baking cocoa
½ cup hot water
½ cup shortening
1½ cups sugar
2 large eggs, room temperature
1 tsp. vanilla extract
2⅔ cups all-purpose flour
1 tsp. baking powder
1 tsp. baking soda
¼ tsp. salt
½ cup buttermilk

FILLING
3 Tbsp. all-purpose flour
Dash salt
1 cup 2% milk
¾ cup shortening
1½ cups confectioners' sugar
2 tsp. vanilla extract

1. Preheat oven to 350°. In a bowl, combine cocoa and water. Cool for 5 minutes. In a large bowl, cream shortening and sugar until light and fluffy, 5-7 minutes. Beat in the eggs, vanilla and cocoa mixture. Combine dry ingredients; gradually add to creamed mixture alternately with buttermilk, beating well after each addition.

2. To form each cookie, drop 2 tsp. dough 2 in. apart onto greased baking sheets. Bake until firm to the touch, 10-12 minutes. Remove to wire racks to cool.

3. For the filling, in a small saucepan, combine flour and salt. Gradually whisk in milk until smooth; cook and stir over medium-high heat until thickened, 5-7 minutes. Remove from heat. Cover and refrigerate until completely cool.

4. In a bowl, cream the shortening, confectioners' sugar and vanilla until light and fluffy, 3-4 minutes. Add milk mixture; beat until fluffy, about 7 minutes. Spread filling on half the cookies; top with remaining cookies. Store in the refrigerator.

NOTE To substitute for each cup of buttermilk, use 1 Tbsp. white vinegar or lemon juice plus enough milk to measure 1 cup. Stir and then let stand 5 minutes. Or use 1 cup plain yogurt or 1¾ tsp. cream of tartar plus 1 cup milk.

1 WHOOPIE PIE 244 cal., 11g fat (3g sat. fat), 19mg chol., 116mg sod., 33g carb. (20g sugars, 1g fiber), 3g pro.

Haystacks

Peanut butter haystacks are one of my favorite treats. I love to share them with guests because they marvel at how something so simple tastes so good!
—*Starrlette Howard, Ogden, UT*

TAKES: 25 min. • **MAKES:** 2 dozen

¾ cup butterscotch chips
½ cup peanut butter
1 can (3 oz.) chow mein noodles
1 cup miniature marshmallows

1. In a microwave or large bowl over simmering water, melt butterscotch chips and peanut butter; stir until smooth. Gently stir in noodles and marshmallows.

2. Drop by rounded tablespoonfuls onto waxed paper-lined baking sheets. Refrigerate until set, 10-15 minutes.

1 COOKIE 95 cal., 5g fat (2g sat. fat), 0 chol., 71mg sod., 10g carb. (6g sugars, 0 fiber), 2g pro.

DIME-STORE
WHOOPIE PIES

Canned Spaghetti Sauce

This DIY spaghetti sauce is a tomato grower's dream come true! Use up your garden bounty and enjoy it later in the year.
—*Tonya Branham, Mount Olive, AL*

PREP: 1½ hours + simmering
PROCESS: 40 min. • **MAKES:** 9 qt.

25	lbs. tomatoes (about 80 medium)
4	large green peppers, seeded
4	large onions, cut into wedges
2	cans (12 oz. each) tomato paste
¼	cup canola oil
⅔	cup sugar
¼	cup salt
8	garlic cloves, minced
4	tsp. dried oregano
2	tsp. dried parsley flakes
2	tsp. dried basil
2	tsp. crushed red pepper flakes
2	tsp. Worcestershire sauce
2	bay leaves
1	cup plus 2 Tbsp. bottled lemon juice

1. In a Dutch oven, bring 2 qt. water to a boil. Using a slotted spoon, place tomatoes, 1 at a time, in boiling water for 30-60 seconds. Remove each tomato and immediately plunge into ice water. Peel and quarter tomatoes; place in a stockpot.

2. Pulse green peppers and onions in batches in a food processor until finely chopped; transfer to stockpot. Stir in next 11 ingredients. Add water to cover; bring to a boil. Reduce heat; simmer, uncovered, 4-5 hours, stirring occasionally.

3. Discard bay leaves. Add 2 Tbsp. lemon juice to each of 9 hot 1-qt. jars. Ladle the hot mixture into jars, leaving ½-in. headspace. Remove air bubbles and adjust headspace, if necessary, by adding or removing hot mixture. Wipe rims. Center lids on jars; screw on bands until fingertip tight.

4. Place jars into canner with simmering water, ensuring that they are completely covered with water. Bring to a boil; process for 40 minutes. Remove the jars and cool.

NOTE The processing time listed is for altitudes of 1,000 feet or less. For altitudes up to 3,000 feet, add 5 minutes; 6,000 feet, add 10 minutes; 8,000 feet, add 15 minutes; 10,000 feet, add 20 minutes.

¾ CUP 118 cal., 5g fat (0 sat. fat), 0 chol., 614mg sod., 17g carb. (11g sugars, 4g fiber), 3g pro. **DIABETIC EXCHANGES** 1 starch, 1 fat.

ENTICING IDEAS
This jarred sauce is so versatile you can use it in several different entrees. Try it as a sauce for homemade pizzas or a dipping sauce for chicken fingers. Stir a bit into your sloppy Joe mixture or make it your secret ingredient in chili. Mix it with softened cream cheese and zap it all in the microwave for a hot appetizer spread, or add a few teaspoons to scrambled eggs at breakfast.

Leftover Rice Pudding

This rice pudding, made with leftover cooked rice, is a delicious classic. We also like to dress it up with English toffee bits, chocolate and toasted coconut.
—*Laura German, North Brookfield, MA*

TAKES: 25 min. • **MAKES:** 4 servings

- 2 cups cooked long grain rice
- 2 cups whole milk
- 3 Tbsp. plus 1 tsp. sugar
- ⅛ tsp. salt
- 1 tsp. vanilla extract
  Optional: Whipped cream, cinnamon and dried cranberries

In a large saucepan, combine the rice, milk, sugar and salt. Cook, uncovered, over medium heat until thickened, stirring often, about 20 minutes. Remove from the heat; stir in vanilla. Spoon into serving dishes. Serve warm. If desired, top with whipped cream, cinnamon and dried cranberries.

⅔ CUP 221 cal., 4g fat (2g sat. fat), 12mg chol., 127mg sod., 39g carb. (17g sugars, 0 fiber), 6g pro.

Favorite Bread & Butter Pickles

I made these pickles while growing up and love them because you can eat them with just about anything. Now, both of my children love these pickles too. I think you'll enjoy them as much as we do!
—*Linda Weger, Robinson, IL*

PREP: 45 min. + standing
PROCESS: 10 min./batch + cooling
MAKES: 11 pints

- 20 cups sliced cucumbers (about 12 medium)
- 3 cups sliced onions (about 4 medium)
- 1 medium sweet red pepper, sliced
- 1 medium green pepper, sliced
- 3 qt. ice water
- ½ cup canning salt
- 6 cups sugar
- 6 cups white vinegar
- 3 Tbsp. mustard seed
- 3 tsp. celery seed
- 1½ tsp. ground turmeric
- ¼ tsp. plus ⅛ tsp. ground cloves

1. Place cucumbers, onions and peppers in a large bowl. In another large bowl, mix ice water and salt; pour over the vegetables. Let stand 3 hours.

2. Rinse vegetables and drain well. Pack vegetables into 11 hot 1-pint jars to within ½ in. of the top.

3. In a Dutch oven, bring sugar, vinegar, mustard seed, celery seed, turmeric and cloves to a boil. Carefully ladle hot liquid over vegetable mixture, leaving ½-in. headspace. Remove air bubbles and adjust headspace, if necessary, by adding hot liquid. Wipe the rims. Center the lids on jars; screw on bands until fingertip tight.

4. Place jars into canner, ensuring that they are completely covered with water. Bring to a boil; process for 10 minutes. Remove jars and cool.

NOTE The processing time listed is for altitudes of 1,000 feet or less. For altitudes up to 3,000 feet, add 5 minutes; 6,000 feet, add 10 minutes; 8,000 feet, add 15 minutes; 10,000 feet, add 20 minutes.

¼ CUP 60 cal., 0 fat (0 sat. fat), 0 chol., 645mg sod., 15g carb. (14g sugars, 0 fiber), 0 pro.

Stained Glass Gelatin

Kids love this sweet, wiggly gelatin and whipped topping dessert. Use different flavors of gelatin to make color versions that are as wild as your imagination.
—Taste of Home *Test Kitchen*

PREP: 25 min. + chilling
MAKES: 15 servings

2 pkg. (3 oz. each) lime gelatin
6 cups boiling water, divided
2 pkg. (3 oz. each) orange gelatin
2 envelopes unflavored gelatin
⅓ cup cold water
1½ cups white grape juice
1 carton (12 oz.) frozen whipped topping, thawed

1. In a bowl, dissolve the lime gelatin in 3 cups boiling water. Pour into an 8-in. square dish coated with cooking spray. In another bowl, dissolve orange gelatin in remaining boiling water. Pour into another 8-in. square dish coated with cooking spray. Refrigerate for 4 hours or until very firm.

2. In a small saucepan, sprinkle the unflavored gelatin over cold water; let stand for 1 minute. Add grape juice. Heat over low heat, stirring until gelatin is completely dissolved. Pour into a large bowl; refrigerate for 45 minutes or until slightly thickened. Fold in whipped topping.

3. Cut green gelatin into ½-in. cubes and orange gelatin into 1-in. cubes. Set aside 8-10 cubes of each color for garnish. Place 2 cups whipped topping mixture in a bowl; fold in remaining green cubes. Spread into a 13x9-in. dish coated with cooking spray. Fold remaining orange cubes into remaining whipped topping mixture; spread over bottom layer. Sprinkle with reserved green and orange gelatin cubes. Refrigerate for 2 hours or until set. Cut into squares.

1 PIECE 122 cal., 4g fat (4g sat. fat), 0 chol., 29mg sod., 18g carb. (16g sugars, 0 fiber), 2g pro.

Homemade Lemon Curd

Lemon curd is a scrumptious spread for scones, biscuits or other baked goods. You can find it in larger grocery stores alongside the jams and jellies or with the baking supplies, but we like making it from scratch.
—*Mark Hagen, Milwaukee, WI*

PREP: 20 min. + chilling • **MAKES:** 1⅔ cups

3 large eggs
1 cup sugar
½ cup lemon juice (about 2 lemons)
¼ cup butter, cubed
1 Tbsp. grated lemon zest

In a small heavy saucepan over medium heat, whisk eggs, sugar and lemon juice until blended. Add butter and lemon zest; cook, whisking constantly, until mixture is thickened and coats the back of a metal spoon. Transfer to a small bowl; cool 10 minutes. Refrigerate, covered, until cold.

2 TBSP. 110 cal., 5g fat (3g sat. fat), 52mg chol., 45mg sod., 16g carb. (16g sugars, 0 fiber), 2g pro.

Pistachio Mallow Salad

This fluffy salad is a real treat since it's creamy but not overly sweet. It's easy to mix up, and the flavor gets better the longer it stands. It's perfect for St. Patrick's Day, served in a green bowl.
—*Pattie Ann Forssberg, Logan, KS*

PREP: 10 min. + chilling
MAKES: 12 servings

- 1 carton (16 oz.) whipped topping
- 1 pkg. (3.4 oz.) instant pistachio pudding mix
- 6 to 7 drops green food coloring, optional
- 3 cups miniature marshmallows
- 1 can (20 oz.) pineapple tidbits, undrained
- ½ cup chopped pistachios or walnuts
  Additional whipped topping, optional

In a large bowl, combine whipped topping, pudding mix and, if desired, food coloring. Fold in the marshmallows and pineapple. Cover and refrigerate for at least 2 hours. Just before serving, top with additional whipped topping if desired, and sprinkle with nuts.

¾ CUP 236 cal., 9g fat (7g sat. fat), 0 chol., 140mg sod., 35g carb. (23g sugars, 1g fiber), 2g pro.

POTLUCK POINTER
Pistachio salad is a foolproof potluck recipe because it can be made ahead. It'll keep in the fridge for up to 2 days but the longer it sits in the fridge, the wetter it may get because of the pineapple juice. Otherwise, you can freeze it for up to 3 months.

Classic Tapioca

My family loves old-fashioned tapioca, but I don't always have time to make it. So I came up with this simple recipe. It lets us enjoy one of our favorites without all the hands-on time.
—*Ruth Peters, Bel Air, MD*

PREP: 10 min. • **COOK:** 4½ hours
MAKES: 18 servings

- 8 cups 2% milk
- 1 cup pearl tapioca
- 1 cup plus 2 Tbsp. sugar
- ⅛ tsp. salt
- 4 large eggs, room temperature
- 1½ tsp. vanilla extract
  Optional: Sliced fresh strawberries and whipped cream

1. In a 4- to 5-qt. slow cooker, combine the milk, tapioca, sugar and salt. Cover and cook on low for 4-5 hours.

2. In a large bowl, beat the eggs; stir in a small amount of hot tapioca mixture. Return all to the slow cooker, stirring to combine. Cover and cook 30 minutes longer or until a thermometer reads 160°. Stir in vanilla.

3. If desired, serve with strawberries and whipped cream.

½ CUP 149 cal., 3g fat (2g sat. fat), 55mg chol., 86mg sod., 25g carb. (18g sugars, 0 fiber), 5g pro.

Pennsylvania Dutch Apple Butter

You can spread this apple butter on thick and still enjoy a breakfast that's thin on calories. For a smoother texture, use tender varieties such as McIntosh or Cortland apples.
—*Diane Widmer, Blue Island, IL*

PREP: 20 min. • **COOK:** 2 hours
MAKES: 2 cups

- ¾ cup unsweetened apple cider or juice
- ⅓ cup sugar
- 1 tsp. ground cinnamon
- ¼ tsp. ground cloves
- 6 medium apples, peeled and quartered (3 lbs.)

1. Place apple juice, sugar, cinnamon and cloves in a blender; cover and process until blended. Adding 3-4 apple pieces at a time, cover and process until smooth.

2. Pour into a saucepan. Bring to a boil. Reduce heat; cover and cook over low heat for 1 hour, stirring occasionally.

3. Uncover and cook 1 to 1½ hours longer or until thickened. Store in airtight containers in the refrigerator.

2 TBSP. 46 cal., 0 fat (0 sat. fat), 0 chol., 1mg sod., 12g carb. (10g sugars, 1g fiber), 0 pro.

Creamy Egg Salad

I love this egg salad's versatility—serve it on a nest of mixed greens, tucked into a sandwich or with your favorite crisp crackers.
—*Cynthia Kolberg, Syracuse, IN*

TAKES: 10 min. • **MAKES:** 3 cups

- 3 oz. cream cheese, softened
- ¼ cup mayonnaise
- ½ tsp. salt
- ⅛ tsp. pepper
- ¼ cup finely chopped green or sweet red pepper
- ¼ cup finely chopped celery
- ¼ cup sweet pickle relish
- 2 Tbsp. minced fresh parsley
- 8 hard-boiled large eggs, chopped

In a bowl, mix the cream cheese, mayonnaise, salt and pepper until smooth. Stir in green pepper, celery, relish and parsley. Fold in eggs. Refrigerate, covered, until serving.

½ CUP 228 cal., 19g fat (6g sat. fat), 264mg chol., 456mg sod., 6g carb. (4g sugars, 0 fiber), 9g pro.

Yummy! This is the best egg salad recipe I have ever had! Definite keeper.
—LOVE_MY_LIFE, TASTEOFHOME.COM

Grandma's Divinity

Every year, my grandmother and I made divinity, just the two of us.
I still make it to this day.
—*Anne Clayborne, Walland, TN*

PREP: 5 min. • **COOK:** 40 min. + standing
MAKES: 60 pieces (1½ lbs.)

- 2 large egg whites
- 3 cups sugar
- ⅔ cup water
- ½ cup light corn syrup
- 1 tsp. vanilla extract
- 1 cup chopped pecans

1. Place egg whites in the bowl of a stand mixer; let stand at room temperature for 30 minutes. Meanwhile, line three 15x10x1-in. pans with waxed paper.

2. In a large heavy saucepan, combine the sugar, water and corn syrup; bring to a boil, stirring constantly to dissolve sugar. Cook, without stirring, over medium heat until a candy thermometer reads 252° (hard-ball stage). Just before the temperature is reached, beat egg whites on medium until stiff peaks form.

3. Slowly add hot sugar mixture in a thin stream over egg whites, beating constantly and scraping sides of bowl occasionally. Add vanilla. Beat until candy holds its shape, 5-6 minutes. (Do not overmix or candy will get stiff and crumbly.) Immediately fold in pecans.

4. Quickly drop by heaping teaspoonfuls onto prepared pans. Let stand at room temperature until dry to the touch. Store between sheets of waxed paper in an airtight container at room temperature.

NOTE We recommend that you always test your candy thermometer before each use by bringing water to a boil; the thermometer should read 212°. Adjust your recipe temperature up or down based on your test.

1 PIECE 61 cal., 1g fat (0 sat. fat), 0 chol., 4mg sod., 13g carb. (12g sugars, 0 fiber), 0 pro.

FRESH IS BEST
Improper storing is one of one of the most commonly made candy mistakes. To ensure divinity stays fresh, simply store it in an airtight container in a cool, dry place for up to 2 weeks.

7UP POUND CAKE, P. 235

Yesteryear Cakes

Spiced Pineapple Upside-Down Cake

Upside-down cakes, which have been around since the 1800s, were once called skillet cakes because they were cooked in cast-iron skillets on the stovetop.
—*Jennifer Sergesketter, Newburgh, IN*

PREP: 15 min. • **BAKE:** 40 min.
MAKES: 12 servings

- 1⅓ cups butter, softened, divided
- 1 cup packed brown sugar
- 1 can (20 oz.) pineapple slices, drained
- 10 to 12 maraschino cherries
- ½ cup chopped pecans
- 1½ cups sugar
- 2 large eggs, room temperature
- 1 tsp. vanilla extract
- 2 cups all-purpose flour
- 2 tsp. baking powder
- ½ tsp. baking soda
- ½ tsp. salt
- ½ tsp. ground cinnamon
- ½ tsp. ground nutmeg
- 1 cup buttermilk

1. In a saucepan, melt ⅔ cup butter; stir in brown sugar. Spread in the bottom of an ungreased heavy 12-in. ovenproof skillet or a 13x9-in. baking pan. Arrange pineapple in a single layer over sugar mixture; place a cherry in the center of each slice. Sprinkle with pecans and set aside.

2. In a large bowl, cream sugar and remaining butter until light and fluffy, 5-7 minutes. Add eggs, 1 at a time, beating well after each addition. Beat in vanilla. Combine flour, baking powder, baking soda, salt, cinnamon and nutmeg; add alternately to batter with buttermilk, beating well after each addition.

3. Carefully pour over the pineapple. Bake at 350° until a toothpick inserted in the center comes out clean, about 40 minutes for skillet, 50-60 minutes for baking pan. Immediately invert onto a serving platter. Serve warm.

1 PIECE 509 cal., 25g fat (13g sat. fat), 91mg chol., 467mg sod., 69g carb. (52g sugars, 2g fiber), 5g pro.

Caramel Pecan Pumpkin Cake

Use your slow cooker as a cake maker for a seriously yummy dessert that is easy enough for any weekday and tasty enough for a holiday meal—and frees up oven space too.
—*Julie Peterson, Crofton, MD*

PREP: 15 min. • **COOK:** 2 hours + standing
MAKES: 10 servings

- 1 cup butter, softened
- 1¼ cups sugar
- 4 large eggs, room temperature
- 2 cups all-purpose flour
- 2 tsp. baking powder
- 1 tsp. baking soda
- 1 tsp. pumpkin pie spice or ground cinnamon
- ½ tsp. salt
- 1 can (15 oz.) pumpkin
- ½ cup caramel sundae syrup
- ½ cup chopped pecans

1. In large bowl, cream butter and sugar until light and fluffy, 5-7 minutes. Add eggs, 1 at a time, beating well after each addition. In another bowl, whisk together the next 5 ingredients; add to creamed mixture alternately with pumpkin, beating well after each addition.

2. Line a 5-qt. round slow cooker with heavy-duty foil extending over sides; spray with cooking spray. Spread batter evenly into slow cooker. Cook, covered, on high until a toothpick inserted in center comes out clean, about 2 hours.

To avoid scorching, rotate the slow-cooker insert a half turn midway through cooking, lifting carefully with oven mitts. Turn off slow cooker; let stand, uncovered, 10 minutes. Using foil, carefully lift cake out of slow cooker and invert onto a serving plate.

3. Drizzle caramel syrup over cake; top with pecans. Serve warm.

1 PIECE 473 cal., 25g fat (13g sat. fat), 123mg chol., 561mg sod., 59g carb. (35g sugars, 2g fiber), 7g pro.

SPICED PINEAPPLE
UPSIDE-DOWN CAKE

Cream Cheese Sheet Cake

This tender, buttery sheet cake with a thin layer of fudge frosting is perfect for a crowd. It's always popular at potlucks and parties. It's not uncommon to see folks going back for second and even third pieces.
—*Gaye Mann, Rocky Mount, NC*

PREP: 20 min. • **BAKE:** 30 min. + cooling
MAKES: 30 servings

- 1 cup plus 2 Tbsp. butter, softened
- 6 oz. cream cheese, softened
- 2¼ cups sugar
- 6 large eggs, room temperature
- ¾ tsp. vanilla extract
- 2¼ cups cake flour

FROSTING
- 1 cup sugar
- ⅓ cup evaporated milk
- ½ cup butter, cubed
- ½ cup semisweet chocolate chips
  Sprinkles, optional

1. In a large bowl, cream the butter, cream cheese and sugar until light and fluffy, 5-7 minutes. Add eggs, 1 at a time, beating well after each addition. Beat in vanilla. Add flour until well blended.

2. Pour into a greased 15x10x1-in. baking pan. Bake at 325° until a toothpick inserted in the center comes out clean, 30-35 minutes. Cool completely on a wire rack.

3. For frosting, in a small saucepan, combine sugar and milk; bring to a boil over medium heat. Cover and cook for 3 minutes (do not stir). Stir in butter and chocolate chips until melted. Cool slightly. Stir frosting; spread over top of cake. If desired, top with sprinkles.

1 PIECE 250 cal., 13g fat (8g sat. fat), 73mg chol., 125mg sod., 32g carb. (23g sugars, 0 fiber), 3g pro.

Lemon Chiffon Cake

This fluffy cake is a real treat drizzled with sweet-tart lemon glaze.
—*Rebecca Baird, Salt Lake City, UT*

PREP: 15 min. • **BAKE:** 45 min. + cooling
MAKES: 16 servings

- ½ cup fat-free evaporated milk
- ½ cup reduced-fat sour cream
- ¼ cup lemon juice
- 2 Tbsp. canola oil
- 2 tsp. vanilla extract
- 1 tsp. grated lemon zest
- 1 tsp. lemon extract
- 2 cups cake flour
- 1½ cups sugar
- 1 Tbsp. baking powder
- ½ tsp. salt
- 1 cup egg whites (about 7 large)
- ½ tsp. cream of tartar

LEMON GLAZE
- 1¾ cups confectioners' sugar
- 3 Tbsp. lemon juice

1. In a large bowl, combine the first 7 ingredients. Sift together flour, sugar, baking powder and salt; gradually beat into lemon mixture until smooth. In a small bowl, beat egg whites until foamy. Add cream of tartar; beat until stiff peaks form. Gently fold into lemon mixture.

2. Pour into an ungreased 10-in. tube pan. Bake at 325° for 45-55 minutes or until cake springs back when lightly touched. Immediately invert pan; cool completely. Remove cake from pan to a serving platter. Combine glaze ingredients; drizzle over cake.

1 PIECE 230 cal., 3g fat (1g sat. fat), 3mg chol., 189mg sod., 47g carb. (33g sugars, 0 fiber), 4g pro.

Hummingbird Cake

This impressive cake is my dad's favorite, so I always make it for his birthday. The beautiful, old-fashioned layered delight makes a memorable celebration dessert any time of year.
—Nancy Zimmerman, Cape May Court House, NJ

PREP: 40 min. • **BAKE:** 25 min. + cooling
MAKES: 14 servings

- 2 cups mashed ripe bananas
- 1½ cups canola oil
- 3 large eggs, room temperature
- 1 can (8 oz.) unsweetened crushed pineapple, undrained
- 1½ tsp. vanilla extract
- 3 cups all-purpose flour
- 2 cups sugar
- 1 tsp. salt
- 1 tsp. baking soda
- 1 tsp. ground cinnamon
- 1 cup chopped walnuts

PINEAPPLE FROSTING
- ¼ cup shortening
- 2 Tbsp. butter, softened
- 1 tsp. grated lemon zest
- ¼ tsp. salt
- 6 cups confectioners' sugar
- ½ cup unsweetened pineapple juice
- 2 tsp. half-and-half cream
  Chopped walnuts, optional

1. In a large bowl, beat the bananas, oil, eggs, pineapple and vanilla until well blended. In another bowl, combine the flour, sugar, salt, baking soda and cinnamon; gradually beat into banana mixture until blended. Stir in walnuts.

2. Pour into 3 greased and floured 9-in. round baking pans. Bake at 350° until a toothpick inserted in the center comes out clean, 25-30 minutes. Cool for 10 minutes before removing from pans to wire racks to cool completely.

3. For frosting, in a large bowl, beat the shortening, butter, lemon zest and salt until fluffy. Add confectioners' sugar alternately with pineapple juice. Beat in cream. Spread between layers and over top and sides of cake. If desired, sprinkle with walnuts.

1 PIECE 777 cal., 35g fat (6g sat. fat), 50mg chol., 333mg sod., 113g carb. (85g sugars, 2g fiber), 7g pro.

> **"**
> *Putting this in the refrigerator overnight really helps it set up. We just love this cake, and my husband makes it all the time. We first heard of this from his boss, whose mother made it for years. Such a good ol' southern cake.*
>
> —SHYGIRL55, TASTEOFHOME.COM

7UP Pound Cake

My grandmother gave me my first cake recipe—a pound cake using 7UP—which her grandmother had given to her. On top of being delicious, this cake represents family tradition, connection and love.
—*Marsha Davis, Desert Hot Springs, CA*

PREP: 25 min. • **BAKE:** 65 min. + cooling
MAKES: 16 servings

1½ cups butter, softened
3 cups sugar
5 large eggs, room temperature
2 Tbsp. lemon juice
1 tsp. vanilla extract
3 cups all-purpose flour
¾ cup 7UP soda

GLAZE
1½ cups confectioners' sugar
1 Tbsp. lemon or lime juice
1 to 2 Tbsp. 7UP soda
½ tsp. grated lemon or lime zest, optional

1. Preheat oven to 350°. Grease and flour a 10-in. fluted or plain tube pan.

2. In a large bowl, cream butter and sugar until light and fluffy, 5-7 minutes. Add eggs, 1 at a time, beating well after each addition. Beat in lemon juice and vanilla. Add flour alternately with 7UP, beating well after each addition.

3. Transfer batter to the prepared pan. Bake until a toothpick inserted in center comes out clean, 65-75 minutes. Cool in pan 20 minutes before removing to a wire rack to cool completely.

4. For glaze, in a small bowl, mix the confectioners' sugar, lemon juice and enough 7UP to reach desired consistency. If desired, stir in zest. Drizzle over cake.

NOTE To remove cakes easily, use solid shortening to grease plain and fluted tube pans.

1 PIECE 457 cal., 19g fat (11g sat. fat), 104mg chol., 177mg sod., 69g carb. (50g sugars, 1g fiber), 5g pro.

FRESH FLAVOR & AIRY TEXTURE
The 7UP in this recipe means you don't need traditional leaveners like baking soda or baking powder. The carbonation in the 7UP actually gives the cake a lift, helping it rise.

Lemon Ricotta Cake

This recipe is a family gem that was passed down from my grandmother and mother. Garnished with shaved lemon peel, the moist four-layer cake is the perfect dessert when you want to impress.
—*Nanette Slaughter, Sammamish, WA*

PREP: 1 hour + chilling
BAKE: 30 min. + cooling
MAKES: 16 servings

- 3 large eggs, room temperature
- 2 large egg yolks, room temperature
- ⅔ cup sugar
- ⅓ cup lemon juice
- ⅓ cup butter, cubed

CAKE BATTER
- 1 cup butter, softened
- 2 cups sugar
- 3 large eggs, room temperature
- 1 cup ricotta cheese
- 1 cup buttermilk
- 1 Tbsp. grated lemon zest
- 1½ tsp. vanilla extract
- 1 tsp. lemon juice
- 3 cups all-purpose flour
- ½ tsp. baking powder
- ½ tsp. baking soda
- ½ tsp. salt

SUGARED LEMON ZEST
- 6 medium lemons
- ¼ cup sugar

FROSTING
- ⅔ cup butter, softened
- 5½ cups confectioners' sugar
- ⅓ cup 2% milk
- 1½ tsp. grated lemon zest
- 1½ tsp. vanilla extract
- ⅛ tsp. salt
- Colored sugar, optional

1. For lemon curd, in a small bowl, combine eggs and egg yolks. In a heavy saucepan, cook and stir the sugar, lemon juice and butter over medium heat until smooth. Stir a small amount of hot mixture into eggs; return all to the pan, stirring constantly. Bring to a gentle boil; cook and stir until thickened, about 2 minutes. Cool slightly. Cover and chill until thickened, about 1½ hours or overnight.

2. Preheat oven to 350°. In a large bowl, cream butter and sugar until light and fluffy, 5-7 minutes. Add eggs, 1 at a time, beating well after each addition. Combine ricotta cheese, buttermilk, lemon zest, vanilla and lemon juice. Combine flour, baking powder, baking soda and salt; add to creamed mixture alternately with buttermilk mixture, beating well after each addition.

3. Pour into 2 greased and floured 9-in. round baking pans. Bake until a toothpick inserted in the center comes out clean, 30-35 minutes. Cool 10 minutes before removing from pans to wire racks to cool completely.

4. Using a citrus zester, remove zest from lemons in long narrow strips; toss with sugar. Let stand for 30 minutes. (Save fruit for another use.) Meanwhile, to make the frosting, in a large bowl, cream butter until light and fluffy. Add the confectioners' sugar, milk, grated lemon zest, vanilla and salt; beat until smooth.

5. Cut each cake in half horizontally. Place 1 cake layer on a serving plate. Pipe a circle of frosting around edge of cake. Spread a third of the lemon curd inside frosting. Repeat layers twice. Top with remaining cake layer. Frost top and sides. If desired, pipe a decorative border of frosting using a star tip, and decorate sides of cake with colored sugar. Garnish with lemon zest strips. Store in the refrigerator.

NOTE To substitute for each cup of buttermilk, use 1 Tbsp. white vinegar or lemon juice plus enough milk to measure 1 cup. Stir, then let stand 5 minutes. Or, use 1 cup plain yogurt or 1¾ tsp. cream of tartar plus 1 cup milk.

1 PIECE 657 cal., 27g fat (16g sat. fat), 172mg chol., 370mg sod., 98g carb. (77g sugars, 1g fiber), 8g pro.

CITRUS CURD
Citrus curd (such as the lemon one used to fill this cake) became popular in England in the 1800s as a sweet spread for scones and filling for desserts. Made from citrus juice, sugar, eggs and butter, this smooth and tangy condiment has become a beloved addition to tarts, cakes and tea trays, where it adds a burst of bright flavor.

German Chocolate Cake

This cake is my husband's favorite! Every bite has a light crunch from the pecans, a sweet taste of coconut and a drizzle of chocolate.
—Joyce Platfoot, Wapakoneta, OH

PREP: 30 min. • **BAKE:** 25 min. + cooling
MAKES: 16 servings

- 4 oz. German sweet chocolate, chopped
- ½ cup water
- 1 cup butter, softened
- 2 cups sugar
- 4 large eggs, separated, room temperature
- 1 tsp. vanilla extract
- 2½ cups cake flour
- 1 tsp. baking soda
- ½ tsp. salt
- 1 cup buttermilk

FROSTING
- 1½ cups sugar
- 1½ cups evaporated milk
- ¾ cup butter
- 5 large egg yolks, room temperature, beaten
- 2 cups sweetened shredded coconut
- 1½ cups chopped pecans
- 1½ tsp. vanilla extract

GLAZE
- 2 oz. semisweet chocolate
- 1 tsp. shortening

1. Line 3 greased 9-in. round baking pans with waxed paper. Grease waxed paper and set aside. In a small saucepan, melt chocolate with water over low heat; cool.

2. Preheat oven to 350°. In a large bowl, cream butter and sugar until light and fluffy, 5-7 minutes. Beat in 4 egg yolks, 1 at a time, beating well after each addition. Blend in melted chocolate and vanilla. Combine flour, baking soda and salt; add to the creamed mixture alternately with buttermilk, beating well after each addition.

3. In a small bowl and with clean beaters, beat the 4 egg whites until stiff peaks form. Fold a fourth of the egg whites into the creamed mixture; fold in remaining whites.

4. Pour batter into prepared pans. Bake 24-28 minutes or until a toothpick inserted in center comes out clean. Cool 10 minutes before removing from pans to wire racks to cool completely.

5. For the frosting, in a small saucepan, heat sugar, milk, butter and egg yolks over medium-low heat until mixture is thickened and golden brown, stirring constantly. Remove from heat. Stir in coconut, pecans and vanilla. Cool until thick enough to spread. Spread a third of the frosting over each cake layer and stack the layers.

6. For the glaze, in a microwave, melt chocolate and shortening; stir until smooth. Drizzle over cake.

NOTE To substitute for each cup of buttermilk, use 1 Tbsp. white vinegar or lemon juice plus enough milk to measure 1 cup. Stir, then let stand 5 minutes. Or, use 1 cup plain yogurt or 1¾ tsp. cream of tartar plus 1 cup milk.

1 PIECE 691 cal., 40g fat (21g sat. fat), 166mg chol., 415mg sod., 78g carb. (58g sugars, 3g fiber), 8g pro.

GERMAN CHOCOLATE ORIGIN & SUBSTITUTES

Perhaps one of the most interesting facts about this cake is that German chocolate is not really from Germany! German chocolate is a sweet chocolate invented by a man named Sam German in 1852 for Baker's Chocolate. The moniker stuck, and we still call it German chocolate to this day. If you can't find German chocolate, either milk chocolate or semisweet chocolate will work just fine.

Aunt Murna's Jam Cake

I remember Aunt Murna telling me that she created her jam cake recipe as a young girl. She made improvements over the years, such as soaking the raisins in crushed pineapple. This cake is a favorite at our annual family reunions.
—*Eddie Robinson, Lawrenceburg, KY*

PREP: 20 min. + soaking
BAKE: 50 min. + cooling
MAKES: 16 servings

- 1 cup raisins
- 1 can (8 oz.) crushed pineapple, undrained
- 1 cup butter, softened
- 1 cup sugar
- 4 large eggs, room temperature
- 1 jar (12 oz.) blackberry jam or 1 cup homemade blackberry jam
- ⅔ cup buttermilk
- 2½ cups all-purpose flour
- ⅓ cup baking cocoa
- 1 tsp. baking soda
- 1 tsp. ground cinnamon
- 1 tsp. ground nutmeg
- ½ tsp. ground cloves
- 1 cup chopped pecans

CARAMEL ICING
- 1 cup butter, cubed
- 2 cups packed brown sugar
- ½ cup 2% milk
- 3½ to 4 cups sifted confectioners' sugar

1. Soak raisins in pineapple and juice several hours or overnight.

2. In a large bowl, cream butter and sugar until light and fluffy, 5-7 minutes. Add eggs, 1 at a time, beating well after each addition. Add jam and buttermilk; beat until well blended. Sift together dry ingredients; add to batter. Beat on low just until combined. Stir in the raisins, pineapple and pecans.

3. Pour into 2 greased and floured 9-in. round baking pans. Bake at 350° until a toothpick inserted in the center comes out clean, about 50 minutes. Cool in pans for 10 minutes before removing to wire racks.

4. For icing, melt butter in a saucepan over medium heat. Stir in brown sugar and milk; bring to a boil. Remove from the heat. Cool just until warm; beat in enough confectioners' sugar for icing to reach spreading consistency. Add more sugar for thicker icing or more milk to thin it. Frost cooled cake.

NOTE To substitute for each cup of buttermilk, use 1 Tbsp. white vinegar or lemon juice plus enough milk to measure 1 cup. Stir, then let stand 5 minutes. Or, use 1 cup plain yogurt or 1¾ tsp. cream of tartar plus 1 cup milk.

1 PIECE 694 cal., 30g fat (15g sat. fat), 116mg chol., 353mg sod., 105g carb. (83g sugars, 2g fiber), 6g pro.

Chocolate Mayonnaise Cake

Mom always made this special chocolate mayo cake for my birthday dessert. It is very moist and has a nice light chocolate taste. Plus, the flavorful frosting is the perfect topping.
—*Deborah Amrine, Fort Myers, FL*

PREP: 15 min. • **BAKE:** 30 min. + cooling
MAKES: 12 servings

- 1 cup water
- 1 cup mayonnaise
- 1 tsp. vanilla extract
- 2 cups all-purpose flour
- 1 cup sugar
- 3 Tbsp. baking cocoa
- 2 tsp. baking soda

BROWN SUGAR FROSTING
- ½ cup packed brown sugar
- ¼ cup butter, cubed
- 2 Tbsp. 2% milk
- 1¾ cups confectioners' sugar

1. In a large bowl, combine the water, mayonnaise and vanilla until well blended. In another large bowl, combine the flour, sugar, cocoa and baking soda; gradually beat into mayonnaise mixture until blended.

2. Pour into a greased 9-in. square or 11x7-in. baking pan. Bake at 350° until a toothpick inserted in the center comes out clean, 30-35 minutes. Cool completely.

3. For frosting, in a small saucepan, cook and stir the brown sugar in butter until bubbly. Remove from the heat; stir in milk. Gradually add confectioners' sugar; beat until smooth. Frost cake.

1 PIECE 416 cal., 19g fat (4g sat. fat), 17mg chol., 354mg sod., 60g carb. (42g sugars, 1g fiber), 3g pro.

MAYONNAISE CAKE CLUES

What does mayonnaise do to a cake?
Mayonnaise can be used in place of fat or oil in cake recipes. It adds moisture, richness and flavor. And don't worry, you won't taste the mayo!

Are there any alternatives to brown sugar frosting?
Brown sugar adds depth of flavor because of its rich taste with a hint of molasses. But you can also use a frosting made with confectioners' sugar, a classic buttercream, or a prepared vanilla or chocolate frosting.

Favorite Pumpkin Cake Roll

Keep this cake roll in the freezer for a quick dessert for family or unexpected guests, to take to a gathering, or to give as a yummy gift.
—*Erica Berchtold, Freeport, IL*

PREP: 30 min. • **BAKE:** 15 min. + freezing
MAKES: 10 servings

3   large eggs, separated,
    room temperature
1   cup sugar, divided
⅔   cup canned pumpkin
¾   cup all-purpose flour
1   tsp. baking soda
½   tsp. ground cinnamon
⅛   tsp. salt

FILLING
8   oz. cream cheese, softened
2   Tbsp. butter, softened
1   cup confectioners' sugar
¾   tsp. vanilla extract
    Additional confectioners' sugar,
    optional

1. Line a 15x10x1-in. baking pan with parchment or waxed paper; grease the paper and set aside. In a large bowl, beat egg yolks on high speed until thick and lemon-colored. Gradually add ½ cup sugar and the pumpkin, beating on high until sugar is almost dissolved.

2. In a small bowl, beat the egg whites until soft peaks form. Gradually add the remaining ½ cup sugar, beating until stiff peaks form. Fold into egg yolk mixture. Combine the flour, baking soda, cinnamon and salt; gently fold into pumpkin mixture. Spread into prepared pan.

3. Bake at 375° until cake springs back when lightly touched, 12-15 minutes. Cool 5 minutes. Turn cake onto a kitchen towel dusted with confectioners' sugar. Gently peel off waxed paper. Roll up cake in the towel jelly-roll style, starting with a short side. Cool completely on a wire rack.

4. In a small bowl, beat the cream cheese, butter, confectioners' sugar and vanilla until smooth. Unroll cake; spread filling evenly to within ½ in. of edges. Roll up again, without towel. Cover and freeze until firm. May be frozen for up to 3 months. Remove from the freezer 15 minutes before cutting. If desired, dust with confectioners' sugar.

1 PIECE 287 cal., 12g fat (7g sat. fat), 85mg chol., 268mg sod., 42g carb. (33g sugars, 1g fiber), 4g pro.

PUMPKIN CAKE ROLL TIPS

How do you keep a cake roll from cracking?
Cracks are the bane of all cake rolls, but they aren't inevitable! The most important thing you can do to prevent cracks is to roll the sponge cake while it's still hot out of the oven. The heat and moisture still in the cake will help keep the sponge intact. Another cause of cracks is if the cake is overbaked. Timing is key—since the cake layer is so thin, you have to remove it from the oven as soon as it's done.

How can you put your own spin on pumpkin cake roll?
Jazz it up by swirling some of your favorite jam or preserves into the filling for a decorative and extra-flavorful effect. We suggest apricot preserves, blackberry jam, apple butter or even a bit of maple syrup to go with the autumnal flavor. Sprinkle the top of the roll with some toasted pecans, toasted sliced almonds or mini chocolate chips.

Southern Lane Cake

I just love this impressive cake, and so do my dinner guests. With the fruit filling and topping, it's reminiscent of a fruitcake, but so much more delicious!
—*Mabel Parvi, Ridgefield, WA*

PREP: 40 min. • **BAKE:** 20 min. + cooling
MAKES: 12 servings

- 6 large egg whites
- ¾ cup butter, softened
- 1½ cups sugar
- 1 tsp. vanilla extract
- 2¼ cups all-purpose flour
- 2½ tsp. baking powder
- ½ tsp. salt
- ¾ cup 2% milk

FILLING
- 6 large egg yolks
- 1 cup sugar
- ½ cup butter, cubed
- ¼ cup bourbon
- 1 Tbsp. grated orange zest
- ¼ tsp. salt
- ¾ cup raisins
- ¾ cup sweetened shredded coconut
- ¾ cup chopped pecans
- ¾ cup coarsely chopped red candied cherries
- 1 cup heavy whipping cream, whipped and sweetened

1. Line bottoms of 3 greased 9-in. round baking pans with parchment. Grease parchment; set aside. Place egg whites in a large bowl; let stand at room temperature 30 minutes.

2. In another large bowl, cream the butter and sugar until light and fluffy, 5-7 minutes. Beat in vanilla. In another bowl, whisk flour, baking powder and salt; add to creamed mixture alternately with milk, beating well after each addition. Beat egg whites until stiff peaks form; fold into batter. Transfer to prepared pans.

3. Bake at 325° until a toothpick inserted in the center comes out clean, 20-25 minutes. Cool for 10 minutes before removing from pans to wire racks; remove paper. Cool completely.

4. For filling, combine egg yolks and sugar in a large saucepan. Add butter; cook and stir over medium-low heat until sugar is dissolved and mixture thickens (do not boil). Remove from the heat. Stir in bourbon, orange zest and salt. Fold in the raisins, coconut, pecans and cherries. Cool.

5. Place 1 cake layer on a serving plate; spread with a third of the filling. Repeat layers twice. Frost sides of cake with whipped cream. Refrigerate until serving.

1 PIECE 677 cal., 36g fat (20g sat. fat), 167mg chol., 469mg sod., 81g carb. (58g sugars, 2g fiber), 8g pro.

Pink Lemonade Stand Cake

If you love a moist and creamy cake, this is it. Lemon juice
and lemonade give the layers a tangy, citrusy punch, and the
cream cheese frosting with pink sprinkles is so pretty.
—*Lauren McAnelly, Des Moines, IA*

PREP: 50 min. • **BAKE:** 20 min. + cooling
MAKES: 12 servings

1   cup buttermilk
2   Tbsp. lemon juice
2   Tbsp. seedless strawberry jam,
    warmed
2   Tbsp. thawed pink lemonade
    concentrate
2   Tbsp. grenadine syrup
1   cup unsalted butter, softened
1¼ cups sugar
3   Tbsp. grated lemon zest
4   large eggs, room temperature
½   tsp. vanilla extract
2½ cups all-purpose flour
1   tsp. baking powder
½   tsp. baking soda
½   tsp. salt

FROSTING
1   cup unsalted butter, softened
1   pkg. (8 oz.) cream cheese, softened
1   Tbsp. grated lemon zest
4   cups confectioners' sugar
⅓   cup plus 3 Tbsp. thawed pink
    lemonade concentrate, divided
    Pink sprinkles

1. Preheat oven to 350°. Line bottoms of
3 greased 8-in. round baking pans with
parchment; grease parchment.

2. In a small bowl, whisk the first
5 ingredients until blended. In a large
bowl, cream butter, sugar and lemon
zest until light and fluffy, 5-7 minutes.
Add eggs, 1 at a time, beating well after
each addition. Beat in vanilla. In another
bowl, whisk flour, baking powder, baking
soda and salt; add to creamed mixture
alternately with buttermilk mixture,
beating well after each addition.

3. Transfer batter to prepared pans.
Bake until a toothpick inserted in center
comes out clean, 20-24 minutes. Cool
in pans 10 minutes before removing to
wire racks; remove parchment. Cool
completely.

4. For frosting, in a large bowl, beat
butter, cream cheese and lemon zest
until smooth. Gradually beat in
confectioners' sugar and ⅓ cup
lemonade concentrate. If necessary,
refrigerate until spreadable, up to 1 hour.

5. Place 1 cake layer on a serving plate.
Brush 1 Tbsp. lemonade concentrate
over cake; spread with ½ cup frosting.
Repeat layers. Top with remaining
cake layer; brush remaining lemonade
concentrate over top. Spread remaining
frosting over top and side of cake.

6. Decorate with sprinkles. Refrigerate
until serving.

NOTE To substitute for each cup of
buttermilk, use 1 Tbsp. white vinegar or
lemon juice plus enough milk to measure
1 cup. Stir, then let stand 5 minutes. Or,
use 1 cup plain yogurt or 1¾ tsp. cream
of tartar plus 1 cup milk.

1 PIECE 732 cal., 39g fat (24g sat. fat),
172mg chol., 291mg sod., 91g carb. (68g
sugars, 1g fiber), 7g pro.

PINK LEMONADE CUPCAKES Make batter
as directed; fill 24 paper-lined muffin
cups three-fourths full. Bake in a
preheated 350° oven for 16-19 minutes or
until a toothpick comes out clean. Cool in
pans 10 minutes before removing to wire
racks to cool completely. Prepare frosting
as directed, omitting 3 Tbsp. lemonade
concentrate for brushing layers; pipe or
spread frosting over cupcakes.

Orange Dream Angel Food Cake

A basic angel food cake becomes a heavenly indulgence thanks to a hint of orange flavor swirled into every bite. The orange color makes slices of the cake look so pretty when arranged on individual dessert plates.
—*Lauren Osborne, Holtwood, PA*

PREP: 25 min. • **BAKE:** 30 min. + cooling
MAKES: 16 servings

- 12 large egg whites
- 1 cup all-purpose flour
- 1¾ cups sugar, divided
- 1½ tsp. cream of tartar
- ½ tsp. salt
- 1 tsp. almond extract
- 1 tsp. vanilla extract
- 1 tsp. grated orange zest
- 1 tsp. orange extract
- 6 drops red food coloring, optional
- 6 drops yellow food coloring, optional

1. Place egg whites in a large bowl; let stand at room temperature for 30 minutes. Sift flour and ¾ cup sugar together twice; set aside.

2. Add cream of tartar, salt, and almond and vanilla extracts to egg whites; beat on medium speed until soft peaks form. Gradually add remaining sugar, about 2 Tbsp. at a time, beating on high until stiff glossy peaks form and sugar is dissolved. Gradually fold in flour mixture, about ½ cup at a time.

3. Gently spoon half the batter into an ungreased 10-in. tube pan. To the remaining batter, stir in orange zest, orange extract and, if desired, food colorings. Gently spoon orange batter over white batter. Cut through both layers with a knife to swirl the orange and remove air pockets.

4. Bake on the lowest oven rack at 375° for 30-35 minutes or until lightly browned and entire top appears dry. Immediately invert pan; cool completely, about 1 hour.

5. Run a knife around side and center tube of pan. Remove the cake to a serving plate.

1 SLICE 130 cal., 0 fat (0 sat. fat), 0 chol., 116mg sod., 28g carb. (22g sugars, 0 fiber), 4g pro. **DIABETIC EXCHANGES** 2 starch.

COOLING TRICK
If your tube pan doesn't have feet for cooling, sling the pan over a sturdy bottle to cool the cake upside down.

Cherry Cola Cake

Cherry cola and marshmallows make a zippy chocolate dessert that is scrumptious topped with vanilla ice cream.
—*Cheri Mason, Harmony, NC*

PREP: 30 min. • **BAKE:** 25 min. + cooling
MAKES: 12 servings

2¼ cups miniature marshmallows
3 cups all-purpose flour
3 cups sugar
1½ tsp. baking soda
1½ cups butter, cubed
1½ cups cherry-flavored cola
4 Tbsp. baking cocoa
3 large eggs, room temperature
¾ cup buttermilk
1½ tsp. vanilla extract

FROSTING
1½ cups butter, softened
2 cups confectioners' sugar
2 jars (7 oz. each) marshmallow creme
4 Tbsp. frozen cherry-pomegranate
    juice concentrate, thawed
    Fresh sweet cherries with stems

1. Preheat oven to 350°. Line bottoms of 3 greased 9-in. round baking pans with parchment; grease paper. Divide marshmallows among pans.

2. In a large bowl, whisk flour, sugar and baking soda. In a small saucepan, combine butter, cola and cocoa; bring just to a boil, stirring occasionally. Add to flour mixture, stirring just until moistened.

3. In a small bowl, whisk eggs, buttermilk and vanilla until blended; add to flour mixture, whisking constantly. Pour into prepared pans, dividing batter evenly. (Marshmallows will float to the top.)

4. Bake 25-30 minutes or until a toothpick inserted in center comes out clean. Cool in pans 10 minutes before removing to wire racks; remove paper. Cool completely.

5. For frosting, in a small bowl, beat butter and confectioners' sugar until smooth. Beat in marshmallow creme and juice concentrate on low speed just until combined; increase to high and beat until smooth.

6. Place 1 cake layer on a serving plate; spread top with 1 cup frosting. Repeat with second layer. Top with remaining cake layer; spread with remaining frosting. Decorate with cherries.

1 PIECE 591 cal., 28g fat (17g sat. fat), 103mg chol., 369mg sod., 83g carb. (60g sugars, 1g fiber), 4g pro.

NOTE To frost sides as well as top of cake, double amounts for frosting.

NOTES

EASY KEY LIME PIE, P. 263

Favorite
Pies

Juicy Peach & Strawberry Crumb Pie

You've had peach pie and strawberry pie, and maybe even peach-strawberry pie. But throw in some garden-fresh basil and you're in for a real treat. Trust me.
—*Lindsay Sprunk, Rochelle, IL*

PREP: 25 min. • **BAKE:** 45 min. + cooling
MAKES: 8 servings

- 1 sheet refrigerated pie crust
- 3½ cups sliced peeled peaches (about 4 medium)
- 2½ cups sliced fresh strawberries
- 2 Tbsp. lemon juice
- ¾ cup sugar
- ¼ cup cornstarch
- 2 Tbsp. minced fresh basil
- ¾ cup all-purpose flour
- ½ cup packed brown sugar
- 6 Tbsp. cold butter

1. Preheat oven to 375°. Unroll pie crust into a 9-in. pie plate; flute edge. In a large bowl, combine peaches, strawberries and lemon juice. In a small bowl, mix sugar, cornstarch and basil. Add to fruit and toss gently to coat. Transfer to crust.

2. In a small bowl, mix flour and brown sugar; cut in butter until crumbly. Sprinkle over filling. Place pie on a foil-lined baking pan.

3. Bake on a lower oven rack until topping is golden brown and filling is bubbly, 45-55 minutes. Cool on a wire rack.

1 PIECE 424 cal., 16g fat (9g sat. fat), 28mg chol., 174mg sod., 69g carb. (41g sugars, 2g fiber), 3g pro.

Honey Lemon Meringue Pie

My husband especially enjoys this lemon meringue pie with condensed milk. His mother made a similar treat for him when he was a child, but it was rewarding for me to create a recipe of my own that he loves so much!
—*Portia Gorman, Los Angeles, CA*

PREP: 20 min. • **BAKE:** 35 min. + chilling
MAKES: 8 servings

- 1 Tbsp. honey
- 3 Tbsp. butter, melted, divided
- 1 graham cracker crust (9 in.)
- 1 can (14 oz.) sweetened condensed milk
- ½ cup lemon juice
- ¼ cup sugar
- 3 large eggs, separated, room temperature

MERINGUE
- ¼ tsp. cream of tartar
- ½ tsp. vanilla extract
- 6 Tbsp. sugar

1. Preheat oven to 350°. Drizzle honey and 1 Tbsp. melted butter in bottom of crust. In a medium bowl, beat sweetened condensed milk, lemon juice, sugar, egg yolks and remaining 2 Tbsp. melted butter until blended. Pour into crust; bake for 20 minutes.

2. Meanwhile, in a small bowl, beat egg whites and cream of tartar until frothy. Add vanilla; gradually beat in sugar, 1 Tbsp. at a time, on high until stiff glossy peaks form and sugar is dissolved. Spread evenly over hot filling, sealing edges to crust. Bake until meringue is golden brown, about 15 minutes. Cool on a wire rack for 1 hour. Refrigerate at least 3 hours before serving.

1 PIECE 458 cal., 17g fat (8g sat. fat), 104mg chol., 268mg sod., 69g carb. (65g sugars, 0 fiber), 9g pro.

JUICY PEACH &
STRAWBERRY CRUMB PIE

Irresistible Coconut Cream Pie

My husband and I grow 500 acres of wheat on the farm his family homesteaded in 1889. I grind my own flour and love to use it in this recipe. The easy pat-in crust has a rich grain flavor. It's irresistible topped with old-fashioned coconut cream and a fluffy meringue.
—Roberta Foster, Kingfisher, OK

PREP: 40 min. • **BAKE:** 15 min. + chilling
MAKES: 8 servings

1½ cups whole wheat flour
2 tsp. sugar
½ tsp. salt
½ cup canola oil
2 Tbsp. whole milk

FILLING
½ cup sugar
3 Tbsp. cornstarch
1 Tbsp. all-purpose flour
½ tsp. salt
2¼ cups whole milk
3 large egg yolks, room temperature
1 Tbsp. butter
½ cup sweetened shredded coconut
1 tsp. vanilla extract

MERINGUE
3 large egg whites, room temperature
1 cup marshmallow creme
¼ cup sweetened shredded coconut

1. Preheat oven to 350°. In a bowl, mix flour, sugar and salt. In another bowl, whisk oil and milk. Gradually add to flour mixture, tossing with a fork until moistened (mixture will be crumbly). Press onto bottom and up side of an ungreased 9-in. pie plate. Bake for 20 minutes. Cool on a wire rack.

2. For filling, in a heavy saucepan, mix sugar, cornstarch, flour and salt. Gradually whisk in milk. Bring to a boil; cook and stir 2 minutes or until thickened. Remove from heat.

3. In a small bowl, whisk a small amount of hot mixture into egg yolks; return all to pan, whisking constantly. Bring to a gentle boil; cook and stir 2 minutes. Remove from heat; stir in butter, coconut and vanilla.

4. For meringue, in a bowl, beat egg whites until soft peaks form. Gradually add marshmallow creme, beating on high speed. Continue beating until stiff glossy peaks form.

5. Transfer hot filling to crust. Spread meringue evenly over filling, sealing to edge of crust. Sprinkle with coconut. Bake 12-15 minutes or until meringue is golden brown. Cool 1 hour on a wire rack. Refrigerate at least 3 hours before serving.

1 PIECE 437 cal., 23g fat (7g sat. fat), 80mg chol., 395mg sod., 51g carb. (29g sugars, 3g fiber), 8g pro.

NOTES

Caramel Pecan Pie

This is hands down the best pecan pie—it's so good, it's scary! I'm making it for Thanksgiving because there will be others around to share it with me. Here's the trick: Toss the bag of caramels to your kid or spouse and promise they can eat whatever is left after they unwrap your 36 caramels.
—*Dorothy Reinhold, Malibu, CA*

PREP: 25 min. • **BAKE:** 35 min. + cooling
MAKES: 8 servings

- 36 caramels
- ¼ cup water
- ¼ cup butter, cubed
- 3 large eggs, room temperature
- ¾ cup sugar
- 1 tsp. vanilla extract
- ⅛ tsp. salt
- 1⅓ cups chopped pecans, toasted
- 1 frozen deep-dish pie crust (9 in.)
  Pecan halves, optional

1. Preheat oven to 350°. In a small heavy saucepan, combine the caramels, water and butter. Cook and stir over low heat until caramels are melted. Remove from the heat and set aside.

2. In a small bowl, beat the eggs, sugar, vanilla and salt until smooth. Gradually add caramel mixture. Stir in chopped pecans. Pour into crust. If desired, arrange pecan halves over filling.

3. Bake until set, 35-40 minutes. Cool on a wire rack. Refrigerate leftovers.

1 PIECE 541 cal., 29g fat (7g sat. fat), 88mg chol., 301mg sod., 68g carb. (49g sugars, 2g fiber), 7g pro.

Easy Grasshopper Ice Cream Pie

This quick pie is such an ego booster! My family compliments me the entire time they're eating it. A big hit at work potlucks, too, it's good to the last crumb.
—*Kim Murphy, Albia, IA*

PREP: 15 min. + freezing
MAKES: 8 servings

- 4 cups mint chocolate chip ice cream, softened
- 1 chocolate crumb crust (9 in.)
- 5 Oreo cookies, chopped
- ⅓ cup chocolate-covered peppermint candies
  Chocolate hard-shell ice cream topping

Spread ice cream into crust. Sprinkle with cookies and candies; drizzle with ice cream topping. Freeze until firm. Remove from the freezer 15 minutes before serving.

NOTE This recipe was tested with Junior Mints chocolate-covered peppermint candies.

1 PIECE 354 cal., 17g fat (9g sat. fat), 15mg chol., 181mg sod., 48g carb. (37g sugars, 2g fiber), 4g pro.

CHOCOLATE CHERRY ICE CREAM PIE
Soften ¾ cup dried cherries in boiling water; drain. Stir into 3½ cups chocolate ice cream with ¾ cup miniature chocolate chips. Spread into crust; freeze. Top with chocolate sauce and maraschino cherries.

MILKY WAY ICE CREAM PIE Finely chop four regular-size Milky Way candy bars; add ¼ cup milk and 2-3 tsp. instant coffee granules. Stir into 4 cups vanilla ice cream. Spread into crust; freeze. Top with additional chopped candy bars.

Classic Sweet Potato Pie

This simple but special deep-dish pie provides a down-home finish to hearty autumn meals served at home. Pecans and pumpkin pie spice make it a comforting seasonal classic.
—*Paul Azzone, Shoreham, NY*

PREP: 25 min. • **BAKE:** 45 min. + cooling
MAKES: 8 servings

- 1⅔ cups pie crust mix
- ¼ cup finely chopped pecans
- 3 to 4 Tbsp. cold water
- 3 large eggs
- 2 cans (15 oz. each) sweet potatoes, drained
- 1 can (14 oz.) sweetened condensed milk
- 1½ to 2 tsp. pumpkin pie spice
- 1 tsp. vanilla extract
- ½ tsp. salt
  Optional: Whipped cream and additional chopped pecans, toasted

1. In a small bowl, combine pie crust mix and pecans. Gradually add water, tossing with a fork until dough forms a ball. Roll out to fit a 9-in. deep-dish pie plate or cast-iron skillet. Transfer crust to pie plate. Flute edge; set aside.

2. In a food processor, combine the eggs, sweet potatoes, milk, pumpkin pie spice, vanilla and salt; blend until smooth. Pour into crust.

3. Bake at 425° for 15 minutes. Reduce heat to 350°; bake 30-35 minutes longer or until a knife inserted in the center comes out clean. Cool on a wire rack. Garnish with whipped cream and toasted pecans if desired.

1 PIECE 417 cal., 17g fat (6g sat. fat), 96mg chol., 436mg sod., 59g carb. (42g sugars, 3g fiber), 9g pro.

Easy Key Lime Pie

You need only five ingredients to create this refreshing pie. It's easy enough to make for a weeknight dessert but special enough for weekend potlucks.
—*Taste of Home Test Kitchen*

PREP: 20 min. + chilling
MAKES: 8 servings

- 1 pkg. (8 oz.) cream cheese, softened
- 1 can (14 oz.) sweetened condensed milk
- ½ cup Key lime juice or lime juice
- 1 graham cracker crust (9 in.)
- 2 cups whipped topping
  Lime slices, optional

In a large bowl, beat cream cheese until smooth. Beat in milk and lime juice until blended. Pour into crust. Refrigerate, covered, at least 4 hours. Just before serving, garnish with whipped topping and, if desired, lime slices.

1 PIECE 417 cal., 22g fat (13g sat. fat), 46mg chol., 274mg sod., 48g carb. (42g sugars, 0 fiber), 7g pro.

Shoofly Pie

My grandmother made the best shoofly pie in the tradition of the Pennsylvania Dutch. Shoofly pie is to the Amish as pecan pie is to a Southerner.
—*Mark Morgan, Waterford, WI*

PREP: 20 min. + chilling
BAKE: 65 min. + cooling
MAKES: 8 servings

Dough for single-crust pie
½ cup packed brown sugar
½ cup molasses
1 large egg
1½ tsp. all-purpose flour
½ tsp. baking soda
1 cup boiling water
1 large egg yolk, lightly beaten

TOPPING
1½ cups all-purpose flour
¾ cup packed brown sugar
¾ tsp. baking soda
Dash salt
6 Tbsp. cold butter, cubed

1. On a floured surface, roll dough to fit a 9-in. deep-dish pie plate. Trim and flute edge. Refrigerate at least 30 minutes.

2. Meanwhile, preheat oven to 425°. For filling, mix brown sugar, molasses, egg, flour and baking soda. Gradually stir in boiling water; cool completely.

3. Line unpricked crust with a double thickness of foil. Fill with pie weights, dried beans or uncooked rice. Bake on a lower oven rack 15 minutes. Remove foil and pie weights; brush crust with egg yolk. Bake 5 minutes. Cool on a wire rack. Reduce oven setting to 350°.

4. In another bowl, whisk together first 4 topping ingredients. Cut in butter until crumbly. Add filling to crust; sprinkle with topping. Cover edge of pie with foil.

5. Bake until filling is set and golden brown, 45-50 minutes. Cool on a wire rack. Store in the refrigerator.

NOTE Let pie weights cool before storing. Beans and rice may be reused for pie weights, but not for cooking.

1 PIECE 540 cal., 22g fat (13g sat. fat), 99mg chol., 630mg sod., 82g carb. (49g sugars, 1g fiber), 6g pro.

DOUGH FOR SINGLE-CRUST PIE (9 IN.)
Combine 1¼ cups all-purpose flour and ¼ tsp. salt; cut in ½ cup cold butter until crumbly. Gradually add 3-5 Tbsp. ice water, tossing with a fork until dough holds together when pressed. Cover and refrigerate 1 hour.

SHOOFLY SECRETS

What is shoofly pie made of?
Shoofly pie is made of brown sugar and molasses as well as flour, eggs, butter and the other basic ingredients you'd most likely find in a crumb cake recipe.

Why is it called shoofly pie?
Many believe that it's called shoofly pie because the Pennsylvania Dutch specialty is so sugary you might need to shoo away the flies. Others believe the pie was deliberately set out to lure flies away from the choicer foods on the table.

How long does shoofly pie stay fresh?
Shoofly pie can be kept tightly covered in the refrigerator up to 5 days.

Old-Fashioned Banana Cream Pie

This fluffy no-bake pie is full of old-fashioned flavor, with only a fraction of the work. Because it uses instant pudding, it's ready in just minutes.
—*Perlene Hoekema, Lynden, WA*

TAKES: 10 min. • **MAKES:** 8 servings

- 1 cup cold 2% milk
- 1 pkg. (3.4 oz.) instant vanilla pudding mix
- ½ tsp. vanilla extract
- 1 carton (12 oz.) frozen whipped topping, thawed, divided
- 1 graham cracker crust (9 in.)
- 2 medium firm bananas, sliced
  Additional banana slices, optional

1. In a large bowl, whisk milk, pudding mix and vanilla for 2 minutes (mixture will be thick). Fold in 3 cups whipped topping.

2. Pour 1⅓ cups pudding mixture into pie crust. Layer with banana slices and remaining pudding mixture. Top with remaining whipped topping. If desired, garnish with additional banana slices. Refrigerate until serving.

1 PIECE 311 cal., 13g fat (9g sat. fat), 2mg chol., 213mg sod., 43g carb. (34g sugars, 1g fiber), 2g pro.

CHOCOLATE & PEANUT BUTTER BANANA CREAM PIE Substitute a 9-in. chocolate crumb crust for the graham cracker crust. Arrange banana slices on crust. In a microwave-safe bowl, mix ¾ cup peanut butter and 2 oz. chopped chocolate; microwave on high for 1-1½ minutes or until blended and smooth, stirring every 30 seconds. Spoon over bananas. Prepare pudding mix filling as directed; pour over the top. Layer with remaining whipped topping. Just before serving, garnish with chopped salted peanuts or chopped peanut butter cups.

Sky-High Strawberry Pie

This pie is my specialty. It's fairly simple to make but so dramatic to serve. The ultimate taste of spring, the luscious pie has a big, fresh berry taste. I've had many requests to bring it to gatherings.
—*Janet Mooberry, Peoria, IL*

PREP: 20 min. • **COOK:** 5 min. + chilling
MAKES: 10 servings

- 3 qt. fresh strawberries, divided
- 1½ cups sugar
- 6 Tbsp. cornstarch
- ⅔ cup water
  Red food coloring, optional
- 1 deep-dish pie crust (10 in.), baked
- 1 cup heavy whipping cream
- 4½ tsp. instant vanilla pudding mix

1. In a large bowl, mash enough berries to equal 3 cups. In a large saucepan, combine sugar and cornstarch. Stir in mashed berries and water. Bring to a boil over medium heat, stirring constantly. Cook and stir for 2 minutes or until thickened.

2. Remove from the heat; add food coloring if desired. Pour into a large bowl. Chill for 20 minutes, stirring occasionally, until mixture is just slightly warm. Fold in the remaining berries. Pile into pie crust. Chill for 2-3 hours.

3. In a small bowl, whip cream until soft peaks form. Sprinkle dry pudding mix over cream and whip until stiff. Pipe around edge of pie or dollop on individual slices.

1 PIECE 350 cal., 13g fat (6g sat. fat), 27mg chol., 82mg sod., 59g carb. (40g sugars, 4g fiber), 3g pro.

Winnie's Mini Rhubarb & Strawberry Pies

Every spring, we had strawberries and rhubarb on our farm outside Seattle. These fruity hand pies remind me of those times and of Grandma Winnie's baking.
—*Shawn Carleton, San Diego, CA*

PREP: 25 min. + chilling
BAKE: 15 min. **MAKES:** 18 servings

- 3 Tbsp. quick-cooking tapioca
- 4 cups sliced fresh strawberries
- 2 cups sliced fresh rhubarb
- ¾ cup sugar
- 1 tsp. grated orange zest
- 1 tsp. vanilla extract
- ¼ tsp. salt
- ¼ tsp. ground cinnamon
- 3 drops red food coloring, optional
   Dough for double-crust pie
   Sweetened whipped cream, optional

1. Place tapioca in a small food processor or spice grinder; process until finely ground.

2. In a large saucepan, combine strawberries, rhubarb, sugar, orange zest, vanilla, salt, cinnamon, tapioca and, if desired, food coloring; bring to a boil. Reduce heat; simmer, covered, until strawberries are tender, stirring occasionally, 15-20 minutes. Transfer to a large bowl; cover and refrigerate overnight.

3. Preheat oven to 425°. On a lightly floured surface, roll half the dough to an 18-in. circle. Cut 9 circles with a 4-in. biscuit cutter, rerolling scraps as necessary; press crusts onto bottoms and up sides of ungreased muffin cups. Repeat with remaining dough, cutting 9 more circles. Spoon strawberry mixture into muffin cups.

4. Bake until filling is bubbly and crust is golden brown, 12-15 minutes. Cool in pan 5 minutes; remove to wire racks to cool. If desired, serve with whipped cream.

NOTE If using frozen rhubarb, measure rhubarb while still frozen, then thaw completely. Drain in a colander, but do not press liquid out.

DOUGH FOR DOUBLE-CRUST PIE Combine 2½ cups all-purpose flour and ½ tsp. salt; cut in 1 cup cold butter until crumbly. Gradually add ⅓-⅔ cup ice water, tossing with a fork until dough holds together when pressed. Divide dough in half. Shape each into a disk; wrap and refrigerate 1 hour.

1 MINI PIE 207 cal., 10g fat (6g sat. fat), 27mg chol., 171mg sod., 27g carb. (11g sugars, 1g fiber), 2g pro.

I wish I could give this recipe 10 stars—it's that delicious. This reminds me of the pies my grandmother would make for me and my sisters.
—LINDAS_WI, TASTEOFHOME.COM

Grandma's Sour Cream Raisin Pie

The aroma of this pie baking in my farm kitchen oven reminds me of my dear grandma, who made this pretty pie for special occasions.
—*Beverly Medalen, Willow City, ND*

PREP: 30 min. • **BAKE:** 10 min. + chilling
MAKES: 8 servings

- 1 cup raisins
- ⅔ cup sugar
- 3 Tbsp. cornstarch
- ⅛ tsp. salt
- ⅛ tsp. ground cloves
- ½ tsp. ground cinnamon
- 1 cup sour cream
- ½ cup 2% milk
- 3 large egg yolks, room temperature
- ½ cup chopped nuts, optional
- 1 pie shell (9 in.), baked

MERINGUE
- 3 large egg whites, room temperature
- ¼ tsp. salt
- 6 Tbsp. sugar

1. In a small saucepan, place raisins and enough water to cover; bring to a boil. Remove from the heat; set aside.

2. In a large saucepan, combine the sugar, cornstarch, salt, cloves and cinnamon. Stir in sour cream and milk until smooth. Cook and stir over medium-high heat until thickened and bubbly. Reduce heat to low; cook and stir for 2 minutes longer. Remove from the heat. Stir a small amount of hot filling into egg yolks; return all to the pan, stirring constantly. Bring to a gentle boil; cook and stir for 2 minutes. Remove from the heat.

3. Drain raisins, reserving ½ cup liquid. Gently stir liquid into filling. Add raisins, and nuts if desired. Pour into pie crust.

4. For meringue, in a small bowl, beat egg whites and salt on medium speed until soft peaks form. Gradually beat in sugar, 1 Tbsp. at a time, on high until stiff peaks form. Spread over hot filling, sealing edge to crust.

5. Bake at 350° for 15 minutes or until golden brown. Cool on a wire rack for 1 hour; refrigerate for 1-2 hours before serving. Refrigerate leftovers.

1 PIECE 381 cal., 15g fat (7g sat. fat), 82mg chol., 253mg sod., 58g carb. (40g sugars, 1g fiber), 5g pro.

PREVENT WEEPING MERINGUE PIES

To prevent that dreaded watery texture, be sure to cook the filling long enough. Keep an eye on the clock and heat the filling for the full time the recipe indicates. Another way to prevent weepy filling is to seal the pie properly. That means spreading the meringue to the very edge of the crust, making sure no filling is exposed. Do this while the filling is hot. Finally, meringue pies and humidity are not friends. If you're serving this pie on a humid day, keep it covered and refrigerated until it's time to serve.

Green Tomato Pie

When frost nips our garden, I quickly gather all the green tomatoes still on the vine and make this old family favorite. It's been handed down from my grandmother, and now my granddaughters are asking for the recipe.
—*Violet Thompson, Port Ludlow, WA*

PREP: 15 min. • **BAKE:** 1 hour + cooling
MAKES: 8 servings

- 1½ cups sugar
- 5 Tbsp. all-purpose flour
- 1 tsp. ground cinnamon
  Pinch salt
- 3 cups thinly sliced green tomatoes (4 to 5 medium)
- 1 Tbsp. cider vinegar
  Dough for double-crust pie
- 1 Tbsp. butter

1. Preheat oven to 350°. In a bowl, combine sugar, flour, cinnamon and salt. Add tomatoes and vinegar; toss to coat. On a lightly floured surface, roll half the dough to a ⅛-in.-thick circle; transfer to a 9-in. pie plate. Trim to ½ in. beyond rim of plate. Add filling; dot with butter.

2. Roll remaining dough to a ⅛-in.-thick circle; cut into 1-in.-wide strips. Arrange over filling in a lattice pattern. Trim and seal strips to edge of bottom crust; flute edge.

3. Bake until tomatoes are tender, about 1 hour. Cool on a wire rack to room temperature. Store in the refrigerator.

DOUGH FOR DOUBLE-CRUST PIE Combine 2½ cups all-purpose flour and ½ tsp. salt; cut in 1 cup cold butter until crumbly. Gradually add ⅓-⅔ cup ice water, tossing with a fork until dough holds together when pressed. Divide dough in half. Shape each into a disk; wrap and refrigerate 1 hour.

1 PIECE 433 cal., 16g fat (7g sat. fat), 14mg chol., 242mg sod., 71g carb. (40g sugars, 1g fiber), 3g pro.

Old-Fashioned Peanut Butter Pie

My mother made a chewy, gooey peanut butter pie I loved as a child. Now I continue the tradition for our generation of peanut butter lovers.
—*Brianna DeBlake, Fremont, MI*

PREP: 20 min. • **BAKE:** 1 hour + cooling
MAKES: 8 servings

  Dough for single-crust pie
- 1½ cups light corn syrup
- ½ cup sugar
- ½ cup creamy peanut butter
- ¼ tsp. salt
- 4 large eggs
- ½ tsp. vanilla extract
  Optional toppings: Chopped peanuts, broken Nutter Butter cookies and whipped topping

1. Preheat oven to 350°. On a lightly floured surface, roll the dough to a ⅛-in.-thick circle; transfer to a 9-in. pie plate. Trim to ½ in. beyond rim of plate; flute edge.

2. In a large bowl, beat corn syrup, sugar, peanut butter and salt until blended. Beat in eggs and vanilla until smooth. Pour into crust. Bake until top is puffed and center is almost set, 60-70 minutes; cover top loosely with foil during the last 30 minutes to prevent overbrowning.

3. Remove foil. Cool on a wire rack. (Top may sink and crack slightly upon cooling.) Serve or refrigerate within 2 hours. Top as desired.

DOUGH FOR SINGLE-CRUST PIE Combine 1¼ cups all-purpose flour and ¼ tsp. salt; cut in ½ cup cold butter until crumbly. Gradually add 3-5 Tbsp. ice water, tossing with a fork until dough holds together when pressed. Wrap and refrigerate 1 hour.

1 PIECE 538 cal., 22g fat (10g sat. fat), 123mg chol., 379mg sod., 82g carb. (65g sugars, 1g fiber), 9g pro.

GREEN TOMATO PIE

Apple Pie

I remember coming home sad one day because we'd lost a softball game. Grandma, in her wisdom, suggested a slice of hot apple pie to make me feel better. She was right!
—*Maggie Greene, Granite Falls, WA*

PREP: 20 min. • **BAKE:** 1 hour
MAKES: 8 servings

Dough for double-crust pie
⅓ cup sugar
⅓ cup packed brown sugar
¼ cup all-purpose flour
1 tsp. ground cinnamon
¼ tsp. ground ginger
¼ tsp. ground nutmeg
6 to 7 cups thinly sliced peeled tart apples
1 Tbsp. lemon juice
1 Tbsp. butter
1 large egg white
Optional: Turbinado or coarse sugar, ground cinnamon, vanilla bean ice cream, and caramel sauce

1. Preheat oven to 375°. On a lightly floured surface, roll half the dough to a ⅛-in.-thick circle; transfer to a 9-in. pie plate. Chill while preparing filling. In a small bowl, combine sugars, flour and spices. In a large bowl, toss apples with lemon juice. Add sugar mixture; toss to coat. Add filling to crust; dot with butter.

2. Roll remaining dough to a ⅛-in.-thick circle; cut into 1-in.-wide strips. Arrange over filling in a lattice pattern. Trim and seal strips to edge of bottom crust; flute edge. Beat egg white until foamy; brush over crust. If desired, sprinkle with turbinado sugar and ground cinnamon.

3. Bake on the lowest rack 60-70 minutes, until crust is golden brown and filling is bubbly, covering with foil halfway if crust begins to get too dark. Cool on a wire rack. If desired, serve with ice cream and caramel sauce.

DOUGH FOR DOUBLE-CRUST PIE Combine 2½ cups all-purpose flour and ½ tsp. salt; cut in 1 cup cold butter until crumbly. Gradually add ⅓-⅔ cup ice water, tossing with a fork until dough holds together when pressed. Divide dough in half. Shape each into a disk; wrap and refrigerate 1 hour.

1 PIECE 467 cal., 25g fat (15g sat. fat), 64mg chol., 331mg sod., 58g carb. (26g sugars, 2g fiber), 5g pro.

EASY APPLE PIE

What are the best apples to use in pies?
At *Taste of Home*, we prefer Granny Smith apples because of their tart flavor and ability to hold their shape. If you want something with a bit more sweetness, consider Braeburn, Golden Delicious or Jonagold.

How many apples are in 6 cups?
Typically, 1 medium apple yields 1⅓ cups sliced. For 6 cups of sliced apples, you will need about 5 medium apples.

How do you keep the bottom of a pie from getting soggy?
Allow the bottom crust to heat more rapidly than the rest of the pie. To do this, place a baking sheet in the oven while preheating and then bake the pie on the sheet.

Is it better to bake a pie in glass or metal?
Metal and glass pie plates work equally well for double-crust pies. For single-crust pies that are prebaked, a metal plate is preferred as it heats quickly, ensuring a crisp crust.

Raspberry-Rhubarb Slab Pie

Slab pie is a pastry baked in a jelly-roll pan and cut into slabs like a bar cookie—or a pie bar, if you will. My grandfather was a professional baker and served pieces of slab pie to his customers back in the day. Here is my spin, featuring rhubarb and gorgeous red raspberries.
—*Jeanne Ambrose, Des Moines, IA*

PREP: 30 min. + chilling
BAKE: 45 min. + cooling
MAKES: 24 servings

3¼ cups all-purpose flour
1   tsp. salt
1   cup butter
¾   cup plus 1 to 2 Tbsp. 2% milk
1   large egg yolk
2   cups sugar
⅓   cup cornstarch
5   cups fresh or frozen unsweetened raspberries, thawed and drained
3   cups sliced fresh or frozen rhubarb, thawed and drained

VANILLA ICING
1¼ cups confectioners' sugar
½   tsp. vanilla extract
5   to 6 tsp. 2% milk

1. In a large bowl, combine flour and salt; cut in butter until crumbly. Whisk ¾ cup milk and egg yolk; gradually add to flour mixture, tossing with a fork until dough forms a ball. Add additional milk, 1 Tbsp. at a time, if necessary.

2. Divide dough into 2 portions so that 1 is slightly larger than the other; cover each and refrigerate 1 hour or until easy to handle.

3. Preheat oven to 375°. Roll out larger portion of dough between 2 large sheets of lightly floured waxed paper into an 18x13-in. rectangle. Transfer to an ungreased 15x10x1-in. baking pan. Press onto the bottom and up sides of pan; trim crust to edges of pan.

4. In a large bowl, combine sugar and cornstarch. Add raspberries and rhubarb; toss to coat. Spoon into crust.

5. Roll out remaining dough; place over filling. Fold bottom crust over edges of top crust; seal with a fork. Prick top with a fork.

6. Bake until golden brown, 45-55 minutes. Cool completely on a wire rack.

7. For icing, combine confectioners' sugar, vanilla and enough milk to achieve a drizzling consistency; drizzle over pie. Cut pie into squares.

NOTE If using frozen rhubarb, measure rhubarb while still frozen, then thaw completely. Drain in a colander, but do not press liquid out.

1 PIECE 247 cal., 8g fat (5g sat. fat), 29mg chol., 159mg sod., 42g carb. (25g sugars, 2g fiber), 3g pro.

WORK-AHEAD OPTION
You can make this pie dough ahead of time and freeze it. Before refrigerating or freezing the dough, shape it into 2 rectangles so it's easier to roll into larger rectangles later. Thaw overnight in the fridge.

Grandma's Chocolate Meringue Pie

My grandmother served chocolate meringue pie after Sunday dinner each week, usually apologizing that it was too runny or that something else was wrong with it. Of course it was never less than perfect!
—*Donna Vest Tilley, Chesterfield, VA*

PREP: 30 min. • **BAKE:** 15 min. + chilling
MAKES: 8 servings

Dough for single-crust pie

MERINGUE
- 4 large egg whites, room temperature
- ¼ tsp. cream of tartar
- ½ cup sugar

FILLING
- ¾ cup sugar
- 5 Tbsp. baking cocoa
- 3 Tbsp. cornstarch
- ¼ tsp. salt
- 2 cups whole milk
- 3 large egg yolks, room temperature, beaten
- 1 tsp. vanilla extract

1. On a lightly floured surface, roll dough to a ⅛-in.-thick circle; transfer to a 9-in. pie plate. Trim to ½ in. beyond rim of plate; flute edge. Refrigerate 30 minutes. Preheat oven to 425°.

2. Line unpricked crust with a double thickness of foil. Fill with pie weights, dried beans or uncooked rice. Bake on a lower oven rack until edges are light golden brown, 15-20 minutes. Remove foil and weights; bake until bottom is golden brown, 3-6 minutes longer. Cool on a wire rack. Reduce oven setting to 350°.

3. For meringue, beat egg whites with cream of tartar until soft peaks form. Gradually add sugar and continue to beat until stiff, glossy and sugar is dissolved.

4. In a saucepan, mix sugar, cocoa, cornstarch and salt; gradually add milk. Cook and stir over medium-high heat until thickened and bubbly. Reduce heat; cook and stir 2 minutes more. Remove from heat. Stir about 1 cup of the hot filling into the egg yolks. Return to saucepan and bring to a gentle boil. Cook and stir 2 minutes. Remove from the heat and stir in vanilla. Pour hot filling into pie crust.

5. Immediately spread meringue evenly over hot filling, sealing meringue to pie crust. Bake until meringue is golden brown, 12-15 minutes. Cool on a wire rack until set, 1-2 hours. Refrigerate leftovers.

DOUGH FOR SINGLE-CRUST PIE Combine 1¼ cups all-purpose flour and ¼ tsp. salt; cut in ½ cup cold butter until crumbly. Gradually add 3-5 Tbsp. ice water, tossing with a fork until dough holds together when pressed. Wrap and refrigerate 1 hour.

1 PIECE 382 cal., 16g fat (9g sat. fat), 105mg chol., 286mg sod., 54g carb. (35g sugars, 1g fiber), 8g pro.

Classic Pumpkin Pie

Nothing says Thanksgiving like a slice of pumpkin pie. And you can relish every luscious bite of this version since the tender crust is made with a mere hint of canola oil and butter.
—Taste of Home *Test Kitchen*

PREP: 20 min. • **BAKE:** 45 min. + cooling
MAKES: 8 servings

- 1 cup all-purpose flour
- 1 tsp. sugar
- ¼ tsp. salt
- 3 Tbsp. canola oil
- 1 Tbsp. butter, melted
- 2 to 3 Tbsp. cold water

FILLING
- 1 large egg
- 1 large egg white
- ½ cup packed brown sugar
- ¼ cup sugar
- ½ tsp. salt
- ½ tsp. ground cinnamon
- ⅛ tsp. each ground allspice, nutmeg and cloves
- 1 can (15 oz.) pumpkin
- 1 cup fat-free evaporated milk
  Whipped cream, optional

1. In a small bowl, combine the flour, sugar and salt. Using a fork, stir in oil and butter until dough is crumbly. Gradually add enough water until dough holds together. Roll out between sheets of waxed paper into an 11-in. circle. Freeze for 10 minutes.

2. Remove top sheet of waxed paper; invert crust into a 9-in. pie plate. Remove the remaining waxed paper. Trim and flute edge. Chill.

3. Roll dough scraps to ⅛-in. thickness. Cut with a 1-in. leaf-shaped cookie cutter. Place on an ungreased baking sheet; bake at 375° for 6-8 minutes or until edges are very lightly browned. Cool on a wire rack.

4. In a large bowl, beat the egg, egg white, sugars, salt and spices until smooth. Beat in pumpkin. Gradually beat in milk. Pour into crust. Bake at 375° for 45-50 minutes or until a knife inserted in the center comes out clean. Cool on a wire rack. Garnish with leaf cutouts. If desired, top with whipped cream. Refrigerate leftovers.

1 PIECE 249 cal., 8g fat (2g sat. fat), 32mg chol., 295mg sod., 40g carb. (26g sugars, 3g fiber), 6g pro.

PIE POINTERS

How can you keep pumpkin pie from cracking?
To prevent pie cracking, make sure to not overbake the pie filling—when you take it out of the oven, there should still be a slight jiggle at the center of the pie. Also, be sure to let the pumpkin pie cool at room temperature—not in the refrigerator.

How do you store pumpkin pie?
Pumpkin pie can be stored in the refrigerator for up to 3 days after baking, and 3 days before baking.

What are some substitutions you can make to this recipe?
Use fresh pumpkin puree instead of canned pumpkin if you want, but know that the texture and flavor will differ slightly.

PECAN TASSIES,
P. 289

Cookie Jar Delights & More

Soft Honey Cookies

This old-fashioned cookie has a pleasant honey-cinnamon flavor and a tender texture that resembles cake. It has been a family favorite for years, and I love sharing this recipe.
—*Rochelle Friedman, Brooklyn, NY*

PREP: 15 min. + chilling • **BAKE:** 10 min.
MAKES: 16 cookies

- ¼ cup sugar
- 2 Tbsp. canola oil
- 1 large egg, room temperature
- 3 Tbsp. honey
- ¾ tsp. vanilla extract
- 1 cup plus 2 Tbsp. all-purpose flour
- ¼ tsp. baking powder
- ¼ tsp. ground cinnamon
- ⅛ tsp. salt

1. In a small bowl, beat sugar and oil until blended. Beat in egg; beat in honey and vanilla. Combine flour, baking powder, cinnamon and salt; gradually add to sugar mixture and mix well (dough will be stiff). Cover and refrigerate for at least 2 hours.

2. Preheat oven to 350°. Drop dough by tablespoonfuls 2 in. apart onto a greased baking sheet. Bake until bottoms are lightly browned, 8-10 minutes. Cool for 1 minute before removing from pan to a wire rack. Store in an airtight container.

1 COOKIE 77 cal., 2g fat (0 sat. fat), 12mg chol., 31mg sod., 13g carb. (6g sugars, 0 fiber), 1g pro. **DIABETIC EXCHANGES** 1 starch, ½ fat.

Cherry Pecan Dreams

Packed with fruit, nuts and vanilla chips, these goodies are sure to please. If you prefer, replace the cherries with cranberries or apricots.
—*Mary Ann Mariotti, Plainfield, IL*

PREP: 25 min. • **BAKE:** 10 min./batch
MAKES: about 3 dozen

- 1 cup butter, softened
- ½ cup sugar
- ½ cup packed brown sugar
- 1 large egg, room temperature
- 1 Tbsp. grated orange zest
- 2¼ cups all-purpose flour
- 1 tsp. baking soda
- ½ tsp. salt
- 2 cups white baking chips
- 1 cup dried cherries, coarsely chopped
- 1 cup chopped pecans

1. In a large bowl, cream butter and sugars until light and fluffy, 5-7 minutes. Beat in egg and orange zest. Combine the flour, baking soda and salt; gradually add to creamed mixture and mix well. Fold in the chips, cherries and pecans.

2. Drop by rounded tablespoonfuls 2 in. apart onto greased baking sheets. Bake at 350° for 10-12 minutes or until edges are golden brown. Cool for 2 minutes before removing to wire racks.

1 COOKIE 166 cal., 10g fat (5g sat. fat), 19mg chol., 108mg sod., 19g carb. (13g sugars, 1g fiber), 2g pro.

Broadway Brownie Bars

I named these dessert bars for Broadway because they're a hit every time I serve them. I especially like to make them for the holidays or for hostess gifts. They're sure to please any sweet tooth!
—*Anne Frederick, New Hartford, NY*

PREP: 20 min. + chilling • **BAKE:** 30 min.
MAKES: 2½ dozen

FILLING
- 6   oz. cream cheese, softened
- ½   cup sugar
- ¼   cup butter, softened
- 2   Tbsp. all-purpose flour
- 1   large egg, lightly beaten
- ½   tsp. vanilla extract

BROWNIE
- ½   cup butter, cubed
- 1   oz. unsweetened chocolate
- 2   large eggs, room temperature, lightly beaten
- 1   tsp. vanilla extract
- 1   cup sugar
- 1   cup all-purpose flour
- 1   tsp. baking powder
- 1   cup chopped walnuts

TOPPING
- 1   cup semisweet chocolate chips
- ¼   cup chopped walnuts
- 2   cups miniature marshmallows

FROSTING
- ¼   cup butter
- ¼   cup 2% milk
- 2   oz. cream cheese
- 1   oz. unsweetened chocolate
- 3   cups confectioners' sugar
- 1   tsp. vanilla extract

1. Preheat oven to 350°. In a small bowl, combine the first 6 ingredients until smooth.

2. In a large saucepan over medium heat, melt butter and chocolate. Remove from heat and let cool. Stir in eggs and vanilla. Add sugar, flour, baking powder and nuts, stirring until blended.

3. Spread batter in a 13x9-in. baking pan coated with cooking spray. Spread filling over batter. For topping, in a small bowl, combine chocolate chips and nuts; sprinkle over filling.

4. Bake until bars almost set, about 28 minutes. Sprinkle marshmallows over the top; bake 2 minutes longer.

5. For frosting, in a large saucepan, heat the butter, milk, cream cheese and chocolate until melted, stirring until smooth. Remove from heat; stir in confectioners' sugar and vanilla. Immediately drizzle over marshmallows. Chill well; cut into bars.

1 BROWNIE 271 cal., 15g fat (7g sat. fat), 46mg chol., 108mg sod., 33g carb. (26g sugars, 1g fiber), 4g pro.

NOTES

_____

_____

_____

_____

_____

_____

_____

_____

_____

_____

_____

Glazed Molasses Cookies

I dreamed up these molasses cookies while sipping coffee and watching snow fall. The aroma from the baking cookies reaches all corners of the house.
—*Faith Ford, Big Lake, MN*

PREP: 40 min.
BAKE: 10 min./batch + cooling
MAKES: about 3 dozen

- ¾ cup butter, softened
- ½ cup packed brown sugar
- ½ cup plus ⅓ cup sugar
- ⅓ cup molasses
- 1 large egg, room temperature
- 1 tsp. vanilla extract
- 2¼ cups all-purpose flour
- 2 tsp. baking soda
- 1½ tsp. ground cinnamon
- 1 tsp. ground ginger
- ½ tsp. ground cloves
- ¼ tsp. ground allspice
- ½ tsp. salt
- 1 cup confectioners' sugar
- ⅓ cup heavy whipping cream
- 1½ tsp. instant coffee granules

1. Preheat oven to 350°. In a large bowl, cream butter, brown sugar and ½ cup granulated sugar until light and fluffy, 5-7 minutes. Beat in molasses, egg and vanilla. In another bowl, whisk flour, baking soda, spices and salt; gradually beat into creamed mixture.

2. Shape the dough into rounded tablespoonfuls; roll in remaining ⅓ cup sugar. Place 2 in. apart on ungreased baking sheets. Bake 8-10 minutes or until edges begin to set. Cool on pans 5 minutes. Remove to wire racks to cool completely.

3. In a small bowl, mix confectioners' sugar, cream and coffee granules until blended; drizzle over cookies. Let stand until set.

FREEZE OPTION Freeze shaped balls of dough on baking sheets until firm. Transfer to airtight containers; return to freezer. To use, roll balls in remaining sugar. Bake and decorate cookies as directed, increasing time by 1-2 minutes.

1 COOKIE 106 cal., 4g fat (3g sat. fat), 15mg chol., 118mg sod., 17g carb. (11g sugars, 0 fiber), 1g pro.

Grandma's Scottish Shortbread

My Scottish grandmother was renowned for baked goods; these chunky shortbread bars are just one example.
—*Jane Kelly, Wayland, MA*

PREP: 15 min. • **BAKE:** 45 min. + cooling
MAKES: 4 dozen

- 1   lb. butter, softened
- 8   oz. superfine sugar (about 1¼ cups)
- 1   lb. all-purpose flour (3⅔ cups)
- 8   oz. white rice flour (1⅓ cups)

1. Preheat oven to 300°. Cream butter and sugar until light and fluffy, 5-7 minutes. Combine flours; gradually beat into creamed mixture. Press dough into an ungreased 13x9-in. baking pan. Prick with a fork.

2. Bake until light brown, 45-50 minutes. Cut into 48 bars or triangles while warm. Cool completely on a wire rack.

1 BAR 139 cal., 8g fat (5g sat. fat), 20mg chol., 61mg sod., 16g carb. (5g sugars, 0 fiber), 1g pro.

Ranger Cookies

These golden brown cookies are crispy on the outside and cakelike on the inside. Their tasty blend of oats, rice cereal, coconut and brown sugar have made them a favorite with our family. You won't be able to eat just one.
—*Mary Lou Boyce, Wilmington, DE*

PREP: 25 min. • **BAKE:** 10 min./batch
MAKES: 7½ dozen

- 1   cup shortening
- 1   cup sugar
- 1   cup packed brown sugar
- 2   large eggs, room temperature
- 1   tsp. vanilla extract
- 2   cups all-purpose flour
- 1   tsp. baking soda
- ½   tsp. baking powder
- ½   tsp. salt
- 2   cups quick-cooking oats
- 2   cups crisp rice cereal
- 1   cup sweetened shredded coconut

1. Preheat oven to 350°. In a large bowl, cream shortening and sugars until light and fluffy, 5-7 minutes. Beat in eggs and vanilla. Combine flour, baking soda, baking powder and salt; gradually add to creamed mixture and mix well. Stir in oats, cereal and coconut.

2. Drop by rounded tablespoonfuls 2 in. apart onto ungreased baking sheets. Bake until golden brown, 7-9 minutes. Remove from pans to wire racks to cool.

1 COOKIE 63 cal., 3g fat (1g sat. fat), 5mg chol., 40mg sod., 9g carb. (5g sugars, 0 fiber), 1g pro.

PEANUT BUTTER RANGER COOKIES
Before creaming the shortening and sugars, add 1 cup peanut butter.

TEST KITCHEN TIP
Cookies made with shortening tend to be taller and more tender. Cookies made with butter tend to be flatter and crispier and have more butter flavor. Either works here depending upon what you're looking for in your perfect cookie. You can also use half butter and half shortening.

Bake-Sale Lemon Bars

The recipe for these tangy lemon bars comes from my cousin, who is famous for cooking up farm feasts.
—*Mildred Keller, Rockford, IL*

PREP: 25 min. • **BAKE:** 20 min. + cooling
MAKES: 15 bars

- ¾ cup butter, softened
- ⅔ cup confectioners' sugar
- 1½ cups plus 3 Tbsp. all-purpose flour, divided
- 3 large eggs
- 1½ cups sugar
- ¼ cup lemon juice
  Additional confectioners' sugar

1. Preheat oven to 350°. In a large bowl, beat butter and confectioners' sugar until blended. Gradually beat in 1½ cups flour. Press onto bottom of a greased 13x9-in. baking pan. Bake 18-20 minutes or until golden brown.

2. Meanwhile, in a small bowl, whisk eggs, sugar, lemon juice and remaining 3 Tbsp. flour until frothy; pour over hot crust.

3. Bake 20-25 minutes or until lemon mixture is set and lightly browned. Cool completely on a wire rack. Dust with additional confectioners' sugar. Cut into bars. Refrigerate leftovers.

1 BAR 247 cal., 10g fat (6g sat. fat), 62mg chol., 88mg sod., 37g carb. (26g sugars, 0 fiber), 3g pro.

Rhubarb Custard Bars

Once I tried these rich, gooey bars, I just had to have the recipe so I could make them for family and friends. The shortbread-like crust and the rhubarb and custard layers inspire people to seek out rhubarb so they can fix a batch for themselves.
—*Shari Roach, South Milwaukee, WI*

PREP: 25 min. • **BAKE:** 50 min. + chilling
MAKES: 3 dozen

- 2 cups all-purpose flour
- ¼ cup sugar
- 1 cup cold butter

FILLING
- 2 cups sugar
- 7 Tbsp. all-purpose flour
- 1 cup heavy whipping cream
- 3 large eggs, beaten
- 5 cups finely chopped fresh or frozen rhubarb, thawed and drained

TOPPING
- 6 oz. cream cheese, softened
- ½ cup sugar
- ½ tsp. vanilla extract
- 1 cup heavy whipping cream, whipped

1. In a bowl, combine the flour and sugar; cut in butter until the mixture resembles coarse crumbs. Press into a greased 13x9-in. baking pan. Bake at 350° for 10 minutes.

2. Meanwhile, for filling, combine sugar and flour in a bowl. Whisk in cream and eggs. Stir in the rhubarb. Pour over the crust. Bake at 350° until custard is set, 40-45 minutes. Cool.

3. For topping, beat cream cheese, sugar and vanilla until smooth; fold in whipped cream. Spread over top. Cover and chill. Cut into bars. Store in the refrigerator.

1 BAR 198 cal., 11g fat (7g sat. fat), 52mg chol., 70mg sod., 23g carb. (16g sugars, 1g fiber), 2g pro.

Buttery Potato Chip Cookies

Can't decide whether to bring chips or cookies to the tailgate? These crisp, buttery cookies make plenty for a crowd and will keep people guessing the secret ingredient.
—*Rachel Roberts, Lemoore, CA*

PREP: 15 min. • **BAKE:** 10 min./batch
MAKES: 4½ dozen

2	cups butter, softened
1	cup sugar
1	tsp. vanilla extract
3½	cups all-purpose flour
2	cups crushed potato chips
¾	cup chopped walnuts

1. Preheat oven to 350°. In a large bowl, cream butter and sugar until light and fluffy, 5-7 minutes. Beat in vanilla. Gradually add flour to creamed mixture and mix well. Stir in potato chips and walnuts.

2. Drop cookie mixture by rounded tablespoonfuls 2 in. apart onto ungreased baking sheets. Bake 10-12 minutes or until lightly browned. Cool 2 minutes before removing from pans to wire racks.

1 COOKIE 126 cal., 9g fat (5g sat. fat), 18mg chol., 67mg sod., 11g carb. (4g sugars, 0 fiber), 1g pro.

Grandma's Spritz Cookies

I use my grandmother's antique cookie press to make these festive cookies. I'm the only one in the family who can still get it to work!
—*Suzanne Kern, Louisville, KY*

PREP: 15 min. • **BAKE:** 10 min./batch
MAKES: 6½ dozen

1	cup shortening
¾	cup sugar
1	large egg, room temperature
1	tsp. almond extract
2¼	cups all-purpose flour
½	tsp. baking powder
	Dash salt
	Optional: Assorted sprinkles and colored sugar

1. Preheat oven to 400°. In a large mixing bowl, cream shortening and sugar until light and fluffy, 5-7 minutes. Add egg and almond extract; mix well. Combine flour, baking powder and salt; add to the creamed mixture until blended.

2. Using a cookie press fitted with the disk of your choice, press dough shapes 2 in. apart onto ungreased baking sheets. If desired, sprinkle with toppings. Bake until set (do not brown), 7-8 minutes.

1 COOKIE 44 cal., 3g fat (1g sat. fat), 2mg chol., 6mg sod., 5g carb. (2g sugars, 0 fiber), 0 pro.

Gingerbread Cookies with Lemon Frosting

When I spread these spicy gingerbread rounds with my lemony cream cheese frosting, I knew I had a hit. Cardamom and allspice add a hint of chai tea flavor.
—*Aysha Schurman, Ammon, ID*

PREP: 25 min.
BAKE: 10 min./batch + cooling
MAKES: 4 dozen

½   cup butter, softened
¾   cup packed brown sugar
2   large eggs, room temperature
¼   cup molasses
3   cups all-purpose flour
1   Tbsp. ground ginger
2   tsp. baking soda
1   tsp. ground allspice
1   tsp. ground cardamom
1   tsp. ground cinnamon
1   tsp. grated lemon zest
½   tsp. salt

FROSTING
4   oz. cream cheese, softened
2½ cups confectioners' sugar
1   Tbsp. grated lemon zest
2   Tbsp. lemon juice
1   tsp. vanilla extract

1. Preheat oven to 350°. Cream butter and brown sugar until light and fluffy, 5-7 minutes. Beat in eggs and molasses. In another bowl, whisk next 8 ingredients; gradually beat into creamed mixture.

2. Shape into 1-in. balls; place 2 in. apart on ungreased baking sheets. Bake until tops are cracked, 8-10 minutes. Cool 2 minutes before removing from pans to wire racks to cool completely.

3. For frosting, beat cream cheese until fluffy. Add remaining ingredients; beat until smooth. Frost cookies. Refrigerate in an airtight container.

1 COOKIE WITH 1 TSP. FROSTING 100 cal., 3g fat (2g sat. fat), 15mg chol., 105mg sod., 17g carb. (11g sugars, 0 fiber), 1g pro.

Buttery Coconut Bars

My coconut bars are an American version of a Filipino coconut cake called bibingka. These are a crispier, sweeter take on the Christmas tradition I grew up with.
—*Denise Nyland, Panama City, FL*

PREP: 20 min. + cooling
BAKE: 40 min. + cooling
MAKES: 3 dozen

- 2 cups all-purpose flour
- 1 cup packed brown sugar
- ½ tsp. salt
- 1 cup butter, melted

FILLING
- 3 large eggs
- 1 can (14 oz.) sweetened condensed milk
- ½ cup all-purpose flour
- ¼ cup packed brown sugar
- ¼ cup butter, melted
- 3 tsp. vanilla extract
- ½ tsp. salt
- 4 cups sweetened shredded coconut, divided

1. Preheat oven to 350°. Line a 13x9-in. baking pan with parchment, letting ends extend up sides.

2. In a large bowl, mix flour, brown sugar and salt; stir in 1 cup melted butter. Press onto bottom of prepared pan. Bake until light brown, 12-15 minutes. Cool on a wire rack 10 minutes. Reduce oven setting to 325°.

3. In a large bowl, whisk the first 7 filling ingredients until blended; stir in 3 cups coconut. Pour over crust; sprinkle with remaining 1 cup coconut. Bake until light golden brown, 25-30 minutes. Cool in pan on a wire rack. Lifting with the parchment, remove from pan and cut into bars.

1 BAR 211 cal., 12g fat (8g sat. fat), 36mg chol., 166mg sod., 25g carb. (18g sugars, 1g fiber), 3g pro.

Fudgy Brownies with Peanut Butter Pudding Frosting

Rich brownies are topped with a peanut butter pudding frosting, making this a recipe that the whole family will love. These are perfect for a potluck, bake sale or after-dinner treat.
—*Amy Crook, Syracuse, UT*

PREP: 20 min. • **BAKE:** 25 min. + chilling
MAKES: 2½ dozen

- 1 pkg. fudge brownie mix (13x9-in. pan size)
- 1½ cups confectioners' sugar
- ½ cup butter, softened
- 2 to 3 Tbsp. peanut butter
- 2 Tbsp. cold 2% milk
- 4½ tsp. instant vanilla pudding mix
- 1 can (16 oz.) chocolate fudge frosting

1. Prepare and bake brownies according to package directions. Cool brownies on a wire rack.

2. Meanwhile, in a small bowl, beat the confectioners' sugar, butter, peanut butter, milk and pudding mix until smooth. Spread over the brownies. Refrigerate 30 minutes or until firm. Frost with chocolate frosting just before cutting.

1 BROWNIE 236 cal., 12g fat (4g sat. fat), 23mg chol., 145mg sod., 31g carb. (23g sugars, 1g fiber), 2g pro.

Grandma Krause's Coconut Cookies

When my daughters were very young, their great-grandma made them yummy cookies with oats and coconut. Thankfully, she shared the recipe.
—*Debra J. Dorn, Dunnellon, FL*

PREP: 40 min. + freezing
BAKE: 10 min./batch
MAKES: about 3½ dozen

- 1 cup shortening
- 1 cup sugar
- 1 cup packed brown sugar
- 2 large eggs, room temperature
- 1 tsp. vanilla extract
- 2 cups all-purpose flour
- 1 tsp. baking powder
- 1 tsp. baking soda
- ¼ tsp. salt
- 1 cup old-fashioned oats
- 1 cup sweetened shredded coconut

1. In a large bowl, beat shortening and sugars until blended. Beat in eggs and vanilla. In another bowl, whisk flour, baking powder, baking soda and salt; gradually beat into sugar mixture. Stir in oats and coconut.

2. Divide dough into 4 portions. On a lightly floured surface, shape each into a 6-in.-long log. Wrap in waxed paper; freeze 2 hours or until firm.

3. Preheat oven to 350°. Unwrap and cut dough crosswise into ½-in. slices, reshaping as needed. Place 2 in. apart on ungreased baking sheets. Bake until golden brown, 10-12 minutes. Cool on pans 5 minutes. Remove to wire racks to cool completely.

1 COOKIE 124 cal., 6g fat (2g sat. fat), 9mg chol., 66mg sod., 17g carb. (11g sugars, 0 fiber), 1g pro.

Easy Old-Fashioned Oatmeal Raisin Cookies

I've been making these cookies for nearly 30 years. The spice cake mix makes an easy yet delicious backdrop to the oats and raisins. They are an all-time favorite with my family.
—*Nancy Horton, Greenbrier, TN*

PREP: 10 min. • **BAKE:** 10 min./batch
MAKES: 7 dozen

- ¾ cup canola oil
- ¼ cup packed brown sugar
- 2 large eggs, room temperature
- ½ cup 2% milk
- 1 pkg. spice cake mix (regular size)
- 2 cups old-fashioned oats
- 2½ cups raisins
- 1 cup chopped pecans

1. In a large bowl, beat oil and brown sugar until blended. Beat in eggs, then milk. Combine cake mix and oats; gradually add to brown sugar mixture and mix well. Fold in raisins and pecans.

2. Drop by tablespoonfuls 2 in. apart onto greased baking sheets. Bake at 350° until golden brown, roughly 10-12 minutes. Cool for 1 minute before removing to wire racks.

1 COOKIE 79 cal., 4g fat (1g sat. fat), 7mg chol., 50mg sod., 10g carb. (6g sugars, 1g fiber), 1g pro.

FLUFFY RAISIN
PUMPKIN BARS

Fluffy Raisin Pumpkin Bars

Chocolate-covered raisins are a fun surprise inside these moist pumpkin bars. The traditional cream cheese frosting never fails to please.
—*Margaret Wilson, San Bernardino, CA*

PREP: 20 min. • **BAKE:** 25 min. + cooling
MAKES: 4 dozen

- 2   cups sugar
- ¾   cup vegetable oil
- 4   large eggs, room temperature
- 2   cups canned pumpkin
- 2   cups all-purpose flour
- 2   tsp. baking powder
- 1   tsp. baking soda
- 1   tsp. ground cinnamon
- 1   tsp. ground nutmeg
- ½   tsp. ground ginger
- ¼   tsp. ground cloves
- 1   cup chopped walnuts
- 1   cup chocolate-covered raisins for baking

FROSTING
- ⅓   cup butter, softened
- 3   oz. cream cheese, softened
- 2   cups confectioners' sugar
- 1   Tbsp. 2% milk
- 1   tsp. orange extract

1. In a large bowl, beat sugar and oil. Add eggs, 1 at a time, beating well after each addition. Add the pumpkin; mix well. Combine the flour, baking powder, baking soda and spices; gradually add to the pumpkin mixture. Stir in walnuts and chocolate-covered raisins.

2. Pour into a greased 15x10x1-in. baking pan. Bake at 350° for 25-30 minutes or until a toothpick inserted in the center comes out clean. Cool on a wire rack.

3. For frosting, in a large bowl, cream the butter, cream cheese and confectioners' sugar. Add milk and orange extract; beat until smooth. Frost bars. Sprinkle with additional cinnamon if desired. Cut into bars. Store in the refrigerator.

1 PIECE 162 cal., 8g fat (2g sat. fat), 23mg chol., 67mg sod., 21g carb. (15g sugars, 1g fiber), 2g pro.

Pecan Tassies

These tiny tarts make a pretty addition to any cookie tray or make a wonderful dessert by themselves. If you don't have miniature tart pans, use miniature muffin pans.
—*Joy Corie, Ruston, LA*

PREP: 25 min. + chilling • **BAKE:** 20 min.
MAKES: 2 dozen

- ½   cup butter, softened
- 3   oz. cream cheese, softened
- 1   cup all-purpose flour

FILLING
- 1   large egg, room temperature
- ¾   cup packed brown sugar
- 1   Tbsp. butter, softened
- 1   tsp. vanilla extract
      Dash salt
- ⅔   cup finely chopped pecans, divided

1. In a small bowl, beat butter and cream cheese until smooth; gradually beat in flour. Refrigerate, covered, 1 hour or until firm enough to roll.

2. Preheat oven to 375°. Shape the dough into 1-in. balls; press evenly onto bottoms and up sides of 24 greased mini tart pans or mini muffin cups.

3. For filling, in a small bowl, mix egg, brown sugar, butter, vanilla and salt until blended. Stir in ⅓ cup pecans; spoon into cups. Sprinkle with remaining pecans.

4. Bake 15-20 minutes or until edges are golden and filling is puffed. Cool in pans 2 minutes. Remove to wire racks to cool.

FREEZE OPTION Freeze cooled cookies, layered between waxed paper, in freezer containers. To use, thaw in covered containers.

1 COOKIE 242 cal., 16g fat (7g sat. fat), 48mg chol., 131mg sod., 23g carb. (14g sugars, 1g fiber), 3g pro.

Sour Cream & Cranberry Bars

I turned sour cream raisin pie into a cookie bar with a crunchy oatmeal crust, custard-style filling and crisp topping.
—*Shelly Bevington, Hermiston, OR*

PREP: 35 min. • **BAKE:** 35 min. + cooling
MAKES: 2 dozen

3 large egg yolks
1½ cups sour cream
1 cup sugar
3 Tbsp. cornstarch
⅛ tsp. salt
1 cup dried cranberries
1 tsp. vanilla extract

CRUST
1 cup butter, softened
1 cup sugar
2 tsp. vanilla extract
1¾ cups all-purpose flour
1⅓ cups quick-cooking oats
1 tsp. salt
1 tsp. baking soda
1 cup sweetened shredded coconut

1. Preheat oven to 350°. In top of a double boiler or a metal bowl over simmering water, whisk the first 5 ingredients until blended; stir in cranberries. Cook and stir until mixture is thickened, 15-20 minutes. Remove from heat; stir in vanilla.

2. Meanwhile, in a large bowl, cream butter and sugar until light and fluffy, 5-7 minutes. Beat in vanilla. In another bowl, whisk flour, oats, salt and baking soda; gradually beat into creamed mixture. Stir in coconut. Reserve half of the dough for topping. Press remainder onto bottom of a greased 13x9-in. baking dish. Bake until set, 8-10 minutes.

3. Spread sour cream mixture over crust; crumble reserved dough over the top. Bake until filling is set and top is golden brown, 25-30 minutes. Cool in pan on a wire rack. Cut into bars.

1 BAR 260 cal., 13g fat (8g sat. fat), 53mg chol., 241mg sod., 34g carb. (22g sugars, 1g fiber), 3g pro.

These are amazing! All my favorite flavors in one delicious bar cookie. Next time, I'll try using dried cherries in place of the cranberries for a different version.

—RN513, TASTEOFHOME.COM

Old-Fashioned Peanut Butter Cookies

My mother insisted that my grandmother write down one recipe for her when Mom got married in 1942. That was a real effort because Grandma was a traditional pioneer-type cook who used a little of this or that until it felt right. This treasured recipe is the only one she ever wrote down!
—Janet Hall, Clinton, WI

PREP: 15 min. • **BAKE:** 10 min./batch
MAKES: 3 dozen

- 1 cup shortening
- 1 cup peanut butter
- 1 cup sugar
- 1 cup packed brown sugar
- 3 large eggs, room temperature
- 3 cups all-purpose flour
- 2 tsp. baking soda
- ¼ tsp. salt

1. Preheat oven to 375°. In a large bowl, cream shortening, peanut butter and sugars until light and fluffy, 5-7 minutes. Add eggs, 1 at a time, beating well after each addition. Combine flour, baking soda and salt; add to creamed mixture and mix well.

2. Roll into 1½-in. balls. Place 3 in. apart on ungreased baking sheets. Flatten with a meat mallet or fork if desired. Bake 10-15 minutes. Remove to wire racks to cool.

1 COOKIE 180 cal., 9g fat (2g sat. fat), 18mg chol., 128mg sod., 21g carb. (12g sugars, 1g fiber), 3g pro.

Almond Toffee Sandies

I knew after sampling these cookies from a friend that I had to add the recipe to my bulging files!
—Vicki Crowley, Monticello, IA

PREP: 15 min. • **BAKE:** 10 min./batch
MAKES: 9 dozen

- 1 cup butter, softened
- 1 cup sugar
- 1 cup confectioners' sugar
- 2 large eggs, room temperature
- 1 cup canola oil
- 1 tsp. almond extract
- 4½ cups all-purpose flour
- 1 tsp. baking soda
- 1 tsp. cream of tartar
- 1 tsp. salt
- 2 cups sliced almonds
- 1 pkg. (8 oz.) toffee bits

1. Preheat oven to 350°. In a large bowl, cream butter and sugars until blended. Add eggs, 1 at a time, beating well after each addition. Gradually beat in oil and extract. Combine the flour, baking soda, cream of tartar and salt; gradually add to the creamed mixture and mix well. Stir in almonds and toffee bits.

2. Drop by teaspoonfuls 2 in. apart onto ungreased baking sheets. Bake until golden brown, 10-12 minutes. Remove to wire racks to cool.

2 COOKIES 178 cal., 11g fat (4g sat. fat), 19mg chol., 134mg sod., 18g carb. (9g sugars, 1g fiber), 2g pro.

Oat Chocolate Chip Cookies

I made this recipe just before we showed our house. Not only did the people buy the house, they requested the recipe! Be sure to try out the variations.
—*Nancy Fridirici, Brookfield, WI*

PREP: 15 min. • **BAKE:** 15 min./batch
MAKES: 4 dozen

- 1 cup butter, softened
- 1 cup sugar
- 1 cup packed brown sugar
- 2 large eggs, room temperature
- 1 tsp. vanilla extract
- 2 cups all-purpose flour
- 1 tsp. baking soda
- ½ tsp. baking powder
- ½ tsp. salt
- 2 cups old-fashioned oats
- 2 cups semisweet chocolate chips

1. In a large bowl, cream the butter and sugars until light and fluffy. Beat in eggs and vanilla. Combine the flour, baking soda, baking powder and salt; add to creamed mixture and mix well. Stir in oats and chocolate chips.

2. Drop by rounded tablespoonfuls 2 in. apart onto ungreased baking sheets. Bake at 350° for 11-12 minutes or until golden brown. Cool on wire racks.

1 COOKIE 136 cal., 6g fat (4g sat. fat), 18mg chol., 91mg sod., 19g carb. (13g sugars, 1g fiber), 2g pro.

OATMEAL RAISIN COOKIES Omit chocolate chips. Stir in 1½ cups raisins.

OATMEAL JUMBLE COOKIES Add 1 tsp. ground cinnamon to flour mixture. Reduce chocolate chips to ¾ cup. Stir in ¾ cup each butterscotch chips, dried cranberries and chopped pecans.

COCONUT OATMEAL COOKIES Add 1 tsp. ground cinnamon to flour mixture. Reduce chocolate chips to 1¼ cups. Stir in 1 cup chopped pecans and 1 cup flaked coconut.

Vanilla Meringue Cookies

These sweet little swirls are light as can be. I think they're all you need after a large, special dinner.
—*Jenni Sharp, Milwaukee, WI*

PREP: 20 min. • **BAKE:** 40 min. + cooling
MAKES: about 5 dozen

- 3 large egg whites
- 1½ tsp. clear or regular vanilla extract
- ¼ tsp. cream of tartar
- Dash salt
- ⅔ cup sugar

1. Place egg whites in a small bowl; let stand at room temperature 20 minutes.

2. Meanwhile, preheat oven to 250°. Add vanilla, cream of tartar and salt to egg whites; beat on medium speed until foamy. Gradually add sugar, 1 Tbsp. at a time, beating on high after each addition, until sugar is dissolved. Continue beating until stiff glossy peaks form, about 7 minutes.

3. Attach a #32 star tip to a pastry bag. Transfer the meringue to bag. Pipe 1¼-in.-diameter cookies 2 in. apart onto parchment-lined baking sheets.

4. Bake until firm to the touch, 40-45 minutes. Turn off oven; leave meringues in oven 1 hour (leave oven door closed). Remove from oven; cool completely on baking sheets. Remove meringues from paper; store in airtight containers at room temperature.

1 COOKIE 10 cal., 0 fat (0 sat. fat), 0 chol., 5mg sod., 2g carb. (2g sugars, 0 fiber), 0 pro. **DIABETIC EXCHANGES** 1 Free food.

PRETZEL GELATIN
DESSERT, P. 312

Classic
Desserts

Contest-Winning Peach Cobbler

I use canned peaches instead of fresh, so I can reserve some of the syrup to add to the warm butterscotch sauce.
—*Ellen Merick, North Pole, AK*

PREP: 20 min. + standing
BAKE: 50 min. + cooling
MAKES: 12 servings

- 2 cans (29 oz. each) sliced peaches
- ½ cup packed brown sugar
- 6 Tbsp. quick-cooking tapioca
- 1 tsp. ground cinnamon, optional
- 1 tsp. lemon juice
- 1 tsp. vanilla extract

TOPPING
- 1 cup all-purpose flour
- 1 cup sugar
- 1 tsp. baking powder
- ½ tsp. salt
- ¼ cup cold butter, cubed
- 2 large eggs, room temperature, lightly beaten

BUTTERSCOTCH SAUCE
- ½ cup packed brown sugar
- 2 Tbsp. all-purpose flour
- ⅛ tsp. salt
- ¼ cup butter, melted
- 2 Tbsp. lemon juice
  Vanilla ice cream, optional

1. Drain peaches, reserving ½ cup syrup for the sauce. In a large bowl, combine the peaches, brown sugar, tapioca, cinnamon if desired, lemon juice and vanilla. Transfer to an ungreased 11x7-in. baking dish. Let stand for 15 minutes.

2. In a large bowl, combine the flour, sugar, baking powder and salt; cut in butter until mixture resembles coarse crumbs. Stir in eggs. Drop by spoonfuls onto peach mixture; spread evenly. Bake at 350° until filling is bubbly and a toothpick inserted in the topping comes out clean, 50-55 minutes. Cool 10 minutes.

3. For butterscotch sauce, in a small saucepan, combine the brown sugar, flour, salt, butter and reserved peach syrup. Bring to a boil over medium heat; cook and stir until thickened, 1 minute. Remove from heat; add lemon juice. Serve cobbler with warm sauce and, if desired, ice cream.

1 SERVING 352 cal., 9g fat (5g sat. fat), 51mg chol., 248mg sod., 67g carb. (51g sugars, 1g fiber), 2g pro.

NOTES

Spumoni Baked Alaska

For a refreshing end to a celebratory meal, try this fabulous finale.
—Taste of Home *Test Kitchen*

PREP: 50 min. + freezing • **BAKE:** 5 min.
MAKES: 12 servings

- ½ cup butter, cubed
- 2 oz. unsweetened chocolate, chopped
- 1 cup sugar
- 1 tsp. vanilla extract
- 2 large eggs, room temperature
- ¾ cup all-purpose flour
- ½ tsp. baking powder
- ½ tsp. salt
- 1 cup chopped hazelnuts
- 2 qt. vanilla ice cream, softened, divided
- ½ cup chopped pistachios
- ½ tsp. almond extract
- 6 drops green food coloring, optional
- ⅓ cup chopped maraschino cherries
- 1 Tbsp. maraschino cherry juice
- 1 Tbsp. rum

MERINGUE
- 8 large egg whites, room temperature
- 1 cup sugar
- 1 tsp. cream of tartar

1. Preheat oven to 350°. In a microwave-safe bowl, melt butter and chocolate; stir until smooth. Stir in sugar and vanilla. Add eggs, 1 at a time, beating well after each addition. Combine the flour, baking powder and salt; gradually stir into chocolate mixture. Stir in hazelnuts.

2. Spread into a greased 8-in. round baking pan. Bake until a toothpick inserted in the center comes out with moist crumbs (do not overbake), 35-40 minutes. Cool for 10 minutes before removing from pan to a wire rack to cool completely.

3. Meanwhile, line an 8-in. round bowl (1½ qt.) with foil. In a smaller bowl, place 1 qt. ice cream; add the pistachios, almond extract and, if desired, food coloring. Quickly spread ice cream over bottom and up side of foil-lined bowl, leaving the center hollow; cover and freeze for 30 minutes.

4. In a small bowl, combine cherries, cherry juice, rum and remaining 1 qt. ice cream. Pack ice cream into hollow center of 8-in. bowl; cover and freeze.

5. In a large heavy saucepan, combine egg whites, sugar and cream of tartar. With a hand mixer, beat on low speed 1 minute. Continue beating over low heat until egg mixture reaches 160°, about 8 minutes. Transfer to a bowl; beat until stiff glossy peaks form and sugar is dissolved.

6. Place brownie on an ungreased foil-lined baking sheet; top with inverted ice cream mold. Remove foil. Immediately spread meringue over ice cream, sealing to edge of brownie. Freeze until ready to serve, up to 24 hours.

7. Preheat oven to 400°. Bake until meringue is lightly browned, 2-5 minutes. Transfer to a serving plate; serve immediately.

1 PIECE 554 cal., 29g fat (13g sat. fat), 94mg chol., 314mg sod., 68g carb. (52g sugars, 3g fiber), 11g pro.

Apricot Cobbler

Call it old-fashioned, comforting or mouthwatering—all those descriptions fit this down-home dessert. It bakes up golden brown and bubbly, with a crunchy crumb topping. The recipe comes from the owner of a popular restaurant in our state's famous Lancaster County.
—*Shirley Leister, West Chester, PA*

PREP: 20 min. • **BAKE:** 30 min.
MAKES: 6 servings

- ¾ cup sugar
- 1 Tbsp. cornstarch
- ¼ tsp. ground cinnamon
- ⅛ tsp. ground nutmeg
- 1 cup water
- 3 cans (15¼ oz. each) apricot halves, drained
- 1 Tbsp. butter

TOPPING
- 1 cup all-purpose flour
- 1 Tbsp. sugar
- 1½ tsp. baking powder
- ½ tsp. salt
- 3 Tbsp. cold butter
- ½ cup whole milk

1. In a saucepan, combine the sugar, cornstarch, cinnamon and nutmeg. Stir in water until smooth. Bring to a boil over medium heat; cook and stir for 1 minute. Reduce heat. Add apricots and butter; heat through. Pour into a greased shallow 2-qt. baking dish.

2. For topping, combine the flour, sugar, baking powder and salt in a bowl; cut in butter until crumbly. Stir in milk just until moistened. Spoon over hot apricot mixture. Bake at 400° until golden brown and a toothpick inserted into the topping comes out clean, 30-35 minutes.

1 SERVING 325 cal., 9g fat (5g sat. fat), 23mg chol., 387mg sod., 61g carb. (42g sugars, 2g fiber), 3g pro.

Creamy Butterscotch Pudding for 2

One day when I had a craving for something homemade, I tried from-scratch pudding. It's much better than the store-bought kind!
—*EMR, Taste of Home Online Community*

PREP: 10 min. • **COOK:** 10 min. + chilling
MAKES: 2 servings

- ¼ cup packed brown sugar
- 1 Tbsp. plus 1 tsp. cornstarch
  Dash salt
- 1 cup fat-free milk
- 1 large egg yolk, lightly beaten
- 1½ tsp. butter
- ¾ tsp. vanilla extract
- 2 Pirouette cookies, optional

1. In a small saucepan, combine the brown sugar, cornstarch and salt. Add milk and egg yolk; stir until smooth. Cook and stir over medium heat until mixture comes to a boil. Cook and stir until thickened, 1-2 minutes longer.

2. Remove from the heat; stir in butter and vanilla. Cool to room temperature, stirring several times. Pour into 2 individual dessert dishes. Cover and refrigerate until chilled, 1-2 hours. If desired, serve with Pirouette cookies.

½ CUP 217 cal., 5g fat (2g sat. fat), 111mg chol., 157mg sod., 38g carb. (33g sugars, 0 fiber), 5g pro.

Chocolate Malt Cheesecake

For a change of pace, substitute pretzel crumbs for the graham cracker crumbs. They make a surprisingly good crust!
—Anita Moffett, Rewey, WI

PREP: 25 min. • **BAKE:** 1 hour + chilling
MAKES: 14 servings

- 1 cup graham cracker crumbs (about 16 squares)
- ¼ cup sugar
- ⅓ cup butter, melted

FILLING

- 3 pkg. (8 oz. each) cream cheese, softened
- 1 can (14 oz.) sweetened condensed milk
- ¾ cup chocolate malted milk powder
- 4 large eggs, room temperature, lightly beaten
- 1 cup semisweet chocolate chips, melted and cooled
- 1 tsp. vanilla extract
  Confectioners' sugar, optional

1. Preheat oven to 325°. Combine the cracker crumbs, sugar and butter. Press onto the bottom of a greased 9-in. springform pan.

2. In a large bowl, beat cream cheese and milk until smooth. Add malt powder; beat well. Add eggs; beat on low speed just until combined. Stir in the melted chocolate and vanilla just until blended. Pour over crust. Place pan on a baking sheet.

3. Bake until center is almost set, 60-65 minutes. Cool on a wire rack for 10 minutes. Carefully run a knife around edge of pan to loosen; cool 1 hour longer. Refrigerate overnight, covering when completely cooled.

4. Remove rim of pan. Sprinkle with confectioners' sugar if desired. Refrigerate leftovers.

1 PIECE 369 cal., 19g fat (11g sat. fat), 101mg chol., 291mg sod., 47g carb. (35g sugars, 1g fiber), 7g pro.

> *So delicious! I baked this for Easter. It was the first time I've ever made cheesecake. It turned out beautifully— no cracking or bubbling. I was asked by 4 people for the recipe. This recipe made me look like a top chef!*
> —MARYHODGES, TASTEOFHOME.COM

QUICK & EASY
TIRAMISU

Quick & Easy Tiramisu

No one can resist this classic cool and creamy dessert. It's quick to prepare but can be made ahead for added mealtime convenience.
—Taste of Home *Test Kitchen*

PREP: 20 min. + chilling
MAKES: 6 servings

- 2   cups cold 2% milk
- 1   pkg. (3.4 oz.) instant vanilla pudding mix
- 1   cup heavy whipping cream
- 3   Tbsp. confectioners' sugar
- 28 soft ladyfingers, split
- 2½ tsp. instant coffee granules
- ½   cup boiling water
- 1   Tbsp. baking cocoa

1. In a large bowl, whisk milk and pudding mix for 2 minutes. Let stand until soft-set, about 2 minutes. In a small bowl, beat cream until it begins to thicken. Add confectioners' sugar; beat until soft peaks form. Fold into pudding; cover and refrigerate.

2. Arrange half the ladyfingers cut side up in an 11x7-in. dish. Dissolve coffee granules in the boiling water; drizzle half over the ladyfingers. Spread with half the pudding mixture. Repeat layers. Sprinkle with cocoa. Refrigerate until serving.

1 PIECE 384 cal., 19g fat (11g sat. fat), 123mg chol., 379mg sod., 47g carb. (33g sugars, 1g fiber), 7g pro.

Buttermilk Peach Ice Cream

My mother's family owned peach orchards in Missouri. I currently live in Tennessee, a top consumer of buttermilk. This summery ice cream combines my past and present.
—*Kim Higginbotham, Knoxville, TN*

PREP: 15 min. + chilling
PROCESS: 30 min./batch + freezing
MAKES: 16 servings (2 qt.)

- 2   lbs. ripe peaches (about 7 medium), peeled and quartered
- ½   cup sugar
- ½   cup packed brown sugar
- 1   Tbsp. lemon juice
- 1   tsp. vanilla extract
      Pinch salt
- 2   cups buttermilk
- 1   cup heavy whipping cream

1. Place peaches in a food processor; process until smooth. Add sugars, lemon juice, vanilla and salt; process until blended.

2. In a large bowl, mix buttermilk and cream. Stir in peach mixture. Refrigerate, covered, 1 hour or until cold.

3. Fill cylinder of ice cream maker no more than two-thirds full. Freeze according to manufacturer's directions, refrigerating any remaining mixture to process later. Transfer ice cream to freezer containers, allowing headspace for expansion. Freeze 2-4 hours or until firm. Let the ice cream stand at room temperature 10 minutes before serving.

½ CUP 137 cal., 6g fat (4g sat. fat), 22mg chol., 75mg sod., 20g carb. (19g sugars, 1g fiber), 2g pro. **DIABETIC EXCHANGES** 1 starch, 1 fat.

ICE CREAM'S ORIGINS
Food historians believe ice cream originated in China, where people made it out of snow instead of cream or milk.

Slow-Cooker Baked Apples

On a cool fall day, coming home to the scent of an apple dessert cooking and then eating it is a double dose of just plain wonderful.
—*Evangeline Bradford, Covington, KY*

PREP: 25 min. • **COOK:** 4 hours
MAKES: 6 servings

- 6 medium tart apples
- ½ cup raisins
- ⅓ cup packed brown sugar
- 1 Tbsp. grated orange zest
- 1 cup water
- 3 Tbsp. thawed orange juice concentrate
- 2 Tbsp. butter

1. Core apples and peel the top third of each if desired. Combine the raisins, brown sugar and orange zest; spoon into apples. Place in a 5-qt. slow cooker.

2. Pour water around apples. Drizzle with orange juice concentrate. Dot with butter. Cover and cook on low for 4-5 hours or until apples are tender.

1 STUFFED APPLE 203 cal., 4g fat (2g sat. fat), 10mg chol., 35mg sod., 44g carb. (37g sugars, 4g fiber), 1g pro.

Bread Pudding with Bourbon Sauce

There's nothing better than this comforting bread pudding on a cold, wintry day. The bourbon sauce tastes extravagant, but it's really simple to prepare. The slow cooker does the most of the work for you!
—*Hope Johnson, Youngwood, PA*

PREP: 15 min. • **COOK:** 3 hours
MAKES: 6 servings

- 3 large eggs, room temperature
- 1¼ cups 2% milk
- ½ cup sugar
- 3 tsp. vanilla extract
- ½ tsp. ground cinnamon
- ¼ tsp. ground nutmeg
- ⅛ tsp. salt
- 4½ cups day-old cubed brioche or egg bread
- 1¼ cups raisins

BOURBON SAUCE
- ¼ cup butter, cubed
- ½ cup sugar
- ¼ cup light corn syrup
- 3 Tbsp. bourbon

1. In a large bowl, whisk together the first 7 ingredients; stir in bread and raisins. Transfer to a greased 4-qt. slow cooker. Cook, covered, on low 3 hours. (To avoid scorching, rotate slow cooker insert one-half turn midway through cooking, lifting carefully with oven mitts.)

2. For sauce, place butter, sugar and corn syrup in a small saucepan; bring to a boil, stirring occasionally. Cook and stir until sugar is dissolved. Remove from heat; stir in bourbon. Serve warm sauce over warm bread pudding.

1 CUP WITH 2 TBSP. SAUCE 477 cal., 12g fat (6g sat. fat), 130mg chol., 354mg sod., 84g carb. (59g sugars, 2g fiber), 8g pro.

HEALTH TIP
This dessert is rich and decadent even without the sauce. If you skip the sauce, you'll save nearly 200 calories and 8 grams of fat per serving.

Easy Apple Strudel

My family loves it when I make this wonderful dessert. Old-fashioned strudel was too fattening and time-consuming, so I changed it up a bit. This revised classic is just as good as the original. It's best served warm from the oven.
—*Joanie Fuson, Indianapolis, IN*

PREP: 30 min. • **BAKE:** 35 min.
MAKES: 6 servings

⅓ cup raisins
2 Tbsp. water
¼ tsp. almond extract
3 cups coarsely chopped peeled apples
⅓ cup plus 2 tsp. sugar, divided
3 Tbsp. all-purpose flour
¼ tsp. ground cinnamon
2 Tbsp. butter, melted
2 Tbsp. canola oil
8 sheets phyllo dough (14x9-in. size)
    Confectioners' sugar, optional

1. Preheat oven to 350°. Place raisins, water and extract in a large microwave-safe bowl; microwave, uncovered, on high for 1½ minutes. Let stand 5 minutes. Drain. Add apples, ⅓ cup sugar, flour and cinnamon; toss to combine.

2. In a small bowl, mix melted butter and oil; remove 2 tsp. mixture for brushing top. Place 1 sheet of phyllo dough on a work surface; brush lightly with some of the butter mixture. (Keep remaining phyllo covered with a damp towel to prevent it from drying out.) Layer with 7 additional phyllo sheets, brushing each layer with some of the butter mixture. Spread apple mixture over phyllo to within 2 in. of 1 long side.

3. Fold the short edges over filling. Roll up jelly-roll style, starting from the side with a 2-in. border. Transfer to a baking sheet coated with cooking spray. Brush with reserved butter mixture; sprinkle with remaining 2 tsp. sugar. With a sharp knife, cut diagonal slits in top of strudel.

4. Bake until golden brown, 35-40 minutes. Cool on a wire rack. If desired, dust with confectioners' sugar before serving.

1 PIECE 229 cal., 9g fat (3g sat. fat), 10mg chol., 92mg sod., 37g carb. (24g sugars, 2g fiber), 2g pro.

Rhubarb Strawberry Cobbler

Mom's yummy cobbler is a truly wonderful finale to any meal. This sweet-tart family favorite is chock-full of berries and rhubarb and has a thick easy-to-make crust.
—*Susan Emery, Everett, WA*

PREP: 20 min. • **BAKE:** 40 min.
MAKES: 8 servings

1⅓ cups sugar
⅓ cup all-purpose flour
4 cups sliced fresh or frozen rhubarb, thawed (½-in. pieces)
2 cups halved fresh strawberries
2 Tbsp. butter, cubed

CRUST
2 cups all-purpose flour
½ tsp. salt
⅔ cup canola oil
⅓ cup warm water
1 Tbsp. 2% milk
1 Tbsp. granulated or coarse sugar
Vanilla ice cream, optional

1. Preheat oven to 425°. In a large bowl, mix sugar and flour. Add fruit; toss to coat. Transfer to a greased 11x7-in. baking dish. Dot with butter.

2. For crust, in a bowl, mix flour and salt. In another bowl, whisk oil and water; add to flour mixture, stirring with a fork until a dough is formed (dough will be sticky).

3. Roll out dough between 2 pieces of waxed paper into an 11x7-in. rectangle. Remove top piece of waxed paper; invert rectangle over filling. Gently peel off waxed paper. Brush pastry with milk; sprinkle with sugar.

4. Bake 40-50 minutes or until golden brown. If desired, serve with ice cream.

NOTE If using frozen rhubarb, measure rhubarb while still frozen, then thaw completely. Drain in a colander, but do not press liquid out.

1 SERVING 479 cal., 22g fat (4g sat. fat), 8mg chol., 181mg sod., 68g carb. (38g sugars, 3g fiber), 5g pro.

APPLE DUMPLINGS
WITH SAUCE

Apple Dumplings with Sauce

These warm and comforting apple dumplings are incredible by themselves or served with ice cream. You can decorate each dumpling by cutting 1-inch leaves and a 1/2-inch stem from the leftover dough.
—Robin Lendon, Cincinnati, OH

PREP: 1 hour + chilling • **BAKE:** 50 min.
MAKES: 8 servings

- 3 cups all-purpose flour
- 1 tsp. salt
- 1 cup shortening
- ⅓ cup cold water
- 8 medium tart apples, peeled and cored
- 8 tsp. butter
- 9 tsp. cinnamon sugar, divided

SAUCE
- 1½ cups packed brown sugar
- 1 cup water
- ½ cup butter, cubed

1. In a large bowl, combine flour and salt; cut in shortening until crumbly. Gradually add water, tossing with a fork until dough forms a ball. Divide into 8 portions. Cover and refrigerate at least 30 minutes or until easy to handle.

2. Preheat oven to 350°. Roll out each portion of dough between 2 lightly floured sheets of waxed paper into a 7-in. square. Place an apple on each square. Place 1 tsp. butter and 1 tsp. cinnamon sugar in the center of each apple.

3. Gently bring up corners of dough to each center, trimming any excess; pinch edges to seal. If desired, cut out apple leaves and stems from dough scraps; attach to dumplings with water. Place dumplings in a greased 13x9-in. baking dish. Sprinkle with half the remaining 1 tsp. cinnamon sugar.

4. In a large saucepan, combine sauce ingredients. Bring just to a boil, stirring until blended. Pour over apples; sprinkle with remaining cinnamon sugar.

5. Bake dumplings until apples are tender and pastry is golden brown, 50-55 minutes, basting occasionally with sauce. Serve warm.

1 DUMPLING 764 cal., 40g fat (16g sat. fat), 41mg chol., 429mg sod., 97g carb. (59g sugars, 3g fiber), 5g pro.

Caramel Pecan Ice Cream Dessert

My mother passed this old-fashioned recipe on to me because she knew I'd want to make it. I love desserts, especially this one!
—Mary Wright, Morriston, ON

PREP: 35 min. + freezing
MAKES: 15 servings

- 1¾ cups all-purpose flour
- 1 cup quick-cooking oats
- 1 cup chopped pecans
- 1 cup packed brown sugar
- 1 cup butter, melted
- 1½ cups caramel ice cream topping
- 2 qt. vanilla ice cream, softened

1. Preheat oven to 400°. In a large bowl, combine the flour, oats, pecans and brown sugar. Add butter; mix well. Spread in a thin layer in a 15x10x1-in. baking pan. Bake for 15 minutes or until golden, stirring occasionally. Crumble while warm; cool.

2. Press half the crumb mixture into a 13x9-in. dish. Drizzle with half the caramel sauce; spread with ice cream. Top with remaining caramel sauce and crumb mixture. Cover and freeze until firm. Remove dessert from the freezer 10 minutes before serving.

1 PIECE 515 cal., 26g fat (13g sat. fat), 64mg chol., 300mg sod., 68g carb. (48g sugars, 2g fiber), 6g pro.

Creme de Menthe Squares

This layered bar hits all the sweet spots: It's airy, creamy, crunchy and the perfect mix of cool mint and rich chocolate. It has an old-fashioned appeal that no one in our family can resist.
—Marilyn Blankschien, Clintonville, WI

PREP: 30 min. + chilling
MAKES: 9 servings

1¼ cups finely crushed Oreo cookies (about 14 cookies)
2 Tbsp. butter, melted
1 tsp. unflavored gelatin
1¾ cups cold 2% milk, divided
20 large marshmallows
3 Tbsp. green creme de menthe
3 oz. cream cheese, softened
1 pkg. (3.9 oz.) instant chocolate pudding mix
1 cup heavy whipping cream

1. In a small bowl, mix crushed cookies and melted butter. Reserve 3 Tbsp. for topping. Press remaining mixture onto bottom of a greased 8-in. square baking dish. Refrigerate 30 minutes.

2. In a large microwave-safe bowl, sprinkle gelatin over ½ cup cold milk; let stand 1 minute. Microwave on high for 30-40 seconds. Stir until gelatin is completely dissolved. Add the marshmallows; cook 1-2 minutes longer or until marshmallows are puffed; stir until smooth. Stir in creme de menthe. Refrigerate 15-20 minutes or until cold but not set, stirring often.

3. Meanwhile, in a small bowl, gradually beat cream cheese until smooth. In another bowl, whisk pudding mix and remaining 1 ¼ cups cold milk. Gradually beat into cream cheese.

4. In a large bowl, beat cream until soft peaks form; fold into marshmallow mixture. Spoon half of the mixture over prepared crust; refrigerate 10 minutes. Layer with pudding mixture and remaining marshmallow mixture; top with reserved crumbs. Refrigerate 2 hours or until set.

1 PIECE 371 cal., 21g fat (11g sat. fat), 58mg chol., 232mg sod., 43g carb. (27g sugars, 1g fiber), 4g pro.

NOTES

Apple Honey Tapioca Pudding

I'm glad that apple season is long, since my family requests this pudding quite often!
—Amy Kraemer, Glencoe, MN

TAKES: 25 min. • **MAKES:** 6 servings

- 4 cups sliced peeled tart apples, cut into eighths
- ¾ cup honey
- 3 Tbsp. butter
- 1 Tbsp. lemon juice
- ½ tsp. salt
- ½ tsp. ground cinnamon
- 2½ cups water
- ⅓ cup quick-cooking tapioca
  Heavy whipping cream, ice cream or whipped cream

1. In a Dutch oven, combine the first 6 ingredients. Cover and simmer just until apples are tender.

2. Using a slotted spoon, transfer apples to a bowl. Add water and tapioca to pan. Cook and stir until thickened and clear. Pour over apples. Serve warm with cream, ice cream or whipped cream.

1 CUP 257 cal., 6g fat (4g sat. fat), 15mg chol., 256mg sod., 55g carb. (42g sugars, 2g fiber), 0 pro.

Pretzel Gelatin Dessert

This is one of my mother's absolute favorite desserts. The salty pretzel crust is the perfect complement to the sweet cream cheese filling.
—Erin Frakes, Moline, IL

PREP: 30 min. + chilling
MAKES: 12 servings

- 2 cups crushed pretzels
- ¾ cup butter, melted
- 2 Tbsp. sugar

FILLING
- 1 pkg. (8 oz.) cream cheese, softened
- 1 cup sugar
- 1 carton (8 oz.) frozen whipped topping, thawed

TOPPING
- 2 pkg. (3 oz. each) strawberry gelatin
- 2 cups boiling water
- ½ cup cold water
  Optional: Fresh strawberries and additional whipped topping

1. Preheat oven to 350°. Mix crushed pretzels, melted butter and sugar; press onto bottom of an ungreased 13x9-in. baking dish. Bake 10 minutes. Cool completely.

2. For filling, beat cream cheese and sugar until smooth. Stir in whipped topping; spread over crust. Refrigerate, covered, until cold.

3. For topping, in a small bowl, dissolve gelatin in boiling water. Stir in cold water; refrigerate until partially set. Pour carefully over filling. Refrigerate, covered, until firm, 4-6 hours.

4. Cut into squares. If desired, serve with strawberries and additional whipped topping.

1 PIECE 401 cal., 22g fat (14g sat. fat), 50mg chol., 401mg sod., 48g carb. (37g sugars, 1g fiber), 4g pro.

Love this recipe. I make it with orange Jell-O and place mandarin oranges on top, then carefully pour on the slightly gelled Jell-O. People can't figure out what's in the crust and are amazed that it's pretzels!

—KAREN, TASTEOFHOME.COM

Grandma's Old-Fashioned Strawberry Shortcake

When my grandma served this shortcake, she usually topped it with homemade vanilla ice cream.
—*Angela Lively, Conroe, TX*

PREP: 30 min. + standing
BAKE: 20 min. + cooling
MAKES: 8 servings

- 6 cups sliced fresh strawberries
- ½ cup sugar
- 1 tsp. vanilla extract

SHORTCAKE
- 3 cups all-purpose flour
- 5 Tbsp. sugar, divided
- 3 tsp. baking powder
- 1 tsp. baking soda
- ½ tsp. salt
- ¾ cup cold butter, cubed
- 1¼ cups buttermilk
- 2 Tbsp. heavy whipping cream

TOPPING
- 1½ cups heavy whipping cream
- 2 Tbsp. sugar
- ½ tsp. vanilla extract

1. Combine strawberries with sugar and vanilla; mash slightly. Let stand at least 30 minutes, tossing occasionally.

2. Preheat oven to 400°. For shortcakes, whisk together flour, 4 Tbsp. sugar, baking powder, baking soda and salt. Cut in butter until crumbly. Add buttermilk; stir just until combined (do not overmix). Drop batter by ⅓ cupfuls 2 in. apart onto an ungreased baking sheet. Brush with 2 Tbsp. heavy cream; sprinkle with remaining 1 Tbsp. sugar. Bake until golden, 18-20 minutes. Remove to wire racks to cool completely.

3. For topping, beat heavy whipping cream until it begins to thicken. Add sugar and vanilla; beat until soft peaks form. To serve, cut shortcakes in half; top bottom half with strawberries and whipped cream. Replace shortcake tops.

1 SHORTCAKE WITH ½ CUP STRAWBERRIES AND ⅓ CUP WHIPPED CREAM 638 cal., 36g fat (22g sat. fat), 102mg chol., 710mg sod., 72g carb. (33g sugars, 4g fiber), 9g pro.

PERFECT SHORTCAKE
For a tender shortcake, make sure the butter is cold and cut it into the flour mixture until it's about the size of peas. As it melts during baking, this will create the small air pockets that give shortcake its signature flakiness.

Cherry Rhubarb Crunch

My husband's grandmother gave me this recipe, along with a bundle of rhubarb, when we were first married.
I had never cared for rhubarb, but after trying this dessert, I changed my mind. Now my children dig in, too!
—*Sharon Wasikowski, Middleville, MI*

PREP: 20 min. • **BAKE:** 40 min.
MAKES: 15 servings

- 1   cup rolled oats
- 1   cup packed brown sugar
- 1   cup all-purpose flour
- ¼   tsp. salt
- ½   cup cold butter, cubed
- 4   cups diced rhubarb
- 1   cup sugar
- 2   Tbsp. cornstarch
- 1   cup water
- 1   tsp. almond extract
- 1   can (21 oz.) cherry pie filling
- ½   cup finely chopped walnuts
     Vanilla ice cream, optional

1. Preheat oven to 350°. In a large bowl, combine oats, brown sugar, flour and salt; stir well. Cut in butter until crumbly. Pat 2 cups mixture into a greased 13x9-in. baking dish; cover with rhubarb. Set aside remaining crumb mixture.

2. In a saucepan, combine sugar and cornstarch. Stir in water; cook until mixture is thickened and clear. Stir in extract and cherry filling; spoon over rhubarb. Combine nuts with reserved crumb mixture; sprinkle over cherries. Bake until filling is bubbly and topping is lightly browned, 40-45 minutes. If desired, serve with ice cream.

1 SERVING 294 cal., 9g fat (4g sat. fat), 16mg chol., 116mg sod., 52g carb. (38g sugars, 2g fiber), 3g pro.

Vanilla Cheesecake

To me, there is nothing better than a simple, elegant cheesecake where the vanilla takes center stage. And when I'm feeling decadent, I'll add the rich chocolate ganache topping.
—*Ellen Riley, Murfreesboro, TN*

PREP: 30 min.
BAKE: 55 minutes + chilling
MAKES: 12 servings

- 2   cups graham cracker crumbs
- ½   cup butter, melted
- ¼   cup sugar

FILLING
- 4   pkg. (8 oz. each) cream cheese, softened
- 1½   cups sugar
- 3   Tbsp. vanilla extract
- ⅛   tsp. salt
- 4   large eggs, room temperature, lightly beaten

1. Preheat oven to 325°. Mix cracker crumbs, butter and sugar; press onto bottom and 1 in. up side of a greased 9-in. springform pan.

2. In a large bowl, beat cream cheese and sugar until smooth. Beat in vanilla and salt. Add eggs; beat on low speed just until blended. Pour into crust. Place on a baking sheet.

3. Bake until center is almost set, 55-60 minutes. Cool on a wire rack 10 minutes. Loosen side from pan with a knife. Cool 1 hour longer. Refrigerate overnight, covering when completely cooled.

1 PIECE 551 cal., 37g fat (21g sat. fat), 159mg chol., 424mg sod., 47g carb. (37g sugars, 1g fiber), 8g pro.

Recipe Index